Policy Design for Democracy

STUDIES IN GOVERNMENT
AND PUBLIC POLICY

Policy Design
for Democracy

Anne Larason Schneider
and Helen Ingram

University Press of Kansas

Published by the University Press of Kansas (Lawrence, Kansas 66049), which was
organized by the Kansas Board of Regents and is operated and funded by Emporia State
University, Fort Hays State University, Kansas State University, Pittsburg State
University, the University of Kansas, and Wichita State University.

Library of Congress Cataloging-in-Publication Data

Schneider, Anne L.
    Policy design for democracy / by Anne Larason Schneider and Helen
Ingram.
        p.   cm.—(Studies in government and public policy)
    Includes bibliographical references and index.
    ISBN 0-7006-0843-5 (alk. paper).—ISBN 0-7006-0844-3 (pbk.: alk.
paper)
    1. Policy sciences.   2. Political planning—United States.
3. Democracy.   4. Democracy—United States.   I. Ingram, Helen M.,
1937–   . II. Title.   III. Series.
H97.S33   1997
320'.6—dc21   97-20360

British Library Cataloguing in Publication Data is available.

Printed in the United States of America

10 9 8 7 6

Contents

Figures and Tables

FIGURES

TABLES

Preface

A decade ago when we first began conversations that eventually led to this book, we were drawn together by a shared conviction that the content of public policy is vitally important to a democratic society. We were concerned, however, that policy content was being largely ignored by political science and treated in narrow, disciplinary-specific ways by policy researchers. We were convinced that public policy scholars could make important contributions to solving public problems, even though the field was fragmented and often at cross-purposes. Policy research and analysis sometimes was atheoretical, revealing interesting stories about power and influence, but contributing little to policy improvement. In other instances, policy analysis was theoretically driven but largely irrelevant to the real world of policy making. The theories that guided policy research seemed deficient in many respects—either too instrumental and inattentive to the important political and democratic implications; or too focused on the flaws in the policy-making or implementation process.

We were frustrated about the chasm that separated different forms of policy analysis from one another and from political science. Neither of us wished to abandon the practical world of democratic problem solving, however frustrating, to pursue policy theory as a mainly intellectual pursuit. We both believed that research and analysis of public policy would have to confront the complexity of policy *designs* (the actual content of policy found in statutes, guidelines, court rulings, and practices of case workers) rather than focus exclusively on policy processes. We were convinced that ideals such as democratic engagement, justice, efficiency, effectiveness, responsiveness, and political compromise were not irresolutely at odds but could be melded together through improved real-world policy choices.

When we began this project in 1987, we believed a taxonomy of policy content was needed to enable descriptions of policy along common dimensions permitting comparisons across time, societies, and different policy arenas. Just as botanists have a language to describe the common characteristics of deserts, wheat fields, and alpine meadows, policy analysts need a language to describe the common characteristics of criminal justice, natural resources, and social welfare policies. The *elements of public policy* became the basic empirical building blocks of our framework and theory. The elements were identified through a review of actual statutes, guidelines, court decisions, and program models. In contrast with elements, which are finite and found in all policy designs, the theoretical *dimensions* of policy designs are much more varied and those considered most important will depend on the purpose of the analysis. The dimensions we focus on throughout our work and in this book are those we believe most conducive to strengthening democracy. They have been derived from our own policy experiences and studies across a wide range of policy areas as well as from surveying, standardizing, and synthesizing the work of other policy scholars. The experiences of our many graduate students in identifying the most important dimensions of policy designs have been especially helpful, as they struggled with us to develop a more comprehensive framework and theory for the study of policy design.

As we learned about the characteristics of policy designs in many different policy areas, we began to recognize distinctive patterns in the form of embedded assumptions and social constructions of reality—some of which have been largely overlooked in the political science literature. More specifically, many policy designs contain implicit or explicit social constructions of target populations, and these constructions tend to be associated with quite distinctive design patterns. Other designs contain the clearly identified imprint of scientific and professional constructions of knowledge, and embody scientifically oriented theories, rationales, tools, and other elements.

Although our work has not progressed in any simple linear fashion, there have been some enduring themes including drawing examples and making comparisons across many different policy areas rather than the more common methodology of single-policy case studies or comparisons of the same policy across time or areas. Our work has always involved the search both for explanation and interpretation as we have sought to understand why and how designs come into being and what their meanings are for democratic life. We have focused rather intently on the analysis of policy flaws, why they occur, and their implications for democracy.

In this book we expand on the central themes of our previous work, but go beyond them to show how the study of policy design builds on and improves on the dominant public policy theories of the twentieth century: pluralism, policy sciences, public choice, and critical theory. We argue that these theories have much to offer but that they have failed to provide an adequate theory of public policy for this era. We provide a causal theory and analysis linking policy design (as a dependent variable) to the social constructions, power, institutional characteristics, and behavioral dynamics found in the policy-making history and context. We then link design characteristics (as an independent variable) to subsequent effects on democracy. The elaboration of the theory focuses on the dynamic processes through which issues are socially constructed and how social constructions interact with political power

to produce opportunities or risks for political leaders. Some issue contexts are dominated by the social constructions of target populations. In other contexts, target
populations are less important (or not important at all) and the social constructions
of knowledge and facts play much more prominent roles in determining design characteristics. We explain the kinds of design flaws produced by each of these issue
contexts and interpret their implications for democracy. Most importantly, we
explain how characteristics of the context become embedded in designs, damage
democracy, and (re)produce themselves in future contexts thereby thwarting the
self-correcting mechanisms assumed by pluralists and policy sciences approaches.

Our work has truly been a joint effort. There have been many times when we
found it difficult to understand one another because of the vast differences between
the policy areas each of us studied. In our case, the comparison of juvenile and
criminal justice policies with environmental policies was not possible on any meaningful level until we discovered the common elements of design and began systematically exploring similarities and differences across many kinds of policies.
Even after we began to find a common language to compare designs, we were
sharply at odds about the appropriate direction to take for meaningful change. What
emerged from our dialogue was a kind of synthesis that incorporated rather than
rejected different strains of policy theory. Because, in retrospect, we could have
made more progress much faster if we had understood the different theoretical perspectives we were each implicitly taking for granted, we begin the book with four
prominent theories that have guided politics and policy during most of the twentieth century: the pluralist theory, policy sciences, public choice, and critical theories. Each has something important to contribute to the pursuit of democratic
policy design, yet alone each provides only partial views, emphasizing as they do
participation, representation, equality, effectiveness, efficiency, or other discrete
and separate values. We came to understand that policy must serve multiple goals
of solving problems, reflecting interests, being accountable, serving justice, and
engaging and enlightening citizens.

We have learned a great deal during the decades-long collaboration that has
led to this book. The lessons garnered from experience across a much wider array
of policy areas and greater variety of policy theory have enriched our understanding. This is a far different and better book than it would have been had either of us
written it alone, or even had written separate chapters. The book has also been
enriched by the many graduate students in our classes who experimented with our
framework while it was under development. We have profited by the corrective
influence of our many colleagues generous with their comments. We are also grateful to each other for learning to listen with an open mind. We feel immeasurably
wiser than when we began this book and are so bold as to hope that when our readers finish they will feel the same.

We have incurred many debts in the development of the ideas and the content of
this book. Especially we want to thank the many graduate students who worked

their way through innumerable earlier drafts of the manuscript and tried out the ideas on their own favorite policy arenas. We learned as much or more from them then they did from us. Each of us owes thanks to long-ago mentors who taught us much of what we know about pluralism, policy sciences, and public choice including Elinor Ostrom, LeRoy Rieselbach, and Ronald Weber at Indiana University; and Aaron Wildavsky, who generously advised his former Oberlin undergraduates throughout his life.

We are grateful to M. A. "Peg" Bortner for having read the entire manuscript and offering many useful suggestions, especially on how critical theory applies to public policy. And we want to thank the several scholars who attended the Udall Center Conference in 1994 on citizenship and public policy and offered very useful comments on earlier versions of parts of the book, especially Deborah Stone, Michael Lipsky, Marc Landy, Richard Valelley, and Steven Rathgeb Smith. We appreciate the continued encouragement and support of Dan Mazmanian and the very early encouragement received from Aaron Wildavsky. Elaine Sharp and John Mollenkopf made very insightful comments that made this a better book than it otherwise would have been.

Helen wishes to acknowledge the help of the staff at the Udall Center for Studies in Public Policy at the University of Arizona. Most of this book was written while she was Udall Center director. She appreciates the support and patience of family members, particularly her husband David Laird. Mrill Ingram provided many insights about science and public policy. Emlyn, Maia, and Seth contributed a sense of balance and reasons for joy.

Anne wants to acknowledge a lifelong debt to her parents, Bert and Margaret Larason, who taught her the basics about American democracy. She appreciates the many hours of discussion prompted by her father, an Oklahoma legislator uniformly admired for his leadership and integrity, and is deeply grateful to her mother, whose compassion, empathy, and fairness exemplify the finest features of democratic citizenship.

1
Policy Design and Democracy

Designs of many different kinds are embedded in everyday experience. Much of what people encounter and think of as natural, normal, and simply the way things were meant to be is in fact "made up" or artificial, and is the consequence of human choice including the product of intentional acts by human beings (Simon 1981). Even such a seemingly "natural" phenomenon as time is actually a creation of people who invented hours and minutes, along with clocks to measure them, in order to bring more regulation and predictability into living. While most people live by the notion of time, and to a large extent are prisoners of this received idea for regulating ourselves, the design is commonly adapted to serve individual preferences. People set their clocks ahead to avoid being late or shed their watches during vacations and imagine time can stand still.

Public policies contain designs recognizable in the text and in the practices through which policies are conveyed and have consequences. Cities contain designs through which streets, buildings, parks, businesses and residential areas relate to one another and together form patterns that have instrumental and aesthetic purposes. This book has a design. The cover, layout of the chapters, the typeface, the index, and the sentences were all designed intentionally and purposefully to serve many different objectives for the reader, the authors, the editors, printers, binders, publishers, book sellers, and others involved. As with books, cities, and time, the creation of public policy is a matter of human agency, both of societies and individuals.

Designs are variously intended to fulfill educative, economic, aesthetic, personal, and other somewhat disconnected aims, some of which may be partially conflicting. A number of different designers are involved at various points in time and each may have different ideas of what constitutes success. People attribute meanings to designs—whether the designs are those of books, cities, time, public policies or any other humanly created object—and people act on their interpretations,

1

which may be quite different than designers' intentions. Through time, the meanings of designs become socially constructed and accepted as a "natural" part of the design itself even though other constructions are possible.

Designs seldom stand in isolation, but rather are part of a larger whole and contain within themselves a multitude of submerged designs. Designs are not fixed and static but constantly evolving. Not all the various parts of designs are physically obvious in the object itself. Books, for example, are written (and read) to impart ideas, interpretations, knowledge, and meaning. Cities contain aesthetic dimensions that exist quite apart from physical features. Public policies contain ideas, assumptions, and symbolism that may not be obvious in the written text.

A design is quite separate from the process of designing and once completed must stand by itself on its own merits. Books may be perceived as logical or illogical; well or poorly researched and written; useful and informative or confusing and irrelevant; an addition to the literature or derivative and redundant. Readers evaluate the success of book designs, not designing. Evaluation and improvement, whether of books or public policies, focus most intently on the product and from an analysis of the product draw lessons about the designing process. Learning simply through examination of the process without due attention to the product itself is impossible. Trial and error learning can hardly make progress if one never examines the results.

POLICY DESIGN

Public policies are the mechanisms through which values are authoritatively allocated for the society (Easton 1965). Policies are revealed through texts, practices, symbols, and discourses that define and deliver values including goods and services as well as regulations, income, status, and other positively or negatively valued attributes. Policy design refers to the content or substance of public policy—the blueprints, architecture, discourses, and aesthetics of policy in both its instrumental and symbolic forms. Policy designs are observable phenomena found in statutes, administrative guidelines, court decrees, programs, and even the practices and procedures of street level case workers as they interact with policy recipients. The texts (provisions) of policy are part of the design as are the practices that reveal who does what, when, with whom, with what resources, for what reasons, and with what kinds of motivating devices.

From an empirical perspective, policy designs contain specific observable elements such as *target populations* (the recipients of policy benefits or burdens), *goals or problems to be solved* (the values to be distributed), *rules* (that guide or constrain action), *rationales* (that explain or legitimate the policy), and *assumptions* (logical connections that tie the other elements together). Designs are not simply instrumental means directed at goals, however, but contain symbolic and interpretive dimensions that are as important as the instrumental aspects. Policy designs are produced through a design process that usually involves many different people at different points in time, often with different or conflicting aims.

Policy design is inherently a purposeful and normative enterprise through which the elements of policy are arranged to serve particular values, purposes, and interests. We contend that policies are not simply the random and chaotic product of a political process, as some other perspectives assume. Instead, public policies have underlying patterns and logic, and the ideas included in policies have real consequences. Policies usually serve several different purposes and interests simultaneously and therefore have consequences on several levels. Many of the consequences depend mainly on the meanings and interpretations that constitute the social construction of the policy in value dimensions.

Policy designs are dynamic. It is a mistake to think of public policy as a fixed and unchanging feature of the political landscape. Even though a specific statute or program may be "fixed" in terms of its language and description at one point in time, policy is constantly evolving through the addition of new statutes, amendments to old ones, agency guidelines and programs, as well as through the changing and multitudinous interpretations given to the policy.

Policies fit into contexts. What may be an excellent design in one context, may well serve poorly in another. Abstract judgments of public policy are likely to be off the mark, and the analysis of designs requires acute sensitivity to context. Designs are nested inside one another and can be analyzed at many different levels. In literature, a reviewer can critique a particular book, or a particular body of literature of which a book is one small part, or even the literature of an entire society during a particular period of time, or over a long period of time. Policy analysts can study a specific policy design, even as small as one local program or one statute, or an entire policy area, or the policy design(s) of an entire society in one or more historical periods.

Policies contain meanings and ideas that are discernible from knowledge of the language, discourse, and personal experiences with the policy. The values and discourses within policy designs are central to their analysis. And, as with books, cities, or any other human creation, policy designs should be evaluated separately and independently from the processes that produced them. Policy formulation processes that appear to meet some standard of fairness or openness, but that do not produce public policy conducive to democracy, cannot forever be considered fair or open.

THE CRISIS OF DEMOCRACY AND CITIZENSHIP

There is a certain irony in the fact that the United States—having made the case for democracy and seemingly vanquished all competing forms of government—is threatened by a legitimacy crisis unprecedented in its history. Disrespect for government, politics, and everything "public" is pervasive (Dionne 1991, 1996; Greider 1992; Henry 1994; Kennon 1995; Phillips 1994; Rausch 1994; Sandel 1996). The term "politics" is associated in the popular vernacular with the strategic manipulation of power to serve personal or narrow special interests at the expense of more legitimate concerns. This construction has eclipsed the classic understanding of politics as the means through which collectivities make decisions to serve the general (public) interests of the entire society. Most ordinary citizens do not expect to be able to hold public officials accountable for the results of public policies. As Greider noted:

> At this moment of history, Americans are in the awkward position of receiving congratulations from around the world for upholding the democratic example when they know, if they are honest, that this adulation is directed at a political system that is not functioning in good faith with its own ideals and principles. (Greider 1992, p. 406)

Drucker was even more caustic as he echoed a common theme of the 1990s:

> The theory on which all governments in the developed world have operated at least since the Great Depression . . . no longer delivers results. It no longer even delivers votes. The "nanny state"—a lovely English term—is a total farce. Government everywhere—in the United States, the United Kingdom, Germany, the Former Soviet Union—has been proved unable to run community and society. (Drucker 1995, p. 61)

Some critics recommend stringent reforms ranging from abandonment of the egalitarian sentiments of democracy (Henry 1994) to the scattering of the federal government throughout the United States with Congress meeting quarterly in different cities, so as to minimize the impact of interest groups (Phillips 1994). Rauch (1994) argues that political leaders must eschew certain kinds of public policies entirely ("pork barrel" and distributive policies) by simply eliminating federal funding and tax breaks for most programs except those intended to protect the poorest and least organized groups in the society.

Discontent with democracy in the United States carries a curious twist in that criticism is not directed at the traditional symbols or mechanisms of democracy. Complaints are seldom heard about persons being denied the right to vote, to express their opinions, or to run for office. Journalists are not being jailed, threatened, or fined for criticizing the government or its policies. Leaders of radical social movements—either right or left—are not being denied the right to speak, demonstrate, or assemble. Criticisms of government in the United States center around *governance*—the capacity of a democracy to produce public policy that meets the expectations of the society—along with the public officials and institutions responsible for devising these policies.

Criticisms of public policy are pervasive. Economic development and work-related policies have not provided the long-term economic security that people want. Incremental adjustments of tax and regulatory policy have exacerbated income inequality. Welfare policies have not ended poverty—nor even reduced it over the long term—and instead appear to be at least partially responsible for the economic dependency that has become a seemingly permanent part of the social structure of the United States. Policies designed to reduce crime and violence consume significant portions of local, state, and federal funds and incarcerate a record high percentage of the population. Yet, these policies have not yielded a safe, peaceful, or just society. Medicare and Medicaid safety nets may not be adequate to provide for the health care of future populations and social security policies will have to be modified to avoid bankruptcy. Public policy has not been able to halt the degradation of the environment, the depletion of natural resources, or the worldwide explosion in population growth. Free public education (K–12) and widely accessible higher education are both highly valued in the United States and believed to be essential to democracy. Nevertheless, educational policies and institutions are under constant attack for their resistance to reform and their apparent inability to graduate people who can think, read, calculate, or write as well as expected by society. In spite of more than a century of public policy initiatives, the society has not been able to eliminate racism or sexism, and income inequality actually accelerated during the last part of the twentieth century.

THE CENTRAL CONTENTION

The central contention of this book is that policy designs—by which we mean the contents of public policy—are strongly implicated in the current crisis of democracy. The policy design problems are not the normal product of a rapidly changing world that will be met by reasonable collective solutions. Instead, they have taken on the character of long-term policy failures. Rather than provide institutions and symbols to ensure that the self-correcting mechanisms of pluralist democracy will be operative, the policies deceive, confuse, and in other ways discourage active citizenship, minimize the possibility of self-corrections, and perpetuate or exacerbate the very tendencies that produced dysfunctional public policies in the first place.

Policy designs are produced through a dynamic historical process involving the social constructions of knowledge and identities of target populations, power relationships, and institutions. Some contexts encourage choices of design elements that reproduce and accentuate antidemocratic tendencies leading to degenerative designs that are detrimental to democracy. There is always the possibility of human agency, however, and opportunities exist to design policies to support democratic values. Policy designs that enable citizens to participate, learn, and create new or different institutions, and that break down divisive and negative social constructions of social groups lay the foundation for self-correcting policy dynamics and a more genuine democratic society. Policy designs reflect the social constructions of knowledge, target populations, power relationships, and institutions in the context from which they emerge, and these are conveyed to citizens through the messages, interpretations, and experiences that people have with public policy. Citizen orientations toward government, their participation patterns, and the extent to which they trust and respect fellow citizens are all affected by the messages and experiences with public policy. Thus, policy designs are a product of their historical context, but they also create a subsequent context with its own form of politics from which the next round of public policy will ensue.

Many policy designs contain the footprints of a degenerative form of politics in which the social constructions of issues and target populations are strategically manipulated for political gain. These designs separate target populations into "deserving" and "undeserving" groups, thereby legitimating the conferral of beneficial subsidies or regulations for the former and neglect or punishment for the latter. The divisive, value-laden social construction of target populations interacts with the power the targets have over the future careers of political leaders. Such interactions produce distinctive patterns (and flaws) in policy designs that are detrimental to democracy. The characterizations of the target populations become embedded in the design itself and send messages to people about whether their interests are legitimate and how much (or little) they are valued by the society. These policy designs serve to reinforce the stereotypes of "deserving" and "undeserving people" so that policies afford privilege to some and stigmatize and disenfranchise others. Such policies distort our understanding of citizenship and pervert the capacity of public policy to solve problems and serve justice. Further, these policy design flaws perpetuate themselves by engendering a process that is sensitive to the interests of the advantaged and inattentive to the plight of the disadvantaged.

We attribute these kinds of flawed policy designs to a degenerative pattern of policy making that legitimates and rewards strategic and even deceptive manipulation of images and arguments in the pursuit of private political gain. Political leaders manipulate social constructions of issues and target populations to create political opportunities and avoid political risks. By promoting one or another social group as "deserving," political leaders create a constituency on whom they can confer benefits and receive the accolades not only of the group itself, but of the broader public who believes the government has achieved a public policy success. Opportunities also are created by socially constructing groups as "undeserving," "deviant," or "demons" and adopting punishment-oriented policy directed toward them.

While some policy design contexts are dominated by a politics that emphasizes the social construction and political power of target populations, other contexts appear to be scientific and professional rather than political. In these contexts, the social constructions of knowledge and facts are more important than the social constructions of potential target populations, and the power relationships and institutional cultures favor a world view focused around the taken-for-granted objectivity of science.

The role of science in policy design, we contend, varies depending on the political risks and opportunities afforded to powerful political leaders as well as with the stance science takes on the issues and the cohesiveness of the scientific and professional perspective. When issues cannot readily be exploited for political gain, or when the risks are high, political leaders are inclined to leave the arena to the expertise of scientific and professional networks and align themselves with whatever the experts suggest. Science can also be used and abused, however. Powerful interests sometimes exploit divisions within the scientific and professional communities to make it appear that the prestige and legitimacy accorded to science in our society is on their side of the issue. There are occasions in which scientific knowledge points toward policy that would benefit the interests of powerless and underserved populations, and in these situations science sometimes aligns itself with the disadvantaged and challenges the policy proposals of powerful groups. But as often, or even more often, scientific and professional theories provide rationales for policy that will benefit the powerful, positively constructed social groups.

The elements and rationales in scientific and professionalized designs reflect the utilitarian rationality of science yet they often confer benefits that further the interests of the scientific and professional communities themselves. Even though scientific designs appear to be logical and based on sound theory, they only correct for the excesses of politics as their proponents hope in some specific circumstances, and have their own kinds of flaws that are detrimental to democracy. Scientific and professional perspectives construct societal problems as exceptionally complex phenomena about which only experts are able to become sufficiently knowledgeable to offer useful advice. Scientific types of policy designs reflect the complexity that scientists see in an issue and almost always call for collecting more information and carrying out more studies to enhance the knowledge base of the scientific community. Ordinary people may construct the issues in quite different ways and believe the complexity is mainly created by the experts themselves. If simple principles were applied, policy solutions could be found. Ordinary people, however, are encouraged to disengage from policy deliberation and therefore find it difficult to press their construction of the issue onto the political agenda. Citizens become spectators—disconnected from government and public policy initiatives—leaving such issues to experts who rely on scientific studies to determine both the ends and means of policy.

Instead of policies crafted to re-energize people and create an educated, enlightened, active citizenship, both types of designs—the degenerative political ones as well as the scientific designs—contribute to a political system of widespread apathy in which citizens vent their frustration through empty and divisive complaints. Conversations about politics and policy seem to have become increasingly symbolic and rhetorical, grounded in image making, polarized arguments, and shallow and illogical lines of thought. Public officials and media play on the images, thereby gaining support for themselves and their careers, often at the expense of well-designed public policy. Government comes to be a conversation among the few that is irrelevant to the many.

POLICY THEORY AND THE CRISIS OF DEMOCRACY

Theories of public policy should be of some assistance in diagnosing the problems with public policy in the United States and offering sound advice for improvement.

Instead, some aspects of the most prominent social science theories that are applicable to public policy may have inadvertently contributed to the crisis of democracy and citizenship. Policy theory and the research that is associated with it can be influential in a number of different ways. Some theories have direct influence on policy making and are used to guide or justify actions taken in legislative, administrative, and judicial arenas. Others influence how Americans think about government and are conveyed through the media as well as through the instructional curricula in high schools and universities that teach each generation the basic norms and operating principles of U.S. policy making. In the next two chapters of this book we examine the most influential perspectives on public policy, documenting their contributions to democratic public policy processes and designs, as well as their limitations.

Without much question, pluralist theories of democracy have served as a dominant framework and have become entrenched in the public consciousness. The pluralist model of liberal democracy is based on the principles of political equality, open participatory political processes, and a society in which the power of the state is checked and balanced by a private market economy and by a strong civic culture. The power of government is limited to arenas of life that are considered "public," leaving to other nongovernmental institutions such as the family and economy control over the "private" world of individual and group relations. Among the fundamental tenets of pluralism is the belief that people and groups should be able to pursue their self-interests through government, just as they do through the market economy. In addition to protecting fundamental rights, the role of government is to be responsive and accountable to the public, reconcile divergent interests, resolve conflicts, and facilitate compromises. Pluralist models of democracy do not expect government to pursue the public interest, because there is no agreement on what actually constitutes the interest of the public. There are only competing interests of a diverse set of "publics." Decisions are made through a process of bargaining and negotiation among persons advocating various points of view. Pluralist doctrines do not have a normative standard that permits some interests to be considered more legitimate than others, and they have not developed adequate standards for judging the merits of public policy designs. Pluralist theory seems to accept as given the assertion that the United States is a democracy; therefore the actual operation of politics in the United States must by definition be consistent with democracy. The pluralist perspective, unfortunately, has been so uncritically accepting of U.S. democracy that it has blunted the vision Americans have of democratic possibilities and curtailed critiques that might otherwise be applied.

Scientific approaches to policy making offer an alternative that has gained considerable credibility, at least in principle. The policy sciences focus on the role of policy analysis, expertise, professionalism, evaluation research, and scientific studies in the policy process, and argue that greater reliance on scientific analysis is needed to improve public policy (Cronbach 1980; Quade 1991; Weimer and Vining 1989). Actual examples present a mixed picture, however, both in terms of the ability of science to make headway in the face of political power and in its ability to actually produce better policy designs (Dahl and Lindblom 1976; Hawkesworth 1988; Stone 1988).

A different strategy for determining what public policy should do and how it should be done is offered by public choice theory, which has gained many adherents beginning in the 1970s. Public choice theory contends that markets almost always outperform government and that the public sector should be strictly limited to the few tasks that public choice theory believes it can perform effectively. The move toward deregulation, downsizing of government, and privatization reflect the influence of public choice on the practical world of politics.

Critical and democratic theorists find fault with each of these perspectives. They share with public choice the contention that public policy is part of the problem rather than part of the solution, but they offer a dramatically different critique and prescription. Critical theorists contend that public policy has disempowered citizens, permitted or encouraged widespread withdrawal of citizens from political discourse and participation, and systematically created more inequalities in power, wealth, and status than should be tolerated in a democracy. Equal opportunity is a myth, according to these perspectives, and the system is far more elitist than commonly acknowledged. Many critical theorists trace the root problems to the instrumental rationality of advanced industrial societies and to fundamental structural ch .racteristics of the social, economic, and political systems in these societies. Critical theory calls to our attention the centrality of social constructions of reality and how social constructions become constraints that limit human insight. Possibilities for fundamental change are thwarted by the near-hegemonic constructions of reality that discourage human agency and by the capacity of political institutions to respond to, co-opt, or thwart oppositional movements without actually making fundamental structural changes (Barber 1984; Dryzek 1990, 1996a, 1996b; Fishkin 1991; Lindblom 1988; Valelly 1993; Young 1990).

Among the reasons for disparity in the theoretical perspectives is that each views the world through its own narrowly focused knowledge orientation that serves as a lens through which values and facts are constructed. These perspectives have different visions of democracy, and they assign differing roles for public policy to play within a democratic society. The theories propose different normative standards for judging public policy. Pluralists envision democracy as a process through which leaders are chosen and policies selected. Societal stability, responsiveness to public preferences, and accountability are among the important criteria for democracy. Thus, the role of public policy is viewed as one in which interests are to be reflected and conflicts resolved. The technical perspectives such as public choice and policy sciences are grounded in utilitarian notions of justice and focus on the instrumental role of policy in solving problems within society. If democracies are to survive, they must be able to solve problems in ways that are effective and efficient. Critical theorists are more interested in social justice, power, social constructions, and how identities are formed. They direct attention to the role policy plays in creating, perpetuating, or reducing inequality and oppression. From a critical perspective, public policy should serve justice, undermine power differentials in society, unmask and deconstruct prevailing ideologies and systems of privilege, and eliminate oppression. Dryzek (1996a) views democracy as an unfinished project that needs always to be improving by expanding the fundamental concepts of democracy into more areas of life (e.g., the workplace and the family), for more people, in a more accessible and authentic manner.

Yet if one asked ordinary citizens about their expectations of public policy, they almost certainly would agree with all these theories: Policy should solve problems in an efficient and effective manner; it should be responsive to public preferences, represent interests, and resolve conflicts when interests clash; and it should promote justice and democracy in all spheres of life by providing equal opportunity, aiding the disadvantaged, reducing oppression, and empowering people to gain greater control of their own lives and environments. Further, most would contend that policy often fails in all these respects.

None of these theories alone is an adequate response to the crisis in democratic governance confronted by the United States at this time. Each was developed during a historical period when it seemed to offer an antidote to one or more ailments of the polity, but each is incomplete. These theories have a constrained view of the role of public policy in society, and each subscribes to a number of basic assumptions that should be questioned. Foremost among the limitations of the dominant theories is the assumption that all contexts are alike and one design fits all. A related limitation is that each grants dominance to a single role of policy, thereby creating an imbalance in the other values that policy must serve. A third is that none of the theories focuses sufficient attention on the substance—the design—of public policy. Without a sophisticated conceptual framework for studying policy design, the theories have produced underdeveloped causal explanations of why certain types of designs are created or what their consequences are, as well as underdeveloped interpretations and critiques of policy design. A fourth is that the theories have not incorporated insights regarding the importance of social constructions in explaining the causes and consequences of policy design. A different approach is needed that will build on the insights from existing theories, but focus attention on policy design, identify the role of social constructions in understanding the causes and consequences of design flaws, and explicate the role public policy design could play in strengthening democracy in the United States.

PURPOSE AND ORGANIZATION OF THE BOOK

The purposes of the book are twofold. First, we summarize the main characteristics of four prominent theories of public policy and assess both their contributions and limitations for democratic policy design. In these chapters we make the case that existing theories have not provided an adequate diagnosis, explanation, or prescription for public policy and that their central failures include a narrow knowledge orientation, insufficient attention to policy design, and a failure to recognize the central role social constructions have in determining the characteristics of policy designs. Second, we present a framework that locates policy designs within the larger study of politics, policy making, and democracy. We develop a theory of how differences in the issue context are systematically related to different design characteristics and flaws, and how these flaws systematically damage citizenship and democracy.

Chapters 2 and 3 contain a discussion of four prominent theories of public policy: pluralist democracy, policy sciences, public choice, and critical theories. The core concepts and theoretical causal logic within each theory are presented, along with the theory's implied or explicit analysis of what is wrong with U.S. public policy and its prescriptions for change.

In Chapter 4 we describe the evolution of a policy design perspective and present the fundamentals of a theory of policy design. This theory consists of a conceptual framework for the empirical study of policy design that focuses on the elements of design and a causal model showing the processes through which policy designs emerge, and the processes through which designs have impacts on democratic values.

In Chapters 5 and 6 we draw on this framework to explicate the role of social constructions in policy design. Chapter 5 focuses on a degenerative policy-making process in which issues are framed in terms of the power and social construction of target populations and the patterns of interaction among policy makers have become highly politicized, strategic, and manipulative. The theory argues that the political power of target populations interacts with the way they have been socially constructed (often as "deserving" or "undeserving") to produce different design patterns. Differences in the power and social constructions of target populations are systematically associated with differences in the distribution of benefits and burdens, the rationales used to justify the policy, tools, rules, implementation structures, and underlying structural logic of the policy design. The theory suggests there are systematic relationships between the characteristics of the target populations and various kinds of design flaws including how logical the policies are, the extent of deception within the policy itself, whether the policy will have universalistic or particularistic eligibility rules, and whether it encourages or discourages citizenship. The designs carry different kinds of symbolic messages that serve to perpetuate or exacerbate the existing inequalities in political power and the existing divisiveness of social constructions. We propose that the differences in policy design patterns are systematically associated with differences in the political orientations, understandings of citizenship, and participation patterns of citizens. The social constructions of target populations, and other value-laden messages, become embedded in the design elements and teach lessons to ordinary citizens that they absorb through their experiences with public policy.

Not all target populations are treated alike, however. When some groups become systematically treated in certain ways by policy, their political identity, orientation, and participation patterns are affected. This theory of policy design offers an important alternative to the pluralist vision of how U.S. politics actually works, because it shows that social constructions of target groups (or potential target groups) as "deserving" or "undeserving" are as important as—or even more important than—traditional sources of political influence. The analysis also shows that the interaction of political power and social constructions of social groups is highly detrimental to democracy. Importantly, it casts doubt on whether there are self-corrective mechanisms inherent in the politics of U.S. democracy unless citizens can learn to unmask both the process and the design of policies it produces.

Chapter 6 contains a similar kind of analysis focused on policy-making processes in which science and professionalism play a much larger role. Scientific and professionalized designs are often offered as strategies to offset the detrimental effects of degenerative policy-making systems, yet the examples we explore show that when designs become overbalanced toward reliance on science and objectivity, they also are detrimental to democracy. The theory argues that the opportunity for science and professionals to influence policy depends, first, on whether political leaders view the issue context as one presenting political risks or opportunities for themselves. When there are opportunities for political gain, science will have a role only if the findings from scientific studies are convergent with the policy options that create political capital for policy makers. Otherwise, science will be ignored if at all possible. The influence also depends, however, on the cohesiveness of the scientific community itself and whether there is a unified, agreed-on body of knowledge that is relevant for public policy. Chapter 6 goes beyond the explanation of when science and professional designs will emerge to critically analyze the characteristics of such designs in terms of the elements and the dimensions most central to linking designs with democracy. In this chapter we also explore the paradoxical idea that when scientists and professionals wield the greatest power they tend to produce design elements that inflict the greatest damage on democracy, but when they are only a small voice in policy, there seems to be a greater likelihood for their preferred types of designs to play a democratizing role.

In the concluding chapter we review the major contributions of studying policy designs from the framework presented in the book and the implications of our theory linking policy design with democracy. We explore some of the similarities and contrasts between designs produced by degenerative policy-making systems and those produced in more scientific and professionalized systems. Both are flawed (although differently flawed). The study of policy design also has a practical and action-oriented focus. We explore the search for alternative policy-making systems and the kinds of policy designs that may reorient the polity toward a more balanced set of knowledge and value orientations and a more balanced democracy.

2

A Pluralist View of Public Policy

The appropriate role of government in society, according to pluralist theories, is to produce public policies that represent interests of the electorate, resolve conflicts, reflect reasonable compromises among competing perspectives, and ensure the continued stability of the collectivity along with its preferred economic and cultural characteristics. Pluralism has been slow to identify problems or crises in governance, except when the society is racked by massive civil unrest. The concept of "flawed" policy design is virtually unknown within pluralist theory. In contrast, pluralism tends to assume that "good" public policies are whatever is produced through a political process that has certain democratic or quasi-democratic characteristics.

Perhaps the best way to characterize pluralist theory is as a body of knowledge drawn from empirical research that is intended to explain how the U.S. political system actually works. Observations and findings have been compiled into a relatively coherent explanation and defense of the public policy process in the United States. Pluralism traces its roots to the writings of Max Weber and to Bentley's group theory of politics, which were offered as alternatives to both Marxist and classical participatory theories of democracy (Bentley 1908, 1949; Weber 1978). Marxist and some non-Marxist theories contend that capitalist nations will have governments dominated by economic elites who govern in their own interests. Classical majoritarian theories envision a society with active, knowledgeable citizens who make their preferences known to elected leaders who, in turn, are responsive to them. The body of knowledge that we call pluralism contends that the United States is neither of these, but instead is a much more complex and chaotic system of governance, buttressed by characteristic institutions and patterns of behavior that have enabled it to be reasonably responsive to the public and remain stable over a long period of time (Dahl 1989; Easton 1991; Key 1961; Lindblom 1988; Truman 1951).

Viewed through a pluralist lens, democracy is a particular type of process through which binding decisions are made for a collectivity. Even though there is no standard definition of what this process entails, one central tenet of all democracies is that ultimate power resides with the people (Barber 1984; Cobb and Elder 1983; Copp, Hampton, and Roemer 1993; Dahl 1989; Held 1987; Manley 1983). Government "of the people, by the people, and for the people" embodies the democratic sentiment. Dahl, in his review of the historical and contextual development of democracy, said (1989, p. 1): "From ancient times some people have conceived of a political system in which the members regard one another as political equals, are collectively sovereign, and possess all the capacities, resources, and institutions they need in order to govern themselves."

CENTRAL CONCEPTS AND THEORETICAL LOGIC

The logic of pluralist theory revolves around several central concepts and causal relationships:

- Institutions that limit the power of government
- Institutions that ensure governments are responsive to public preferences, are not dominated by simplistic notions of majority rule or by any single interest group, and are held accountable for their actions
- An incremental "self-correcting" process of policy change
- Multiple sources of identity and overlapping social memberships that reduce conflict and provide a context within which compromises can be made
- A "civic culture," a "realistic" view of citizenship, and a rejection of the concept of "public interest" that legitimate the U.S. system of policy making and allow it to be called "democratic."

Limiting the Role of Government

Most pluralist writings place great importance on preventing the emergence of concentrated power within a society, whether that power is in the hands of the state, the economy, or any specific sector of society (such as religious leaders, class-based groups, or the military). Power should be fragmented, according to pluralist doctrine, because it is more likely to be used for mischief than for a good cause. Even though concentrated power enables government to devise and implement public policies that might solve important problems in a much quicker and more efficient manner, concentrated power also could be used to gain totalitarian control and infringe on individual liberties. Thus, pluralism views the fragmentation of power as having a central function within democracy as it curtails the strength of government and prevents it from dominating other institutions or limiting the freedom of individuals beyond that consistent with democratic principles.

The state—usually understood as governing institutions and the policies they produce—is only one of several powerful groups that competes with others such as business, labor, religion, or media for control of resources, status, and influence. None enjoys hegemony or overarching control across different arenas of societal concern. The state is not monolithic and is not an autonomous source of authority.

Evidence of the fragmentation of power in the United States rests on more than a half century of empirical research, but debate still continues about whether the distribution is sufficiently dispersed that the United States should be considered "democratic" by some absolute standard. Community power studies conducted by political scientists typically find that several different groups exercise influence over government decisions (Dahl and Lindblom 1953; Stone 1993), and that no group holds ultimate power even in a few issue areas. Others, using a broader understanding of what constitutes political power and an expanded view of the policy process, disagree and contend that the United States and most of its local communities are far more elitist than pluralism acknowledges (Bachrach and Baratz 1961; Gaventa 1980; Manley 1983; Mills 1956).

Pluralist theory explains the fragmentation of power in the United States as partly a product of constitutional and institutional design. The existence of multiple units of government at local, state, and national levels and the separation of power among the legislative, executive, and judicial branches of government provide numerous access points enabling those who lose in one arena the opportunity to contest the issues at other points in the system. Fragmentation ensures that there is no one institutional structure or decision-making body that can ensure a policy victory by any group or person, no matter how powerful the group or individual may be.

Responsiveness, Accountability, and Groups

Pluralism posits that public policy should be responsive and accountable to citizen preferences. This is not a naive call for self-government, which is considered to be unrealistic in a large nation-state, nor is it a normative claim that democracies should translate majority opinion into policy outputs. In a pluralist democracy, citizen preferences are articulated and aggregated by intermediate groups such as interest groups, professional associations, and political parties. These groups help organize elections and exercise influence in the interelection period on behalf of persons with shared interests within the electorate. Through their activities, citizens are more likely to have their preferences reflected in public policy. In a pluralist democracy, no group always gets what it wants because groups are expected to compete with one another for power and influence. Whenever one group emerges to press its claims on government, others are expected to mobilize and contest its authority. No groups are always left out. Government and public policy carry benign or positive connotations as a "mutual benefit society," as Lindblom (1982a) put it, in which the political system serves critical societal functions for everyone. Pluralists point to the fact that even disadvantaged populations are able to obtain beneficial public policy, as is apparent from the gains made during the twentieth century by minorities, women, the poor, and disabled persons, as an indication that virtually all interests are able to be heard and able to gain benefits from government at least some of the time. Intermediate institutions such as interest groups, parties, media, professional associations, and the like also are central to the capacity of the policy-making system to hold government accountable for what it does. Pluralism provides considerable latitude for leadership, and the heterogeneity of preferences often means that leaders must choose directions without specific mandates from the public. If policy results are unsatisfactory, however, these leaders can be replaced.

Certain political institutions are typically viewed as necessary (but not alone sufficient) to ensure responsive and accountable government. Drawing from Dahl's characterizations (1989), responsive pluralist democracy requires that people who have the authority to make public policy must be chosen through elections that are frequent, free, and fair. Citizens must be able to participate in these elections without coercion or fear. People must be free to articulate their interests and have broad access to public officials during the interelection periods. Elections must be contested, with virtually all adults having the right to run for office, so that the electorate is offered a choice among competing perspectives. Suffrage needs to be inclusive and virtually universal among adults, with registration to vote available without taxation or tests of various kinds.

In addition to these institutional characteristics, pluralist theory suggests that responsiveness in the United States is facilitated by the fact that people are connected to political leaders in many different ways, and there are a large number of different types of political resources that can be brought to bear. Voting strength, wealth, political organization, staging of dramatic media events, direct contact with officials, access to the courts, and bureaucracy are examples. Responsiveness is enhanced by the competitive two-party system that helps organize elections and ensure opposition. As Arnold has pointed out, the anticipation by elected officials that almost any misstep could provide the ammunition needed by an opponent is powerful motivation for attentiveness to the electorate (Arnold 1990). Groups not only have a variety of resources to draw on, but there also are many different strategies for influencing policy. Those who are not effective in one arena or with one type of strategy may be more competitive in another. Persons or groups who fail to convince elected officials at the state level to take seriously their point of view can engage in direct democracy and place the items on the ballot through initiative petitions. Courts are available for various kinds of remedies when legislative or executive branches are unresponsive. Demonstrations, strikes, and politically motivated violence have characterized the process in the United States throughout its history. Policies are almost never "finished," but can be changed if persons who are disadvantaged by them are sufficiently intense and persistent.

In spite of the considerable criticism that conventional wisdom has always directed toward "special interest groups," pluralism has posited a positive role for these groups, as well as for individuals who personally seek advantages or redress from government. In this respect, pluralism differs from Madisonian democracy and rejects the contentions that factions (groups) should be feared and restrained as they will seek their own private gains rather than act in the public interest. In contrast, pluralism views groups as the bedrock of democratic activity. There should be numerous interest groups, and citizens should be free to create new ones at any time. Individuals and groups alike should have unrestricted access to political leaders. People and groups should be free to use their wealth to promote their points of view. Interest groups are not viewed with alarm, but instead are believed to have a central function in a democracy of assisting in the articulation and aggregation of citizen interests and applying pressure on elected officials that will result in responsive legislation. Decision-making processes should be open to public scrutiny so that interest groups can monitor the activities of government, and not even legislative committees should operate in secret. Interest groups are believed to provide information to policy makers that will enable them to create more responsible policies. Interest groups are watchdogs that hold officials accountable and alert the public when their interests are threatened.

Several other characteristics of the contemporary policy-making process in the United States, that are considered problematic by many observers, find a defense within traditional pluralist doctrine. The fact that most elected officials make a career out of politics and hold their positions for long periods of time is not viewed as necessarily detrimental to democracy, because it can be an indication that the public is satisfied with their performance. Having a professionalized legislature composed of persons with many years of service and relevant training (such as law degrees) may be useful because it helps maintain legislative parity with the expertise found in the bureaucracy. If elected officials are not as knowledgeable about policy as bureaucrats, then power and influence is likely to flow from legislative bodies to the bureaucracy. On the other hand, even bureaucracies are expected to be responsive because of pressure from the executive branch of government and legislative oversight, especially the control of agency budgets. The fact that elected representatives are distinctly atypical of the U.S. public in terms of race, income, gender, occupation, and education is not necessarily a problem because, if pluralism is working the way it should, elected officials will be responsive to the electorate not by virtue of their personal characteristics and experiences, but through the incentives built into the policy-making process itself. Foremost among these incentives is the desire for re-election.

Elected leaders who fit the behavioral model of "self-interested utility maximizer" are not criticized for their lack of independence from special interest groups or their lack of political courage. Instead, self-interested pursuit of re-election is viewed as a positive attribute of individuals because it helps ensure responsiveness to the public. Even the excessive costs of campaigns has to be weighed against the infringement on liberty and the enforcement costs that would be involved to eliminate wealth as a form of political influence. In any case, wealth is only one form of political power—voter turnout and organizational strength are more important. Even the reliance on image making and the media's "eight-second sound bites" are more acceptable than the problems of regulating the media. And these are only a few of the ways that voters learn about candidates.

Pluralist theory proceeds as if it is on solid ground with its contention that elected leaders are responsive and accountable to citizens, at least to citizens who actually have a stake in the policy or who have intense opinions. There is another point of view, however. Much of the criticism directed against pluralism has come from persons initially working within the pluralist tradition, but who interpret current conditions and the results of studies in quite a different way. They contend that pluralist theory and research have provided an idealized view of policy making that no longer exists or has never been realized in the United States. Some criticize the responsiveness studies as having a truncated view of the policy process and focusing excessively on roll call votes or legislative outputs. Neopluralists and critical pluralists conceptualize the phases of the policy process with greater precision and have developed a more sophisticated understanding of how power and influence are exercised. Agenda setting refers to the process through which problems come to public attention and then appear on the political agenda for possible resolution through public policy (Bachrach and Baratz 1961; Cobb and Elder 1983; Kingdon 1984). Formulation refers to the gathering of ideas and crafting alternative policies that might serve as solutions. Adoption is the formal decision, usually by elected officials, that approves the policy and makes it part of the official legal system. Implementation includes the actions of agencies as they put the policy into effect (Mazmanian and Sabatier 1983).

Most of the studies documenting the supposed responsiveness of the system have concentrated on the "first face of power"—whether a group has the power to influence elected officials, policy outputs, or agency behavior (R. Brown 1995; Grogan 1994; Quinn and Shapiro 1991; Wood and Waterman 1991). The "second face of power" is the ability to keep issues important to the have-nots of society completely off the political agenda, and this form of power is not taken into account in most of the opinion-policy linkage studies done within political science (Bachrach and Baratz 1961). Even less attention is given to the near-hegemonic "third face of power" through which dominant ideologies shape the belief systems of the public, thereby precluding recognition that certain kinds of social, economic, or political processes are "issues" and needing the attention of government (Lukes 1974). Studies that focus only on who wins or loses in legislation have missed the larger issues of whose concerns even come to the attention of government and whose beliefs shape expectations about what government should do and for whom. During the formulation phase, "iron triangles" of interest groups, policy analysts, and legislative staff often control the options that will be considered (Lowi 1979). Again, the interests of the less powerful may lose out in this process, as the shaping of policy content usually reflects the way others have framed the problems. Legislation may be packaged in such a way during the deliberations within the legislative body that preferences of persons who are less attentive lose to those that have full-time lobbyists.

Even after policies are adopted, powerful groups and individuals may undermine the legislative intent by influencing the agency during implementation, whereas the less powerful have little control over the rules adopted or the kinds of exceptions granted within the bureaucracy. Research on these other parts of the process does not deny that the system is "responsive," but contends that it is responsive to the few rather than the many and has degenerated into a system Lowi (1964, 1979) described as "interest group liberalism."

Social Membership and Political Identity

From a pluralist perspective, the central role of public policy in society is to resolve conflicts and facilitate compromises among competing interests. The capacity of a society to perform this role effectively depends on the nature of social memberships and political identity. One of the most enduring findings from pluralist research is that most U.S. citizens identify with a large number of different groups including those based on race, religion, language, ethnicity, economic class, geographic region, occupation or profession, gender, sexual orientation, and so forth. Social class is only one source of identity, and not even a very important one to most people. Most observers of the United States contend that class identity has not evolved into capitalist and working-class, with distinct and oppositional interests as Marxist theory predicts, nor have any other divisions become so central that all political issues divide the public along predictable lines. Race, gender, ethnicity, religion, class, and region are sources of identification and group solidarity that at some moments in history may serve as mobilizing forces, but they are only a few of the many cleavages found in advanced technological democratic societies, and none is the dominant source of social membership or identity. This system of overlapping membership, multiple identities, and crosscutting cleavages makes it possible for government to facilitate compromises and produce public policies that are acceptable to the society.

Citizenship, the Public Interest, and the "Civic Culture"

Traditional views of democracy rested on the contention that government was supposed to pursue the *public* interest and advance the *public* welfare. Citizens were expected to have a conception of the public interest and no one was supposed to use government simply to gain advantages for themselves or the groups to which they belonged. Citizens should be well-informed and knowledgeable about issues. They were expected to be able to link their interests to political parties and candidates, exhibiting considerable rationality in voting and other political actions.

As might be expected from the pluralist tradition, empirical (behavioral) research was undertaken to assess the accuracy of these contentions. When the studies demonstrated that these conditions did not exist in the United States, the theory of U.S. democracy was reformulated to show that such expectations were either unrealistic or actually dysfunctional in certain respects. Studies on political opinions of the electorate were unable to find any "public interest" that government could pursue. Instead, research indicated that people disagreed on even fundamental principles. Pluralists concluded that there is no conception of a "public interest" that should be pursued by elected officials because interests invariably conflict and there is no basis for granting greater legitimacy to some interests than others.

Behavioral research also undermined the conventional notion that majority opinion is a reliable guide to policy making when it found that most people, most of the time, are not interested in politics and are too ill-informed to provide useful guidance. The closest a society can come to uncovering the public interest and achieving true responsiveness to the people is through the weighing and balancing of private interests that compete with one another for advantages through government. Thus, pluralist theory completely recast the role of public policy in society from the "pursuit of the public welfare" to the weighing and balancing of competing interests.

Research in the 1960s indicated low levels of interest, low levels of knowledge about politics, yet high degrees of allegiance and trust in government, along with considerable pride in U.S. political institutions (Almond and Verba 1963). These results generated considerable debate within political science, with some showing great concern about the apathy, lack of knowledge, and generally low levels of participation. Others contended that these characteristics reflected satisfaction with government rather than alienation from it (Almond and Verba 1963), and that a mixture of "activist" citizens and "apathetic" citizens was essential for the stability of a democracy.

The Civic Culture argued that this rationality-activist model of democratic citizenship could not logically sustain a *stable* democratic government. Only when combined in some sense with its opposites of passivity, trust, and deference to authority and competence was a viable, stable democracy possible (Almond 1989, p. 16).

This is still a fundamental tension, with some contending apathy is necessary to permit democracies to govern whereas others are concerned that it permits powerful, organized groups to dominate. Arnold (1990) and others (Goodin 1993, for example) have argued that even with an apathetic public, however, pluralist democracy can work reasonably well because of the types of institutions and processes that exist in the United States. Public officials, so the argument goes, know that people can become aroused and mobilized easily and over a wide range of seemingly unimportant issues that the media or an opponent might choose to emphasize. Thus, the openness of the system and the self-interested behavior of elected officials (i.e., their desire for re-election) ensure responsiveness and accountability even if most citizens, most of the time, are quite apathetic.

On the whole, pluralist theory suggests that democracies do not need to expect much from citizens (Pateman 1989). Good citizens of a pluralist democracy are those who pursue their own interests through government, act as a countervailing power when needed to check undue attention to the interests of others, and otherwise leave matters in the hands of public officials.

Democratic Change and Political Stability

Pluralist theory builds on the enlightenment view of steady human progress through incremental change and increasing rationality among the electorate. The process of policy change is incremental and emulates the automaticity of a capitalist economic system (Lindblom 1959, 1979, 1988; Lowi 1979). The theory of democratic pluralism assumes an "invisible hand" that guides a democratic process to produce policy that reflects reasonable, responsible compromises among competing perspectives. Designs that are ineffective or unresponsive to public concerns are expected to result in citizens mobilizing and removing from office those leaders who persist in pursuing unwanted directions. If policy content is flawed, people are expected to recognize the problems and take action to bring about changes. If elites control too much power and generate policies that grant them too many advantages, countervailing groups are expected to emerge and contest these advantages. Policies that have detrimental impacts are expected to generate political activity by those who are negatively affected, and political leaders, motivated by desires for re-election, are expected to revise policies accordingly. Such changes will usually be small, however, because it is rarely the case that all the affected interests will support substantial changes. If policies do not address important issues, the negatively affected groups are expected to mobilize and bring the issues to the attention of government.

Essentially, pluralist theory contends that the United States has a built-in self-corrective mechanism that will prompt political action to bring about necessary changes in public policy whenever government is not meeting the expectations of the public. The system will remain stable because incremental change is a viable way for groups that have been displeased with government to obtain changes that they want.

The self-correcting features of pluralism depend on citizens who pay enough attention to politics that they can mobilize when their interests are threatened and who have open access through elections, interest groups, and political parties. Self-interest is an important feature of pluralist democracy not only because it ensures the responsiveness of elected leaders to the electorate, but also because self-interested behavior by citizens provides the motivation needed for them to organize, participate, and ensure that their preferences will be articulated.

THE CRITICS: NEO, REFORM, AND CRITICAL

Even though pluralism is predominately a political science theory of public policy, not all political scientists have accepted its premises, conclusions, or normative implications. Many of the most persistent and insightful criticisms have emerged from within the pluralist tradition as observation of the U.S. policy process increasingly departed from the pluralist vision of democracy. Not all who have studied public policy from within a pluralist perspective have remained silent about the deficiencies of the U.S. form of governance. They sometimes have been referred to as "neopluralist," "reform-pluralist," or "critical pluralist."

Ted Lowi was one of the first and most persistent critics (Lowi 1964, 1979). During three decades of writings Lowi has argued that the competition among interest groups that pluralist theory holds as a necessary feature of democracy does not exist in the United States. Lowi (1964) contended that the pluralist vision of democracy as a competition among a large number of relatively equal groups has been replaced with "interest group liberalism" in which powerful groups capture the policy-making and implementation processes. Interest group liberalism cannot achieve rational policy results (because it is unable to say "no" to anyone) nor can it address issues of justice (because the state is mainly the tool of powerful interests). But Lowi does not blame the public (Lowi 1972, 1979, 1985). Instead, he places the blame with political leaders ("the state"). Policy causes politics, Lowi argues, therefore responsibility for achieving a true pluralist democracy resides squarely with political leaders.

Lowi's historical analysis of American politics led him to the conclusion that the current version of pluralism has left the United States in a state of "permanent receivership," on the verge of dissolution because it cannot possibly meet its debts (Lowi 1964, p. 279). The public interest, Lowi complains, is "defined by the satisfaction of the voters. . . . The test of the public interest is reelection" (p. xii). But policy is not actually derived from voter preferences or from Congress, Lowi asserts, but "from a process of tripartite bargaining between the specialized administrators, relevant members of Congress, and the representatives of self-selected organized interests" (p. xii).

His critique is summarized by his description of governments that are in a state of receivership:

> The state of permanent receivership is a state whose government maintains a steadfast position that any institution large enough to be a significant factor in the community may have its stability underwritten. It is a system of policies that sets a general floor under risk, either by attempting to eliminate risk or to reduce or share the costs of failure. The stress here is on organizational stability, not upon the stabilization of a particular class or power elite. It is biased not so much in favor of the rich as in favor of the established and the organized. (1964, p. 280)

His initial indictment of the U.S. system of government was written more than 30 years ago and not only has become a widely accepted critique, but has sparked several generations of research on how special interests subvert public policy (see Greider 1992, for example). Lowi extended his critique to include political science and policy analysis. Interest group liberalism, he said, produces "an apologetic political science," in which descriptions of political reality are not critiqued or held up to normative scrutiny (1979, p. 312). The pluralist notion that they could study public policy purely from a factual basis without any reference to standards for judging policy has led to an apologetic discipline that inadvertently embraces the reality of politics as a normative standard. In other words, the unwillingness to critique a flawed system produces a rationalization and affirmation of it.

There are, of course, many other critics. (See especially, Barber 1984; Cobb and Elder 1983; Dahl 1989; Dahl and Lindblom 1953; Dryzek 1990; Edelman 1988; Gaventa 1980; Habermas 1975; Lindblom 1983 response to Manley, 1977, 1988; Manley 1983; Paris and Reynolds 1983; Pateman 1989.) Critical theorists and many democratic theorists disagree with the pluralist assumption that public opinion and citizen participation are independent forces, largely unaffected by government, that influence public officials and lead to public policies that are responsive to preferences. This perspective is grounded in the liberal notion of social contract in which people grant to the state certain power and authority but retain ultimate control over government through democratic processes. Critics argue that this assumption is no longer warranted: The state shapes public opinion, channels participation in ways that commonly benefit powerful interests, and has relegated citizenship to choosing between candidates or parties that offer only a narrow range of alternatives.

Manley approaches the issue from a neo-Marxist perspective and notes that pluralism blames the victim (the public) for accepting inequalities and poor performance by government (Manley 1983). Dahl and Lindblom (1953) have couched their critique mainly in terms of the dominance of business interests. Lindblom (1977) argues that the privileged position of business leads to a "circularity through indoctrination" that is inherent within pluralist systems, and pluralist-type reforms are not likely to make any difference.

Lowi's diagnosis emphasizes the excessive power and influence of interest groups, but he looked to policy itself as the source of the problem (1979). Lowi says that public policies (or "the state") create arenas of power that provide certain types of access and mobilization potential. In other words, actions of the state structure the stage on which politics will be played. Lowi asserted that the patterns of political relationships in the society—such as who will mobilize and what types of conflicts will emerge—have underlying policy conditions and that politics can be changed by changing the types of public policies produced by the regime.

Lowi's argument rests on the notion that the types of policy arenas made available by the state serve as magnets to attract certain types of political participation and competition. To put it another way, regimes create a space that pulls to itself the types of political processes that can "play" successfully within the space.

Lowi's approach implies that the regime has a choice of what kinds of policies it will choose to adopt. If a regime wants to end the politics of interest group liberalism, it could do so by focusing on regulatory policy and avoiding distributive, redistributive, and constituent policies. Lowi (1979) argues for juridical democracy, a form of government with strong regimes that pass strong statutes containing clear rules of law and eschew the delegating of authority into arenas captured by special interests. The logic here is that regulatory policy and juridical democracy will produce pluralist types of mobilization and generate competition among interest groups, thereby ensuring that the U.S. policy process comes closer to the one envisioned in traditional pluralist theory. But this position assumes that elected officials (the "regime") are free agents who can do whatever they want. The U.S. system punishes public officials who disregard the interests of powerful groups and removes them from office. Where are these leaders to come from? Dahl, Lindblom, and others take issue with Lowi's juridical democracy as it seems to assume that all persons have equal capacity to mobilize. Lowi's approach might produce pluralist competition among middle-class groups, but would not empower the disadvantaged. Lindblom argues that this type of "self-correcting" mechanism will not work because those who are better off indoctrinate those who are worse off, thereby thwarting their ability to mobilize in their own behalf.

Lindblom says:

> A principal weapon of the advantaged groups, which have always been more educated and have had instruments of communication available to them (ranging from the Church in times past to the mass media today), is indoctrination of the disadvantaged groups to induce them to believe in the rightness of their disadvantaged position and of the difficulty, in any case, of doing anything about it. Hence, the principal purpose of most members of the disadvantaged groups is no more than to protect such gains as are already won and to pursue others only timidly and fitfully. (Lindblom 1982a, p. 11)

Many persons from both the left and the right of the political spectrum agree that the form of democracy practiced in the United States is not very democratic, not very effective, and, many contend, far removed from the idealized version advanced by pluralist theory. Many traditional conservatives draw different conclusions, however, from the ineffectiveness of government. They contend that democracy is a fundamentally flawed idea because most people are not able or willing to govern themselves. Instead, political power should be held by elites who have a stake in the society, are well educated, committed to the principles of liberty, and able to devise public policies that will protect the society from demagoguery and excesses that would prove detrimental in the long run. Goodin (1993) argues that democratic elitism permits the system to pay attention to those preferences that deserve to be respected. Traditional conservatives typically believe power is a positive factor if it is held by educated elites who are able to understand the long-term interests of society. The public disinterest in politics in the United States, exemplified by the markedly low rates of voting especially among less educated and poorer persons, is not considered a problem but as a positive indicator that elites are providing wise guidance to the society. This type of critique accepts limited citizen involvement, the ethic of self-interest, and finds no problem in strong leadership even when it borders on domination of some parts of the population by others.

Many traditional leftists also take issue with pluralism's distrust of centralized power and argue that political power must be used to transform society and enable disadvantaged people to control the state (Gaventa 1980); or protect the environment from destruction (Heilbroner 1993). There is nothing to be feared from power; the problem is that the wrong people hold it. Power is not to be widely dispersed or neutralized, as pluralists believe, or concentrated in privately operated economic systems, because it will be needed to change the structure of society and enable new leaders to take actions that elected officials in a pluralist democracy are unwilling to risk.

PLURALIST THEORY AND POLICY DESIGN

The policy analysis and research traditions within pluralism have contributed significant information about some of the variables that influence policy outputs and have addressed important questions. Policy research in the pluralist tradition typically focuses on the distribution of power in society and on the policy-making process: Who has influence? To whom are elected leaders responsive? Who benefits and loses from public policy? Whose preferences are reflected in public policy? Do political institutions or processes—such as competitive elections—have any bearing on whose interests are served by government? Does the distribution of power in society reflect pluralist competition, or is the system mainly elitist? Who participates, and does participation increase the likelihood of favorable policy? These are very important questions with significant normative implications. Unfortunately, much of the political science research and theorizing is carried out in a "value-free" stance. The analyst is a passive observer who notices, but withholds judgment, about the system's ability to produce policies that are responsive to preferences, reflect interests, resolve conflicts, and support system stability. Too often, researchers do not even interpret their findings in terms of democracy and leave it to the reader to draw any judgments about whether the policy process is producing "good" results and whether it inherently satisfies minimal conditions of democracy.

Wood and Waterman (1991), for example, took a very traditional approach to the values issue in their study of whether the democratically elected executive branch actually is able to exercise effective control over policies implemented by the nonelected members of the bureaucracy:

> We would not presume here to decide what the role of the executive and legislatures should be with respect to political control of the bureaucracy. This is a normative question that cannot be settled by empirical research. Moreover, those issues are best left to the courts or political philosophers. Still, empirical

research can offer evidence as to the consequences of political control of the bureaucracy by various constitutional actors. (p. 825)

This position is essentially one of delegating the normative issues to political philosophy—or, in the case of Wood and Waterman, to the philosophers or the judges. In either case, this delegation of responsibility relieves them of the need to discuss the various normative positions.

An important implication of the nonevaluative posture adopted by many of the policy process researchers is that pluralist theory has not developed an external standard against which policy designs can be judged. Furthermore, most political philosophers are not sufficiently interested in public policy to offer normative standards. The strong impact that John Rawls's theory of justice had on the social sciences is an indication of the dearth of meaningful writings on critical normative issues that are in any way relevant to public policy (Rawls 1971). The renewed interest in critical theory and some of the postmodern theorizing also speaks to the void created by the abandonment of normative issues by most of the pluralist scholars.

Another problem with pluralist theory of U.S. democracy is that it minimizes the role of citizenship and essentially replaces citizenship with the doctrine of self-interest. Self-interest has been elevated to a normative standard, thereby undermining conceptions of public interest, altruism, or even long-term self-interest, that tends to blur into broader collective interests (Kelman 1987; Landy 1993; Pateman 1989). Petracca makes the point persuasively when he argues that Lowi's critique of pluralism does not go far enough and Lowi's solution (juridical democracy) will not solve the problems (Petracca 1990, p. 568):

> Juridical democracy and interest group liberalism face the same problem— neither has a theory of democratic citizenship commensurate with the ambition of transforming self-regarding individuals into other-regarding individuals. ... A polity constituted by self-interested individuals is incompatible with the promise of democratic citizenship ... juridical democracy is only a bandage for a deep and festering wound: a political culture that intellectually and politically celebrates the pursuit of self interest.

The typical pluralist suggestion for improvement in the policy process is for people to mobilize and take action. Traditionally, this meant that people voted, wrote letters to public officials and newspapers, attended political party precinct meetings, sought to have their position incorporated in their political party platform, and sometimes joined with others in a concerted lobbying effort through a formal organization. In the post-modern society, the exercise of influence is different. To be effective, people must learn to use the new tools of influence through which they disguise their self-interests behind carefully constructed versions of a "public problem," create some type of dramatic event to attract media attention, and construe their issue so that it offers appealing political opportunities to public officials who are intent on their own re-elections.

Exerting influence in the United States today means that people may need to create the appearance of "grassroots" uprisings through carefully orchestrated public opinion marketing strategies that can generate hundreds of letters or telephone calls to elected officials. People today may have to find expert policy analysts who will conduct studies surrounded by the aura of scientific respectability, but whose results will support policies advantageous to the interests of those who contracted with them. By carefully structuring the study and putting the best possible "spin" on the results, science can be made to serve political interests. This misuse of policy analysis destroys the ability of science to serve democracy because it politicizes the standards of objectivity, credibility, fairness, and truthfulness that should be observed by the policy analysis profession.

Powerful individuals and groups sometimes are able to exert influence without mobilization or grassroots support—real or orchestrated. Constituency and client politics has risen to a new height; powerful people are able to ask for special favors or line-item legislation that will benefit only them. The putatively democratic process through which interests are articulated and influence exerted too often abandons principles and fair play. It is deceptive and corrupt. Even if pluralism were more adept at pointing out the deficiencies in the policy-making process, it would not serve as an adequate guide to citizen action because it fails to deal with the issue of action for what? There is no theory of policy design; hence, there is no advice for those who wish to improve public policy.

The pluralist prescriptions for citizen mobilization and action will damage democracy unless they are accompanied by a much better developed normative theory of the role of citizens and the role of public policy in a democracy. Mobilization that simply intensifies the pursuit of narrow special interests through increasingly deceptive and manipulative practices will exacerbate the problems of governance.

A third shortcoming stems directly from the inattention to policy design. Without looking more closely, those working in the pluralist research tradition have not noticed the influential role of science and professionalism on policy designs and have remained largely unaware of the differences in the way target populations are treated by policy—differences that rest on socially constructed images of target groups.

Among the most perverse problems, however, is the fact that pluralist theory *appears* to have brought a greater sense of reality to democratic politics in the United States because it departs from the civics-oriented, textbook view of majoritarian democracy. However, the pluralists' "realism" is itself a myth—the system does not usually work the way the theory says. This seemingly "realistic" view of U.S. democracy is wedded to the pluralist notion of how democracy might work, and the flaws and problems are rationalized as being less serious than side effects of proposed solutions. The pluralist vision of democracy—limited as it is—has become ingrained in the public consciousness and has had a prominent role in shaping the instructional content of political science curricula. Several generations of students have been educated in the pluralist tradition who expect very little of politics and view it as simply another arena for individuals to seek improvement in their own personal situation or groups to seek special advantages that will increase their profits, status, power, control, and opportunities. Pluralism has not equipped students with tools of critique that could be directed at the existing or proposed public policies of the United States.

The modern university has not taken its responsibilities seriously for educating students in their roles as citizens of a democratic society. The pluralist contention that citizens should recognize policy failures and other problems in democracy, mobilize, and change the system is seriously flawed because pluralism has not taught people what should be expected of democracy.

There is a case to be made for many of the principles of pluralism, especially those that emphasize the importance of fair and open democratic processes, equality before the law, and freedom of all persons and groups to make their claims. Policy should contribute to democratic processes and should be at least partially judged by whether it represents interests, provides open and fair access to the political arena, is responsive to public preferences, enables people to hold leaders accountable, and resolves conflicts peacefully. Nevertheless, pluralism is only a partial perspective.

3
Alternatives to Pluralism

There is quite a different view of public policy found in policy sciences, public choice, and critical theory. In contrast with the pluralist theories that focus on the role of policy in promoting political stability, being responsive and accountable to various interests, and resolving conflicts among competing perspectives, these alternatives have other values in mind. This chapter describes the policy-relevant aspects of these alternative theories and assesses their contributions as well as their limitations for understanding, explaining, and improving policy design.

THE POLICY SCIENCES

The unifying theme among various approaches within the policy science framework is that policy analysis, conducted in accord with appropriate scientific standards, will provide information enabling public policy to solve problems and achieve goals. If grounded in principles of instrumental rationality, public policy would be able to reduce crime, defeat an enemy in wartime, clean up the environment, and provide health care for all of the nation's citizens. The policy crisis that exists in the United States is caused by an excess of "politics" characterized by self-interest, bargaining, partisanship, competition, corruption, demagoguery, ideology, and policies that serve narrow special interests rather than the public interest.

Evolution of the Policy Sciences

The idea of applying scientific principles to policy and administration dates at least to the late 1800s when political science first became recognized as a distinctive discipline (Farr and Seidelman 1993). Dewey and the spirit of Progressivism championed the introduction of rationality and science in the study of social issues. The role of science in public policy was bolstered substantially by World War II when government investment in research was widely acknowledged as critical to winning the war. World War II also marked the beginning of the influence of science in bureaucratic decision making. Scientists were hired in leadership positions in federal agencies including the forest service and the corp of engineers (Price 1965). Scientific disciplines developed their own idea of rationality in standards and values, such as the concept of sustained yield for the forest service and biodiversity for fish and wildlife.

The early adherents to the vision of a policy science believed the social sciences could contribute to democracy through the rigorous analysis of societal problems and systematic assessment of policy alternatives. Karl Popper's work, *The Open Society,* was directed at understanding how Fascism could have emerged in a presumably civilized world, and how scientific knowledge and information could prevent this type of totalitarian regime from gaining legitimacy (Popper 1966). Popper articulated an understanding of democracy as an open society in which decisions are based on discussions grounded in the "critical and rational" information gained from empirical scientific research. Continual testing and critique of ideas, he believed, could thwart those who sought to rule through passion, ideology, power, or violence.

The evolution of the policy sciences was delayed for several decades when the intense interest of social sciences in the search for general laws of politics and society crowded out most of the "applied" world of policy analysis. Although Dewey, Merriam, and Popper laid the foundation for the policy sciences, most commentators trace the roots of the modern policy science movement to Harold Lasswell (1971) and Yzekial Dror (1971). Lasswell had decided that political science and the other social sciences were unlikely to turn their attention to the more practical and interdisciplinary work of the policy sciences, and Dror argued that the normal social sciences had an inadequate normative basis for policy-relevant work. The normative intent of both Lasswell and Dror was obvious and a marked contrast with most social science writings of the times: "The main test of policy science is better policy making, which produces better policies; these, in turn, are defined as policies which provide increased achievement of goals that are preferred" (Dror 1971, p. 51).

Lasswell was equally explicit (1971, p. 10): "The goals and principles of policy science . . . are to establish and maintain a structure of authority and control that exemplifies and contributes to the realization of the public order of human dignity on the widest possible scale."

Donald Campbell refined the methodologies and rationales for an "experimenting society" in which policies would be piloted and studied prior to implementation (Campbell 1969). Insofar as possible, science and factual information about the actual effects of public policies on public interests should replace the politics of bargaining and negotiating that characterize pluralist democracy (see also Cronbach 1980; Miller 1984). Decision theorists documented the shortcomings of human judgment and argued that scientific studies could produce decision-making models or guidelines that would remove much of the error found in discretionary decisions by bureaucrats, program specialists, and even highly trained professionals such as judges or engineers (Kahneman, Slovic, and Tversky 1982). Many evaluators, declaring which programs worked and which ones did not, expected public officials to allocate funds accordingly. Scientific studies within specific disciplines determined safe levels of carcinogens, the amount of fat in a proper diet, and the types of seat belts that should be installed, thereby permitting legislators and administrators to make very specific rules, reducing discretion at lower levels.

As scientific policy analysis made its way into the administrative and executive branches of government, the tools of science began to replace the tools of management and bureaucratic decision making. Science introduced new language, methodologies, and ways of thinking about public policy that empowered scientifically oriented professionals and policy analysts at the expense of traditional managers and politicians.

Central Concepts and Theoretical Logic

From a policy science perspective, the purposes of policy analysis are to provide scientifically reliable, useful information that will enable decision makers to make better decisions. Better decisions are those that result in rational, efficient, effective public policy that will solve important problems and improve societal conditions. Quade's rendition of the purposes of policy analysis exemplifies the perspective (1991, p. 45):

1. To help the decision makers determine what is wanted
2. To find possible ways of achieving those goals
3. To work out the consequences that follow a decision to adopt each of the alternatives
4. To rank the alternatives according to criteria specified by the decision makers or to present them . . . for ranking along with the pertinent information

Scholars working from the perspective of policy implementation and evaluation research add two additional purposes:

5. To assist implementing agencies in developing the technologies for proper implementation and rational decision making
6. To provide reliable and valid information about the impacts of the policies on society

This process can be characterized as a series of analyses that accompany each step in a rational decision process (Schneider 1986b): determine goals and objectives, create or identify policy alternatives, assess the probable effects of each alternative on each goal, adopt the most efficient or effective policy, implement the policy, and evaluate the results. The central concepts within this paradigm are rational decision making, efficiency, and effectiveness.

The theories of rational decision making developed in economics and psychology (see Wright 1984 for a general overview) define a "rational" decision as selection of the alternative, from among those known to the decision maker, that will maximize his or her utility (value). When decisions are made under conditions of uncertainty, the person also needs to have an estimate of the probability that the decision actually will lead to the gains or losses anticipated. Rational choice theory does not assume people are self-interested or that goals are instrumental rather than valuative. Further, the theory does not assume that people actually behave in accord with the model. On the contrary, research has identified numerous deviations and shortcuts from the self-interested utility maximizing assumptions of rational choice theory (Kahneman, Slovic, and Tversky 1982; Simon et al. 1992). The model of rational decision making is a normative one, not an empirical model: The instrumentally rational decision is the one that maximizes utility.

An efficient public policy is one in which the benefits of the policy are greater than the costs. Conceptually, benefit cost analysis is quite simple: The benefits and the costs of policy alternatives are estimated, relying on the best possible scientific information, and the policy with the greater difference between benefits and costs is chosen. If there is uncertainty about the actual likelihood of achieving the benefits or incurring the costs, then these should be weighted with an estimate of their probability—derived from scientific studies or estimates made by expert decision makers. If none of the alternatives yields more benefits than costs, then government intervention is viewed as inefficient, compared with the value that would have been achieved if the money had remained in the private sector. Risk analysis is a particular form of benefit cost study in which the probability of some type of risk (such as the incidence of cancer per 100,000 persons exposed to a particular level of toxic waste) is multiplied by the losses (the cost of treating the cancer; the number of lives lost) and then weighed against the cost of preventing the risk.

In practice, however, benefit cost analysis and risk analysis are very complicated. Gramlich (1981) explains that benefit cost studies must not simply assess the costs or benefits to the government, but must examine the gains and losses in welfare for all members of the society. Further, many of these gains or losses occur in nonmonetary units, such as changes in pollution, health, safety, education, and the like. Although there are strategies for measuring benefits and costs in nonmonetary units (e.g., shadow prices), actual studies often simply omit variables that are difficult to measure in monetary units (Gray et al. 1991; Lewis et al. 1992). Risk analyses must estimate such values as pain, suffering, environmental degradation, and loss of life. Even when assessing the value of tangible items, such as water, market prices may not be a good indicator of the actual value. Government policies usually impact not just one narrowly defined problem, but may spill over and have effects far beyond the specific problem they were addressing. Careful benefit cost analysis has to include all the positive and negative effects, as well as the actual monetary costs of these effects, for every alternative that is being considered.

Evaluation research is a less ambitious form of policy analysis than cost benefit studies and usually is undertaken to assess the effectiveness of public policy. Evaluation studies examine whether the policy is being implemented properly and seek to provide reliable information on the actual impacts of the policy on society. Evaluation sometimes draws on benefit cost principles, but usually limits itself to designing studies that will provide a more reliable causal estimate of the actual effects of a policy without trying to combine different kinds of effects into a common measure such as a benefit cost difference or ratio.

Evaluation research has come to be viewed by many agencies as a critical management task that should become part of the normal routines of the agency. Evaluations are distinguished by type. Process evaluations (also called formative evaluation or implementation studies) focus on how the policy or program has been put in place by the agencies and on the immediate outputs of the program. These evaluations often pay close attention to whether agencies are complying with statutes and guidelines in terms of costs, scope, rules, and so on. But they also examine the policy or program from the point of view of the lower-level agencies, the caseworkers, and the target populations, thereby providing considerable insight about the program. Process evaluations usually rely on a mixture of qualitative and quantitative data and usually do not attempt to determine whether the program has had causal impacts beyond those that are ascertainable through simple logic.

Outcome evaluations (also called summative evaluations or impact assessments) are designed to assess the causal effects of the policies or programs on the broader society. These types of evaluations employ experimental, quasi-experimental, or time series research designs in an effort to determine the causal linkage between the program or policy and various changes in societal conditions, holding constant other variables that may also be influencing those conditions.

In addition to studies that assess efficiency or effectiveness, specialized scientific analysis has developed in virtually every policy area. These studies have specialized language, characteristic methodologies, prediction formula, and scientific standards that define categories into which people or events are placed. Stone (1993) discussed the use (and misuse) of what she calls "clinical reason" in education, criminal justice, and the regulation of gender roles. She described how the 1975 act, "Education for All Handicapped Children," provides special rules and additional funding to schools based on the number of disabled children they serve. The act led to a virtual explosion of tests and diagnostic procedures for expanding the definition of "disabled" as this permitted schools to qualify more of their students for financial assistance. Because individual judgment by teachers that a student was "disabled" would not be considered valid under the act, scientific definitions and studies that could objectively diagnose disabilities and place children into the correct categories were needed. In criminal justice, Stone (1993, p. 57) described how psychologists, psychiatrists, rape counselors, and legal advocates came together to create the diagnosis called "rape trauma syndrome" that can be used in legal reasoning to "bolster the truth claims of women."

Specialized studies also are quite common in policy areas that are more technical in nature. Scientists study the causal relationship between pollutants and death rates in an attempt to identify safe levels or target specific ones for more severe regulations. The 1970 National Environmental Policy Act directed administrators contemplating actions affecting the environment to document a rational decision process in which the choice between proposed and other alternatives is explained and justified. Courts interpreting the legislation applied high standards for thoroughness of the research undergirding impact statements. Consequently, the charge to prepare environmental impact statements related to federal actions has led to untold thousands of specific technical studies tracing the likely consequences of alternative actions. Federal actions such as setting grazing limits on federal lands have been held up until complete site-specific investigations of the impact of domestic animals on habitat and wildlife have taken place.

Perspectives on Process, Design, and Values

Policy science enthusiasts envision a much expanded role for policy analysis in the policy-making process. Regular monitoring of social indicators, such as income, unemployment, death rates, air and water quality, crime, and literacy, could be used to determine trends in the quality of life and guide the policy agenda. The distribution of quality of life indicators also could be used to help target public policy to the populations most in need. Causal analysis could be used to identify factors that detract from the quality of life, and these could then be regulated or outlawed by public policy. Policy analysis conceivably could create a more rational (and less political or bureaucratic) policy agenda by production and publication of data.

Arguments might even be made to replace voting and elections with carefully constructed public opinion polling of the general public. Properly designed surveys do not suffer from the kinds of selection bias that exist in voting, which is decidedly tilted toward representation of the more advantaged portions of society. Randomly selected citizen panels called together as focus groups might prove a better guide to policy making than hearings, which tend to be stacked by special interests. Studies, conducted by objective and unbiased scientists, might replace lobbyists for the more in-depth information that public officials need. Comparative policy modeling could be used to expand the range of ideas that public officials are aware of and thereby introduce greater innovation in the alternatives that are considered (Schneider and Ingram 1988). Theoretical thinking can be used to identify variables with "policy handles" that might be helpful in solving problems. The types of training and technical assistance needed to ensure good implementation also could become a much expanded topic for policy analysts. Quantitative decision tools based on models of expert decision makers or models drawn from research can be introduced to ensure consistency and effectiveness in the implementation phase.

The policy process envisioned by policy analysis is one in which elected officials rely mainly on scientific studies rather than on interest groups, media, or their personal preferences to establish the agenda, generate alternatives, determine the optimal choice, write the guidelines, and assess the effects. Courts should rely on scientific evidence and social scientific studies whenever relevant. Bureaucracy should rely on analysis rather than on hierarchy or individual judgment to make decisions. In the ideal rational policy process, analysis and evaluation eventually identify program models that seem to have more promise than others for achieving goals that benefit society, and these are widely diffused.

The policy science perspective offers considerable advice about policy design, but most of it is unique and specialized within a single policy arena. Generic principles, however, take a predictable form. Good designs should be clear, specific, have consistent rather than conflicting goals, and contain measurable objectives. Good designs should contain a logical causal theory linking the program to the behavior of target populations and through target populations to desired outcomes. Quantitative decision aids should replace individual discretion wherever possible. Policy should have instruments or tools strong enough to achieve the behavioral changes that are needed. And good designs should mandate benefit cost studies of policy alternatives for agencies and lower-level governments and should mandate evaluations of all programs. Good designs will incorporate strategies of organizational learning at the lower levels, by requiring studies to be used by the lower-level managers, but which also can be called on when needed to hold agencies accountable for results.

Critics of the policy sciences sometimes complain about their technical orientation and lack of attention to normative matters or principles of justice. These critics are correct in that the policy sciences do not deal with an appropriate range of values that policy should serve, but they are wrong in contending that there are no normative standards contained within the policy sciences. The efficiency standard used in benefit cost studies and implied in evaluation research is based on a specific principle of justice—the utilitarian principle "the greatest good for the greatest number." In effect, the policy science orientation defines a just public policy as one that provides a greater differential of benefits over costs than other alternatives.

Because of the great difficulties in actually measuring costs and benefits and the seeming impossibility of aggregating individual preferences to achieve a measure of the public welfare, *Pareto optimality* and *Pareto improvement* have been proposed as the standards of justice for policy choices. Pareto improvement occurs if there is a change in public policy that will make at least one person better off and no one worse off. Such a change clearly is indicated, as it contributes to the total public welfare without having to judge the relative improvement to person A against the relative loss to person B. Pareto optimality is a state of affairs such that no change can be found that will make anyone better off without making someone worse off. This situation is efficient because no change in the use of resources can produce a greater output.

The Pareto principles are quite conservative, as they assume the current distribution of resources should not be changed if anyone is to be made worse off as a result. The compensation principle refers to the possibility that those who gain from a particular public policy could, in principle, compensate those who lose. That is, changes can be justified if they produce a *potential Pareto improvement*. This criterion, sometimes called the Kaldor-Hicks adjustment, specifies that a policy proposal is justified if its aggregate benefits outweigh its aggregate costs. Thus, the principle of cost benefit analysis is usually defended on grounds of potential Pareto improvement.

Effectiveness, the standard usually used in evaluation research, is more flexible and can be defined in terms of distributive justice as well as utilitarianism. Evaluations, for example, sometimes assess how policies impact different subsections of the population, including assessments of impacts by race, age, gender, social class, and the like.

Assessment of Policy Sciences

Although scientific analysis has without question found a secure niche in the policy process, the policy science perspective is not the panacea for democratic societies that initially was expected by its proponents (Tribe 1972). Some contend it has not lived up to its promise (but still has potential), whereas others believe it is fundamentally flawed and will undermine rather than contribute to true democracy. There are two primary areas of criticism: One depicts the dangers of a society in which science and technocracy become privileged, replacing other forms of knowing and decision making; and the other is more narrowly focussed on the normative and practical limitations of the instruments of scientific policy analysis.

Long before the policy science approaches were well established, Max Weber (1978) warned of the dangers to democracy of a bureaucracy that legitimizes its authority on the grounds of instrumental rationality and codified rules that are purpose-oriented rather than based on moral norms. Weber's particular concern was the relative powerlessness of legislators whom he viewed as dilettantes in comparison with bureaucrats. Weber was concerned that the instrumental rationality advocated by scientific policy analysis can have the effect of disempowering political leaders and citizens alike. Bureaucracy, Weber contended, invented the idea of official secrets and intentionally keeps knowledge about strategies, programs, and intentions exclusively to itself. Politicians are not only deprived of the information necessary to frame laws independently of government agencies, but they also must depend on the agencies to implement laws.

Since Weber's warnings, most political scientists have reassured themselves that mechanisms exist to maintain political control of policy making. In the view of these scholars, political control of the purse strings, appointments, and the absence of an elite class from which policy actors including agency officials are drawn all operate to assure the dominance of democratically elected leaders. However, other scholars have documented the extent to which scientific and professional perspectives have colonized all institutions involved in policy, including legislative staffs as well as government agencies, and separated them from democratic influences (Beer 1977; Fischer 1990; Page 1992).

Policy communities made up of highly educated and trained specialists in the science and technology of particular policy areas dominate the setting of the agenda, terms of debate, and alternatives being considered. These experts operate through fairly closed networks to make policy. Laypersons who lack specialized knowledge and command of the appropriate jargon are treated as outsiders. We argue in Chapter 6 that the influence of tightly knit scientific communities is extending into an increasing number of policy arenas. Science now provides the legitimation for authoritative actions across a wide range of policy issues. When policy-making situations offer few political opportunities and many political risks, politicians defer to experts. In other cases they simply use science as a rationale for doing whatever is politically expedient. The dominance of policy areas by scientific and professional communities extends beyond the military industrial complex that Eisenhower worried about in the 1950s to include the health syndicate, the space enterprise, the electronic communications internet, and many other policy areas.

In fairness to the policy science perspective, it must be noted that its proponents never intended politics to be completely dominated by scientific interests; rather, they envisioned a process in which science informed and enlightened political leaders and citizens alike. This perspective has been the subject of intense scrutiny within political science and public administration in terms of its practicality and implications for citizenship. Lindblom (1959, 1979) pointedly noted that it would be impossible for administrators to know enough about any policy area to follow the prescriptions of the rational model. In its place he advocated incrementalism in policy making followed by democratic scrutiny of policy effects from target populations who have direct experiences with the policies. Feedback from relevant target populations would provide a better and faster corrective mechanism, Lindblom argued, than would planning and analysis. When science becomes the privileged form of knowledge, however, policy no longer needs to afford arenas for discussion and no longer needs to rely on the experience of citizens to assess whether the policy is effective.

The interpretive approach to policy analysis (see, for example, Dunn and Kelly 1992; Fischer 1990, 1995; Hawkesworth 1988; Yanow 1995, 1993) builds from Weber's critique and challenges the presumed objectivity of the policy sciences. From an interpretive perspective, the rational analytical (positivist) approach to policy analysis should be replaced with studies of the meanings that different persons bring to the policy process, the arguments used to legitimate policies, and the hidden assumptions or implications of the policy. Policy analysis should not assume that there is scientifically discoverable truth about the efficiency or effectiveness of public policies. Instead, there are simply arguments, legitimations, and rationales.

Among the most detrimental effects of scientific analysis in policy making is the fact that it creates another group of experts who further denigrate the role of the ordinary citizen. Instead of counterbalancing interest group claims or curbing the excesses of self-interest politics, it has created a new privileged class that damages citizenship and democracy. Policy sciences, like pluralism, have not seen it as part of their responsibility to educate citizens about policy complexities so that informed citizen judgment—rather than scientific expertise—can guide public policy. When science replaces the voice of ordinary people, it disempowers them just as much as any other form of elitism.

Carried to its extreme, public policy becomes a scientific enterprise dominated by experts who discover the public interest, find optimal policies to achieve it, and develop decision instruments to ensure control over the implementation process. People are simply the targets of policy, available to be manipulated through inducements or penalties to achieve policy goals, rather than citizens who are integral to the democratic process and to the production of socially desirable results.

PUBLIC CHOICE

Public choice is a highly developed rigorous social science theory with broad applicability to public policy (Buchanan and Tullock 1962; Downs 1957; Mueller 1981; E. Ostrom 1991; V. Ostrom 1989; Sproule-Jones 1984). Public choice is defined as the application of economic principles to politics and has both a positive theory that is axiomatic and deductive, and a normative theory of value. The common features that unite (and to some extent, identify) public choice scholars are the acceptance of the microeconomic assumption that human beings are self-interested utility maximizers, and the systematic, logical, mathematically oriented deductions from that premise. These deductions usually take into account the type of phenomena that individuals value (wealth, power), their perceptions of the situation, the amount of information they have, uncertainty and probability of various outcomes, constraints, expectations of others, and other contextual features. Mathematical modeling probably is the most common form of research, with actual empirical tests of the results from models being somewhat less common. From the self-interest axiom, one can deduce an impressive array of propositions about individual behavior under a wide variety of different conditions. Thus, public choice can be applied to almost every aspect of individual and social life and to every type of public policy.

Most public choice theorists do not view government positively and prescribe only a limited role for it in society, namely, to correct for market failure and provide goods that are not likely to be produced at all by the market. Democratic governments are viewed as excessively inefficient and as growing inevitably until they are seeking to provide far more than people want. The movement to privatization is one of the major impacts of public choice theory in the United States.

The Evolution of Public Choice

Public choice made its first inroads in political science through the work of Kenneth Arrow (1951), James Buchanan and Gordon Tullock (1962), Anthony Downs (1957), Mancur Olson (1965), and Riker and Ordeshook (1968). Its first application to public administration and to the delivery of public policy can be traced to Vincent Ostrom (see V. Ostrom 1973; V. and E. Ostrom 1971; V. Ostrom et al. 1961). Much of the initial work was grounded in democratic theory and intended as a response to the way political scientists approached the study of politics and policy. Most of the topics of interest to pluralists and to behavioral political scientists were also central to public choice, but they studied them with far more attention to the principles of positive science. Within political science, the growth and influence of this theory has been documented by Green and Shapiro (1994) who point out that public choice articles first appeared in the *American Political Science Review* in 1952 and by 1992 accounted for almost 40 percent of all articles in political science's leading journal. Public choice theory has attracted considerable interest in other disciplines, including sociology, law, and philosophy.

Kenneth Arrow explored the taken-for-granted view of traditional liberal democracy that there was such a thing as the "public welfare" or the "public interest," which reasonably could be pursued by government. He concluded that there is no guarantee of a democratically derived public interest when there are more than two sides to an issue (Arrow 1983). Anthony Down's pioneering work postulated that elected officials, following the self-interest dictum, would align themselves with the preferences of the median voter in competitive two-party elections, thereby explaining not only why the parties become very much alike, but also determining whose preferences, under what conditions, will be reflected in policy (Downs 1957). This reasoning explains why and how even small groups can become critically important "swing votes" thereby ensuring that the system will be responsive to a wider array of preferences than otherwise might be expected.

Buchanan and Tullock in *The Calculus of Consent* (1962) proposed a unitary human nature (based on the concept of a utility-maximizing individual) that guided choice across all domains, including economics and politics, and from which a unified social science with universal applicability could be devised. Riker and Ordeshook (1968) applied public choice theory to voting behavior of citizens and elected leaders, influencing much of the research on political behavior to the present. Mancur Olson in *The Logic of Collective Action* (1965) applied the concepts of individual rationality to show that there are insufficient incentives to ensure that persons will join interest groups and engage in the kinds of political mobilization that pluralism essentially takes for granted. These ideas have since been applied to understand the emergence of revolutionary movements and new social movements. Vincent Ostrom (1973) initiated the frontal attack that public choice theory has made on the conventional notion that hierarchy and centralized control are the preferred form of administration. In *The Intellectual Crisis in Public Administration* he argued for a democratic form of administration characterized by responsiveness of administrators to citizens and competition among policy-delivery agencies that would give citizens a choice. He exposed the illogic and fallacies of always calling for "more coordination" or "more controls" when confronted with policy or administrative failures. More recently, Elinor Ostrom has taken public choice theory into the field to study strategies for governing common pool resources and has pioneered a much more optimistic view of the capacity of people to create self-governing institutions that will provide for the collective good (1990, 1992a 1992b, 1996).

Some of these concepts will be explored below within a general discussion of the two issues most relevant to this discussion: public choice perspectives on what the proper role of government is and how institutions (policies, rules) can be devised to ensure that government carries out its responsibilities.

Central Concepts and Theoretical Logic

Most public choice theorists attribute the current policy crisis to the fact that government is attempting to do things that are better suited to other institutions, especially economic markets, and to the problems in the design of public institutions. The principle of self-interest utility maximization is combined with principles of utilitarian justice to develop a deductive theory of what government should and should not do and a theory of the types of institutions that are needed to deliver public policy.

Why Is Government Inefficient?

Public choice envisions a far more limited role for public policy than any of the other perspectives. In public choice theory the market is the central institution of society and can be relied on more than any other to provide for a just, fair, and free society. Markets are granted the central place because they encompass voluntary exchanges among all parties, and each is assumed to be better off as a result. Otherwise, so the theory goes, the person would not have participated in the exchange. To public choice theorists, markets are free and uncoerced, whereas public policy is coercive. Thus, the only just role for public policy is to correct for market failures and provide goods that the market is not able to deliver (Savas 1982, 1987).

These conclusions are derived from the public choice contention that rational action by individuals (that is, self-interested utility maximization) will lead to collectively irrational results (see Miller 1989; and E. Ostrom 1992b), unless institutions are developed to alter the incentive structure so that self-interested behavior will produce collectively optimal results. This, then, becomes the central problem: Can institutions be designed so that individuals and groups—who it is assumed will pursue their own self-interests—can avoid producing collective outcomes that result in no one being better off?

There are several ways in which individual rationality produces collective irrationality. Garrett Hardin (1968) in *The Tragedy of the Commons* poses the classic problem through an analogy of a common property meadow on which herdsmen graze their sheep. Each herdsman, pursuing individual self-interest, will be motivated to add additional sheep to the pasture, thereby ensuring greater personal profit. As all farmers will pursue this strategy, the meadow becomes overgrazed, the grass dies, the meadow is destroyed, and the sheep die. No one makes any profits. Hardin's example has been extended to show what will happen to "common pool resources" such as water, air, fish, wilderness, public lands, or any other commonly held good that is used for private purposes. Simple deductions from public choice axioms show that pluralist democracies cannot protect common pool resources because self-interested individuals will not elect people who will protect the common interests, nor can they organize for self-governing institutions that will protect such resources. Some scholars contend that democracy will result in the ruination of the environment and that dictatorship or rule by elites (of the left or the right) is needed to impose the necessary discipline on the public (Hardin 1982).

Others, such as Savas (1987), argue that privatization is the answer. Commonly held resources should be privatized, thereby ensuring that each person bears the costs, as well as receives the benefits, of his or her own actions. A third point of view has been developed from an institutional branch of public choice that emphasizes the ability of people to take a longer view, organize for their own collective interests, and engage in cooperative behavior that will save the commons (see especially the work of Elinor and Vincent Ostrom, John Orbell, and Robyn Dawes). Institutional public choice is discussed separately below.

The second example that public choice scholars frequently use to show how individual self-interest produces suboptimal collective results is called the "prisoner's dilemma." The prisoner's dilemma is usually represented as a game in which two individuals have a choice of cooperating or defecting. Suppose that there are two prisoners (Jack and Joe, for this example) who have been arrested for kidnapping and murder. They have both been charged with kidnapping, but the authorities have not decided which should be charged with the murder, or whether to charge them both. They have agreed with each other to remain silent about the murder. The authorities, however, offer each the opportunity to implicate the other and in exchange to be granted his freedom. Each now believes that he can accuse the other, thereby gaining his own freedom albeit at the expense of his friend. Public choice theory posits that, in the absence of constraining institutions, each will accuse the other and both will be executed. If only one accuses the other, then the one who broke his promise to remain silent wins and the one who kept his word loses. When applied to public policy, the prisoner's dilemma suggests that people will not be able to join together in collective enterprises, even if this would result in a collective good, because people cannot reach agreements they will keep. Absent such agreements, competition among individuals or groups, each seeking its own interest, will not produce an optimal outcome, as the pluralists seem to assume, but in fact will result in everyone being worse off.

The third example involves the fundamental question of what is meant by the "public interest," or the "public welfare," and whether it is even possible for a collectivity to reach decisions that are fair and just rather than arbitrary and oppressive. The issue is how a collectivity (through government or other means) can aggregate individual preferences so that there is some decision that will reflect the "public interest" or the "public welfare." As a point of departure, it is assumed that actions with which everyone agreed would be considered "fair," and that actions that are approved by the majority would be considered more fair than actions agreed to only by a minority of the population. Any action agreed to only by a minority would be considered arbitrary and therefore unjust.

Arrow's paradox, or the principle of circular majorities, shows that even when a collectivity (or government) attempts to reflect majority preferences, there may not be any policy outcome that actually does so. The paradox of circular majorities is illustrated with the following example, which poses the question of whether the city council should develop its next bus service in the north, south, or west part of the city. Each council member ranks his or her first, second, and third choices.

	North	South	West
Voter 1	1	2	3
Voter 2	2	3	1
Voter 3	3	1	2

The votes are then taken by first comparing north to south, with the winner contesting against west. Here are the results of the pairs:

North vs. south: North is ranked ahead of south by voters 1 and 2, and north therefore wins.

North vs. west: North is ranked ahead of west by voter 1, but west is ranked ahead by voters 2 and 3. Thus, west wins.

Is west the majority choice? The answer is no, because:

West vs. south: South is ranked ahead of west by voters 1 and 3, thus south is the apparent winner.

As already shown, however, north defeats south when paired head to head. Thus, there is a circular majority and none of the choices has any more reason to be selected than any other. Any choice that is made is arbitrary and is imposed against the wishes of two out of three council members. This example could be extended beyond the council members to allow a vote by every person in the city or country. A circular majority can occur any time the electorate is offered more than two alternatives. In any policy situation there are almost always more than just two options. Unless policy preferences are narrowed to two options, a process that itself is arbitrary, circular majorities are actually quite common.

One of the implications of Arrow's paradox is that collective choices, even when based on majority principles, will not reflect the true preferences of a majority. Individuals who act rationally in their voting, then, will not necessarily produce a collectively rational choice. Thus, to most public choice theorists, there is no "public interest" or "public welfare" to be achieved because it is impossible to aggregate individual preferences to ascertain the collective good. Except for situations of Pareto optimality, then, public choice departs from the utilitarian principle of "greatest good for the greatest number," and believes, instead, that there are only individual interests to be pursued through government.

Arrow's contention that there is no collectively rational goal for public policy in the form of a "public interest" or "public welfare" that can be justified under even majoritarian principles undermines pluralist and policy sciences approaches. Pluralists seem to take for granted that the compromises worked out through the countervailing power of interest groups is a reasonable approximation of what government legitimately should do. Arrow's argument suggests that government, itself, may need to ensure its own legitimacy through propaganda or more subtle forms of legitimation and control. For the policy sciences, the common assumption is that there is a legitimate political process that produces the goals toward which policy is directed, and rational scientific analysis can be used to pursue those goals. If the goals themselves are not legitimate, however, policy science in the service of democracy is an illusion, and science is used to legitimate the will of those who hold political power.

A fourth insight from public choice theory that illustrates the disjunction between individual and collective rationality is the principle of "free riders." Olson's classic work (1965) showed that collective action of all types, ranging from social movements to organized political lobbying, is costly. Olson argued that people usually will not organize to protect or pursue their self-interests through government because the costs of doing so are higher than the results are worth to one individual. Furthermore, even though the collective result might make it worth the effort, individuals will be motivated to be "free riders" in the sense that they can gain the benefits of organized action without themselves having to share the costs. In other words, if people mobilize and pursue their interests through government, then all who share those interests will benefit, even if they did not participate. The organizers cannot deny the benefits to nonparticipants; hence there is insufficient motivation for organization to occur.

Pluralism, as we have seen above, assumes that individuals will pursue their individual preferences through government and will organize, collectively, to protect their interests. The self-correcting mechanisms of pluralism require that citizens organize (mobilize) whenever their interests are threatened and that elected officials are motivated by their desire for re-election to pay attention to them. The public choice theory of free riders holds that these self-correcting mechanisms central to pluralism *will not occur* except under constrained conditions. Obviously, one might argue that Olson is wrong in some fundamental sense, as indicated by the very large number of lobbyists who are paid for by organized groups and by the fact that people often mobilize politically and new groups are formed all the time. On the other hand, Olson's point is an important one as it suggests that organizing for political action is not something that can be taken as given.

The Proper Role of Government

Public choice analysis indicates there is no way to determine what the public interest actually is because there is no way to aggregate individual preferences into a collective social welfare or a "public interest." They also are uncomfortable with the contention that one can base policy decisions on benefit cost comparisons, as if those who benefit would compensate those who lose as a result of the policy. Because these compensations virtually never occur, it is hard to argue that such policies meet a strong standard of justice. For these reasons public choice theorists show a preference for Pareto optimality as the standard for determining whether a policy is just (Buchanan and Tullock 1962). Judgments about whether a person gains or loses from a transaction must be made by the individual, as no one else is as capable of this determination. Free and competitive markets are both efficient and just because they involve transactions among individuals that leave both parties better off. If the markets are, in fact, open, free, and competitive, then it is reasonable to assume individuals would not engage in the transaction unless each believed that he or she was better off as a result.

Government actions, however, often fail to meet the Pareto principle. Public policies extract money from some, through taxes, to provide goods and services to others. Public policies regulate or coerce some persons to do things they otherwise would not do, so that others may gain. These actions do not meet the Pareto principle and therefore are not as fair and just as markets.

There are some types of goods that markets do not produce, however, and markets often cannot control externalities (side effects). In particular, markets are not able to provide for *public goods* (also called collective goods) because there is no incentive to produce them. Public goods have a very specific definition within public choice theory and must not be confused with a generic definition of goods provided by government. Instead, public goods are those characterized by nonexclusion and joint consumption. Nonexclusion means that no one can be excluded from consuming the good. For example, no one can be excluded from the provision of national defense—if this service is provided, then everyone enjoys it and there is no way to "package" national defense and require persons to pay for it if they wish to enjoy it. Joint consumption means that the consumption by one person does not detract from consumption by another. With national defense, for example, the "consumption" by one person does not detract at all from the amount available for another. Markets will not produce public goods because they cannot package and sell such goods. Thus, one appropriate role for government, according to public choice theorists, is to provide public goods.

A second appropriate role for government is to regulate or assist in the provision of common pool resources and toll goods. Common pool resources are goods such as air, fisheries, minerals, water, and others that are usually held in common (publicly owned) but are consumed by individuals. Without constraints, the self-interested actions of individuals will lead to the permanent ruination or depletion of these resources, thereby denying them to others. Collective action in the form of rules and regulations usually is needed to prevent depletion or damage to the goods. Toll goods refer to services such as libraries or cable television that can be produced by the market but that often are not because of the high initial costs and the natural monopolies that commonly occur. Government action is needed here to ensure that these services are available and provided at reasonable costs.

All other goods are considered to be "private" goods, best provided by the market in which each person is able to decide whether to engage in a transaction or not. The role of government is to provide the goods that the market cannot handle adequately: that is, the role of government is to correct for "market failures."

Public Choice Critique of U.S. Public Policy

These principles provide public choice theorists with the tools to critique public policy in the United States. The standard critique generally runs as follows: (a) Government provides many goods and services that could be provided and/or produced more efficiently through the market; (b) government often is not organized for the efficient delivery of those functions that it should carry out; (c) government grows and spends more than the public wants and more than is efficient due to the dynamics of self-interest, which, in politics, leads to continued growth of government budgets, bureaucracies, and interventions in the economy whereas in markets self-interest leads to fairness and efficiency; and (d) government provides services that foster dependency because, since individuals operate on the basis of self-interest, they will come to rely on government rather than incur the costs of self-sufficiency.

Education is an example of the first point. Education could be provided through the market (even if government continued to pay for it, through vouchers, for example). Public choice proponents argue that private production of education would increase quality and reduce costs. Consumers would have a choice among schools, thereby creating competition that would force schools to increase quality and reduce costs to attract consumers.

A number of public choice scholars have used the principles of self-interest to show, through deductive logic, that government will grow virtually unchecked even when the people do not want it to grow (Savas 1987; Wilson 1989). Wilson's theory begins with characteristics of the goods being provided and how the costs are allocated. When benefits are heavily concentrated on only a few and costs are widely dispersed among many taxpayers, then those who benefit will have sufficient incentives to mobilize and protect their interests whereas taxpayers will not, due to the relatively small amount that each pays. Similarly, when benefits are large and widely dispersed but the costs are concentrated, as in taxing the rich, then those who receive benefits will be able to prevail. The result is continual government growth beyond what anyone really wants.

The fourth critique is that government spending fosters dependency. This argument is most often framed in terms of welfare recipients, pregnant teenagers, and other disadvantaged populations who are the recipients of redistributed wealth (Murray 1984). The public choice contention is that, for example, such policies create incentives for women to have children to gain the welfare payments. If a second child will increase the size of the welfare payment, they assume that the single mother will have an incentive to conceive and bear a second child to receive the payment. This argument could, of course, be applied equally as well to groups such as tobacco farmers who can be expected to continue producing tobacco so long as it is subsidized heavily; or to persons who live in floodplains and will have an incentive not to carry insurance so long as emergency relief will be available.

Probably the best known prescriptions emerging from public choice theory are to privatize government functions, privatize the delivery of services through contracting when it is necessary for public funds to be used, to develop competitive arrangements among the agencies that remain within the public sector, and to charge full market value for toll or public goods (Savas 1982, 1987). The movement to "choice" in educational policy, contracting for social services, the development of private prisons, the development of water policy based on market prices for water, and so forth indicate the persuasiveness of the public choice perspective on public policy during the past several decades.

Public Choice Theory of Institutional Design

Public choice scholars have used the principles of self-interest and rationality to challenge the conventional wisdom about how government should be organized to deliver goods and services. Here public choice takes issue with the long-standing notions that centralization, coordination, and hierarchical control are the most efficient form of organization. Instead, public choice theory asserts that decentralization, competition among agencies, and privatization of production (under most conditions) are preferred to centralized authority. The rationale again draws on the market as an analogy: competition encourages organizations to be efficient; therefore competition among government agencies should be preferred to consolidation.

An analysis of the appropriate institutional design, according to public choice methodologies, should start with an understanding of the type of good that is being produced. Much of the analysis has focused on common pool resources, such as water, air, fisheries, forests, or land. Capitalist economic theory generally holds that common pool resources will be overexploited, as illustrated with the tragedy of the commons metaphor unless the resource is subject to private property rights or is heavily regulated by an outside authority that is not subject to the will of the voters. E. Ostrom (1985, 1990) has challenged these contentions. She argues that other solutions exist and that hundreds of communities throughout the world have proven that rules can be developed through self-government that will be efficient, acceptable to the community, and will prevent destruction of the common resource. These do not require private property rights:

> The villagers in both settings have *chosen* to retain the institution of communal property as the foundation for land use. . . . One cannot view communal property in these settings as the primordial remains of earlier institutions evolved in a land of plenty. If the transaction costs involved in managing communal property had been excessive, compared with private-property institutions, the villagers would have had many opportunities to devise different land-tenure arrangements for the mountain commons. (E. Ostrom 1990, p. 61)

Outside authorities such as external governments sometimes contribute to the development of these rules, sometimes detract, and usually are not necessary to their evolution. The fundamental tenet of her argument is based on a concept of human agency in which individuals are able to escape the prisoner's dilemma, the tragedy of the commons, and other apparently inevitable negative consequences that result from self-interested behavior, because they are able to reach agreement among themselves that the rules of the game are detrimental and should be changed. People can design institutions that facilitate "enlightened self-interest" rather than the blind pursuit of individual interests that result in collective calamity. Further, she argues that there is no one "right" solution to institutional design; but instead that there are many different solutions, contingent on local social norms and historical circumstances. The case studies she has examined reveal that:

> "Getting the institutions right" is a difficult, time-consuming, conflict-invoking process. It is a process that requires reliable information about time and place variables as well as a broad repertoire of culturally acceptable rules. New institutional arrangements do not work in the field as they do in abstract models unless the models are well specified and empirically valid and the participants in a field setting understand how to make the new rules work. (1990, p. 14)

The empirical studies of how communities throughout the world have dealt with common pool resources show that the models based on the tragedy of the commons, prisoner's dilemma, and Olson's theory of collective action simply were not applicable. E. Ostrom says that they may be useful for predicting behavior in large-scale [situations] where no one communicates, everyone acts independently, no attention is paid to the effects of one's actions, and the costs of trying to change the structure of the situation are high. They are far less useful for characterizing the behavior of appropriators in the smaller-scale CPRs that are the focus of this inquiry. In such situations, individuals repeatedly communicate and interact with one another. . . . It is possible that they can learn whom to trust, what effects their actions will have on each other and on the CPR, and how to organize themselves to gain benefits and avoid harm. When individuals have lived in such situations for a substantial time and have developed shared norms and patterns of reciprocity, they possess social capital with which they can build institutional arrangements for resolving CPR dilemmas. (1990, pp. 183–84)

One of the important insights of her work is that policy and institutional designs are nested within one another; and local, grassroots-initiated designs may be among the most effective in solving common pool resource problems. To assume that all designs must come from an external "government" or "bureaucracy" overlooks much of what has happened at the local level.

Ostrom (1990, pp. 90–102) suggests a limited number of design principles that, at least in the context of relatively small common pool resource situations, seem to distinguish between stable, fragile, and failed institutions. These are:

1. Clear boundaries for the CPR that delimit those eligible to use it
2. Congruent rules that are designed to fit the local circumstances
3. Collective choice arenas that permit all or almost all the persons who are impacted by the CPR or its use to participate in the design and change of the rules
4. Monitoring for compliance by persons accountable to the appropriators (those who take resources from the CPR), or by the appropriators themselves
5. Graduated sanctions so that the number, severity, and context within which the infraction occurred are taken into account
6. Conflict resolution mechanisms to which appropriators and officials have rapid, low-cost access
7. Recognized rights to organize
8. For CPRs that are part of a larger system, there should be nested units and multiple layers to handle the various tasks

Institutional analysis also posits multiple values for assessing institutions including economic efficiency, equity (based on equality of input and receipts or equality of need), accountability, consistency with public morality, and adaptability (E. Ostrom 1996).

Several other scholars have argued that the study of politics and policy should pay more attention to institutions (Lieberman, Ingram, and Schneider 1995; March and Olson 1989; Moe 1990; Skocpoll 1985). As Lieberman argued (1995), institutions not only regulate access to power, but also shape "the formation and expression of political sentiments" (p. 438). Putnam (1993, 1995) has emphasized the central role that institutions have in creating the trust and social capital needed for successful democracy, or alternatively, thwarting and undermining the cultural ties that sustain democratic possibilities.

The institutional perspective departs in important ways from the standard public choice approach. It recognizes that public policy has purposes beyond simply correcting for market failure and providing for the supply and distribution of public goods that the market is not able to handle efficiently. Instead, people working within institutional frameworks that they have created and can change are able to specify the roles that policy should play in their society. The standard posture of public choice has been to assume self-interested utility maximizing behavior is endemic regardless of the characteristics of the institutional setting in which it occurs and that such behavior will always produce inefficient (suboptimal) collective outcomes. The new institutionalists contend that people are capable of altruistic behavior, keeping their promises, and enlightened self-interest in which they recognize that their long-term interests will be served only by short-term decisions of cooperation for the benefit of the collectivity (Orbell, van de Kragt, and Dawes 1988; E. Ostrom 1990, 1992; Ostrom, Walker, and Gardner 1992). Trust and social capital within the institutional settings are essential for democratic governance (Putnam 1993).

Assessment of Public Choice

Critics of mainstream public choice have addressed the adequacy of its normative stance (the Pareto principle), the empirical accuracy of its basic assumption of self-interest utility maximization and propositions derived from it, and its implications for democracy (Elster 1986; Green and Shapiro 1994; Kelman 1987; Mansbridge 1990b; Schaff and Ingram 1986; Wright 1984). The primary challenge to the Pareto principle is that it assumes a just distribution of value within the society. To argue that actions must make one person better off and no one worse off, by their own interpretations, renders as "unjust" all redistributions in society no matter how unequal the initial distributions actually are.

The second challenge is empirical: An enormous body of experimental research has shown, repeatedly, that self-interest is not the dominant motivation for human decisions (Deutsch 1985; Green and Shapiro 1994; Wright 1984). Values and ideas are important components; decisions often belie self-interest in an effort to achieve greater fairness or to produce better results for the group. Orbell and others have shown that people keep their promises, even when not threatened with sanctions (Orbell et al. 1984; Ostrom, Walker, and Gardner 1992); people act as good Samaritans under a variety of conditions for which there is no expectation of any return. To recommend such sweeping prescriptions regarding the role of government and the institutional arrangements from a premise of self-interest that commonly is shown deficient in empirical studies is extraordinarily risky. Institutions that presume self-interest as a motivation are likely to produce such motivations, as the institutions legitimate self-seeking behavior and, furthermore, seriously disadvantage anyone who attempts to engage in more cooperative or collaborative efforts (Petracca 1991). It is not likely that societies can survive if self-interest overwhelms collective considerations ("long-term" self-interest, as some public choice scholars call it). In an especially thorough review of the empirical evidence relevant to public choice theory, Green and Shapiro noted:

> Our reviews of the literatures on voter turnout, collective action, legislative behavior, and electoral competition reveal that the empirical contributions of rational choice theory in these fields are few, far between, and considerably more modest than the combination of mystique and methodological fanfare surrounding the rational choice movement would lead one to expect. (Green and Shapiro 1994, p. 179)

The third point pertains to the impact of public choice theory on democracy. Some believe that the underlying assumptions of public choice theory are anathema to democratic governance (Mansbridge 1990b; Petracca 1991). The individualism of the theory, as Petracca notes, "nurtures the normative belief that politics should attend and respond to the needs, wants, and preferences of individuals. This stands in sharp contrast to the Platonic view that political life is about the pursuit of wisdom, knowledge, virtue, justice, and other qualities intrinsic to the 'good society'" (Petracca 1991, p. 293).

The standard public choice theory labels public-spirited behavior, whether by citizens or public officials, as "irrational" (Kelman 1987; Reich 1991). By focusing scholarly attention on the self-serving behavior of political leaders, Kelman argues, the extent of public-spirited behavior has been greatly underestimated. The theory of public choice legitimates self-interested behavior as if such actions are "natural" and therefore inevitable in the political life of a society. When institutions and public policies are designed as if self-interest is the motivating factor, then such designs not only legitimate this behavior, but actually encourage and produce it. Petracca (1990, p. 311) makes a compelling argument that public choice theory thwarts the "transformation of self-regarding individuals into public-spirited citizens" and also fails to transform private-regarding political regimes into those that can achieve the public good.

Other values of democracy simply have no place in most of the public choice theories. The role or characteristics of citizenship are not a part of public choice theory or research. There is essentially no concern about unequal distribution of power, status, or economic well-being. Values such as citizenship, community, self-development, and so on are excluded from consideration. Oppression, whether attributable to gender, race, ethnicity, religion, social class, or other values that historically have divided societies, is hidden from view.

E. Ostrom's model of institutional designs for common pool resource allocations corrects many of the deficiencies in the standard public choice paradigm, and similar contributions are made by others writing under the broad framework of "new institutionalists." In place of the self-interested egoistic individual assumed in much of the game theory literature, Ostrom posits a human being capable of self-reflection, innovation, self-interest, and artisanship (1992b, p. 83) who, through communication with others, can change the rules underlying the tragedy of the commons and the prisoner's dilemma thereby permitting cooperative behavior and self-governing institutions. Such institutions result in reasonably acceptable and durable allocation of scarce resources. Without using the same language, her premises have much in common with the communicative rationality and communicative ethics suggested by critical theory.

CRITICAL THEORIES

Critical theories have in common an overriding concern with oppression and domination in modern advanced societies and a commitment to radically participatory, nonhierarchical forms of political, economic, and social interaction. The philosophical and methodological orientations of critical theory stand in sharp contrast to the three theories of policy already presented. Critical theory posits a different understanding of what is meant by "rationality" and challenges many of the taken-for-granted tenets of modern society. Critical perspectives challenge the contention that scientific knowledge is superior to other forms and raise serious questions about whether scientific and technological discoveries will lead to a better society. The struggle to create a society without oppression and domination where all people can be free to realize their potential has been a central concern of critical theorists from Marx, who is generally credited as being the first critical theorist, through the Frankfurt School to modern-day writers (Dryzek 1990, 1996a, 1996b; Fay 1987; Habermas 1975; Held 1980; Leonard 1990; Young 1990). Unlike public choice and pluralist theories whose goal is to produce new knowledge, and unlike policy sciences whose goal is to improve public policy, the goal of critical theory is to produce social change that will empower, enlighten, and emancipate all people.

Fay defines critical perspectives as those theories that "want to explain a social order in such a way that it [the theory] becomes itself the catalyst which leads to the transformation of this social order" (1987, p. 28). Critical theories need to offer their audience (those who are oppressed) an alternative conception of who they are, providing them with a new and radically different picture of their political, economic, and social order. Critical social science also aims to empower its audience to take action which, in turn, may lead to their emancipation from oppression.

Leonard (1990, p. 4) specifies the parameters of a critical theory that can "inform an emancipatory practice" as follows:

It must locate the sources of domination in actual social practices; it must project an alternative vision (or at least the outline) of a life free from such domination; and it must craft these tasks in the idiom, so to speak, of its addressees—or risk seeing the practical-emancipatory project recede ever further into the distance of abstract philosophical speculation far removed from the concerns of daily life.

Bernstein (1995) points out that critical theory portends a different way of knowing in which philosophical thinking and self-reflection are joined with social scientific knowledge providing a theory that is both critical and practical. Critical theory takes its cues from opposition to the injustices in society and places itself in opposition to the theories and methodologies that sustain and legitimate injustice.

Of all the theories considered here, critical theory has developed the broadest, most extensive critique encompassing positivism, instrumental rationality, technology, secularism, science, consumerism, media, mass culture, and other attributes of modernity. Their critique of the U.S. political system rejects explanations that emphasize individual failures as the source of social problems. Instead, critical theorists focus on macrostructural and institutional explanations for the pathologies of the society. Culture, ideology, distribution of power and wealth, fundamental economic relationships within the workplace, and the structural characteristics of political institutions are viewed as more important than individual decisions and behavior in understanding social problems ranging from mental illness and violence to environmental degradation. Critical theorists argue that people are born into cultures and institutions from which they gain their identity and characteristic patterns of thinking and acting. Inequality and discrimination are deeply ingrained in identities. Even though human agency over time may alter the culture and institutions, it is difficult for human beings to see through the dominant beliefs of their society.

In public policy, critical theory is often associated with postpositivist, interpretist, interactionist, and neo-Marxist perspectives. Direct applications of critical theory to public policy in the United States are found in Edelman (1964, 1988), whose work unmasks and deconstructs the political process, showing how symbols are used to confuse and deceive the public. John Gaventa (1980) analyzes power and alienation in an Appalachian community whose residents are blind to the hidden systematic controls that rule their lives. Critical theorists are found across many policy domains including public administration (Denhardt 1984; Fischer 1990; Forester 1985; Yanow 1993), environmentalism (Dryzek 1987), education (Freire 1993, 1994; Giroux and McClaren 1989; McClaren 1995), criminal and juvenile justice (Bortner 1988; Bortner and Williams 1997; Currie 1985; Simon 1993), welfare policy (Piven and Cloward 1988; Schram 1993), and family and women's policies (Diamond 1983; Hawkesworth 1988; Young 1990).

Policy scholars with a critical frame of reference have critiqued the policy science movement, pointing out that the increased reliance on policy analysis, science, and technological approaches discourages citizen discussion of issues, thereby producing alienation and low levels of citizen participation (Dunn 1982; Fischer

1990, 1992, 1995; Fischer and Forester 1993; Hawkesworth 1988; Schram 1993; Stone 1988). New forms of policy analysis and research have been developed that draw on the normative principles of critical theory (Dryzek 1990; Dryzek and Berejikian 1993; Fischer 1985; White 1986). There also is considerable common ground between critical theory and theories of participatory democracy. Lance deHaven-Smith (1988) compares Lindblom's radical pluralism with Habermas's critical theory in an analysis of U.S. welfare policy. Benjamin Barber (1984) advocates "strong" forms of democracy to replace the "weak" forms found in liberal democracy. An extended application of critical theory to public policy in the United States is found in John Dryzek's work, especially *Discursive Democracy* (1990) and *Democracy and Capitalism* (1996), where he draws on principles of critical theory to construct a vision of politics, policy making, governance, and policy analysis for an advanced democratic society.

Most critical theorists view government and the public policies it produces as part of the problem in the United States, rather than as potentially positive means for reducing domination and oppression. Government and policy are part of the institutional structures of society that have created and maintained systems of privilege, domination, and quiescence among those who are the most oppressed (deHaven Smith 1988; Dryzek 1990, 1996a; Fay 1987; Habermas 1975; Hawkesworth 1988; Schram 1993). The fundamental problem with public policy is that it controls, coerces, deceives, and then is legitimized by being linked (often illogically) to widely held normative beliefs.

Critical theory is not a homogenous set of principles, research questions, or propositions, but is a broadly drawn theory with far more central concepts and theoretical logics than can be covered here. Those selected for inclusion are the ones most relevant for public policy and democracy:

- Communicative rationality and the ideal speech situation
- A critical theory of democracy that is variously called discursive, deliberative, communicative, or participatory
- A critical theory of administration, and postpositivist methodologies for planning, policy analysis, and social science research

From Instrumental Rationality to Communicative Rationality

Communicative rationality is posed as an alternative to instrumental reason and technological rationality, both of which critical theorists believe have become sources of domination and oppression within society. Critical theorists have essentially the same operational definition of instrumental rationality as public choice and other scholars: An instrumentally rational action is one in which optimal means are used to achieve clearly defined goals. There is an important difference, however, in that critical theorists believe the ideology of modern societies has privileged instrumental rationality to the extent that it has displaced other forms of rationality. To a critical theorist, an instrumentally rational person is one whose thoughts, actions, and being are dominated entirely by the means/ends nexus. An instrumentally rational person is one who is always engaged in calculation, acquisition, consumerism, and self-interest. The potential of human reason is much greater than this, according to critical theorists, and instrumental rationality truncates and subverts the potential for true human emancipation.

Instrumental rationality is considered to be dehumanizing because it defines as "nonrational" much of the cognitive processes normally included in human action, deliberation, and decision making. Instrumental rationality can be juxtaposed against normative or philosophical standards of behavior in which a person does what is "right" rather than what is the most efficient means toward a given end. Thus, instrumental rationality undermines the moral and philosophical beliefs of a society. Other forms of knowing, such as emotion, understanding, and intuition, are devalued by instrumental reason unless they can be "used" to promote instrumental ends. Human attributes such as joy, love, friendship, creativity, and discovery, are displaced into the "irrational" or "nonrational" aspects of human behavior and are not valued as ends in themselves. As instrumentally rational behavior becomes highly valued in some spheres of life—such as economic activity—it gradually moves into other spheres, creating what Weber called an "iron cage" around human existence, and what Habermas referred to as "colonization of the life-world" where even the most personal interactions become distorted due to instrumental and strategic behavior.

Critical theorists also contend that instrumental rationality has distorted our understanding of what it means to be human and our relationship to other species and to the earth. When instrumental rationality is viewed as the highest form of reason, it grants to human beings a justification for dominating other species, the earth, and the environment. Science and technology, which embody the principles of instrumental reason, are valued more than other forms of knowledge because of their potential for enabling human control of the earth, environment, and behavior, as well as promoting economic and military superiority. Scientific knowledge and technology become a dominating ideology, as illustrated by the language associated with science. For example, scientific and technical discoveries or inventions are invariably referred to as scientific "advances" or technological "progress." It is almost impossible to think of any scientific or technological discovery that people believe should not have occurred, or any topic that should not be studied. New knowledge seems immune from criticism. Even the controversy over nuclear energy and the nuclear bomb focuses on political decisions about how it should be used rather than the wisdom of it having been discovered.

Instrumental action also is considered to be dehumanizing because it privileges strategic, success-oriented behavior and legitimates efforts by people to gain for themselves at the expense of others. It legitimates some people exercising control and influence over others, as needed, to pursue the most efficient means toward a goal.

Instrumental rationality undermines democracy because it disempowers ordinary people. As scientific expertise increasingly dominates policy contexts and policy designs, ordinary people are shut out of the discussions about both means and ends. Even the goals of policy become the province of experts who choose those that the scientific and technical communities believe are achievable with current technologies and mechanisms of social control. Means are selected not because they are the ones most preferred by people who will be impacted, but because they maximize benefits over costs, as determined by scientific policy analysis conducted by highly trained social scientists using the methodologies of modern policy analysis. Instrumental rationality is used to justify hierarchical control. With expertise located at the top of an organization, orders can be given to those below, enabling coordination and control of all activities that presumably will eliminate wasteful duplication and poor coordination across the many complex parts of the organization. Even if this organization is efficient—a contention that is increasingly challenged by social scientists and laypersons alike—it falls far short of most understandings of democracy.

Another charge against instrumental rationality is that it cannot resolve complex public policy problems nor can it coordinate social interaction. Dryzek (1990) makes a solid case that even the most complex scientific models cannot produce acceptable policy solutions in complex policy situations. Complex problems involve multiple goals that often conflict and must be balanced against one another. The means also carry values quite apart from their contribution to goal achievement. Attempts to find optimal solutions fail when goals have to be balanced against one another and when the values attached to means have to be weighed against the value of the goals themselves. Science, without extensive interaction and communication among persons who will be impacted by the policy, simply cannot justify one solution over another. Instrumental rationality also cannot coordinate social interaction to produce decisions acceptable to those participating. Both the positive (deductive) versions of public choice and the empirical studies of games show that the rational self-interested pursuit of individual goals in the absence of communication among participants leads to collective results that are disastrous for all concerned or at least far below the optimum that the collectivity could have achieved. When communication is allowed, however, the group is far more likely to arrive at a collectively "rational" or optimal result (Johnson 1993; Orbell, van de Kragt, and Dawes 1988).

Communicative rationality is proposed by critical theorists as an alternative to instrumental rationality. Communicative rationality refers to attempts to reach understanding among persons who are not attempting to control one another but are coming to an understanding among themselves (Seidman 1989, p. 157).

Communication, however, will not necessarily produce understanding or collectively desired outcomes because communication often is distorted by power, hegemonic ideologies, wealth, and status. Distorted communication is a form of control rather than a form of liberation. Habermas posited four standards that communication should meet if it is to be considered rational rather than distorted. These differ somewhat from one translation to another, but the four refer generally to whether the communication is *comprehensible, sincere, right (ethical, legitimate),* and *true* (Forester 1985a; Seidman 1989).

The standards are relevant for face-to-face communication as well as for macrolevel or structural communication. At the face-to-face level, comprehensible refers to clarity, lack of confusion, and lack of misunderstanding in the communication. Sincerity is the absence of deceit, self-deceit, hidden agendas, and misrepresentation of the motives of the speaker. The rightness, or ethical, dimension refers to how the communication fits into the prevailing norms and understandings of what is "right" to do or say. Truthfulness refers to whether the communication contains correct information and whether the information can be validated. At a macrostructural level, such as in a public policy statute, comprehensibility could be judged by the complexity and extent to which jargon mystifies and confuses the meaning of the policy. Sincerity might be judged in terms of whether the public interest has been adequately expressed and whether the stated goals and rationales are an accurate reflection of the actual reasons for the policy. The ethical or legitimate aspects of the policy might be assessed in terms of whether the person or groups that promulgated the policy had the right to do so, or whether it violates constitutional or other norms. The truthfulness could be judged by whether the stated goals or problems to be solved have been accurately analyzed, whether the internal logic within the policy is based on accepted theories, or whether expected results have been concealed, misrepresented, or based on incorrect assumptions.

The context within which undistorted communication can occur and consensus reached on what should be done is called an ideal speech situation. In it, all individuals are equally competent and are able to express their points of view, discuss, understand each other, and reach consensus. The communication in an ideal speech situation should meet the four standards of communicative rationality noted previously. In an ideal speech situation, agreements will be reached on the basis of the best arguments rather than on the basis of power, wealth, status, intimidation, or any other factors.

Dryzek (1990, p. 14), writing more explicitly with public policy in mind, said that communicative rationality requires a context "free from deception, self-deception, strategic behavior and domination through the exercise of power." Communicative rationality, he continued, "is a property of intersubjective discourse, not individual maximization, and it can pertain to the generation of normative judgments and action principles rather than just to the selection of means to ends." Dryzek further argued (p. 15) that communicative rationality obtains to the degree social interaction is free from the exercise of power, strategizing by the actors, and self-deception.

In a public policy context, the ideal speech situation and communicative rationality need to take into account both the access of persons to the arena and their communicative competence (Dryzek 1990; Young 1996). All actors and persons potentially impacted by the policy should be included. All should be equally and fully capable of making and questioning arguments—that is, they should be communicatively competent. "The only remaining authority," Dryzek said (p. 15), "is that of a good argument, which can be advanced on behalf of the veracity of empirical description, explanation, and understanding and, equally important, the validity of normative judgements."

The empirical underpinnings of arguments should be based on accepted factual information that is free of distortion, bias, and error. Such information should be accessible and comprehensible to all parties. The normative dimension of communicative rationality must be backed up with good reasons. Arguments can be made on behalf of normative positions by showing consistency with a broader system of values or membership in a set of beliefs to which almost all members of the community adhere. Communicative rationality does not imply an absolute principle of a substantive nature; but instead it defines a context within which issues can be discussed and consensus achieved. The procedures are discursive and tolerate many different values, beliefs, and practices. Dryzek (1990) argued that the discussions do not generate any universal normative or empirical theory that is independent of the context in which the discussions are taking place.

Communicative rationality is closely aligned with the concept of *practical reason* (Anderson 1993; Hawkesworth 1988). Practical reason traces its roots to Aristotle's *phronesis*—the capability for self-consciously and self-reflectively finding the best course of action within the given situation, taking into account values and cultural understandings that cannot readily be separated from the "facts." Practical reason implies that people can reason together and take into account goals, purposes, value judgments, right and wrong conduct, and so forth rather than simply self-interest or who pays and who benefits (Anderson 1993). Through discursive practices, people can conceptualize the common good and arrive at policies or practices that they believe will promote the common good. It is possible through communicative rationality to conceptualize a public interest that should be served by public policy.

Communicative rationality presents a different set of standards for judging public policy processes and designs than those found in the other three theories discussed earlier. All three of the other theories assume that most public policy will be made by formal governments composed of elected officials who appoint professionals to serve as implementing and service delivery personnel. Pluralism and policy sciences especially seem to assume a representative (republican) form of government whereas communicative rationality implies direct self-governance. Even though one could apply the standards of communicative rationality to a legislative or administrative body (and it would be useful to do so), it is difficult to argue that policy making or implementation by these groups would be as communicatively rational—using the standards of communicative rationality—as policy making by the group for whom the policy will be binding. The other three perspectives all assume that one of the principle functions of government is to deal with conflict among constituent groups and that conflicts often will have to be resolved through negotiation, bargaining, and eventually an authoritative decision made by an outside administrative or legislative body. Critical theory implies that consensus should be the goal, that consensus usually can be reached, and that the decision should be made by direct democracy among the persons impacted by it, not by "outside" authorities. In this sense, critical theorists and the institutional branch of public choice should find a close alliance.

The styles of interaction implied by communicative rationality differ markedly from pluralist and policy science assumptions about interactions. Pluralism legitimates bargaining and negotiating among the various interests, with each attempting to structure the context so that they "win" and gain resources or favorable rules from public policy. In its most degenerative form, pluralism involves confrontations among groups, each of whom wants to ensure that the other loses and wants to inflict as much discredit and dishonor on the other as possible. Policy sciences envision that goals should be chosen by political processes, but the means should be chosen by experts. In contrast, critical theory suggests that interactions should focus on building understanding about how the problem should be framed, what goals should be pursued, and which strategies will be most acceptable to the collectivity. There is a role here for instrumental rationality in the sense of providing information to the group and insisting on the principles of logical reasoning about the relationship of means to ends. The information provided by scientific policy analysis, however, is only one source and is subject to discussion, challenge, and various interpretations. In addition, it is only one kind of information, as participants also draw on their own experiences, values, perspectives, causal thinking, and so forth.

Strengthening and Deepening Democracy

Critical theory has focused mainly on critique and on uncovering the many different forms of domination in society. The test of the theory, however, lies in whether oppressed people are better off as a result of the theory. This places considerable importance on having a practical program of action that can be carried out consistent with the principles of critical theory. Many critical theorists focus on democracy as the forum within which modern societies might be transformed (Barber 1984; Dryzek 1990, 1996a; Pateman 1970, 1989; Young 1990). There is, however, considerable disagreement about the locus of the transformation (e.g., state, economy, public sphere), the means for the transformation (e.g., reconstructed democratic politics, revolution, deconstructive/reconstructive policy analysis, creation of alternative rhetorics to challenge dominant discourses), or the people who might lead the way (e.g., students/academics, working-class people, feminists, environmentalists).

Dryzek's work (1990, 1996a, 1996b) represents perhaps the best-developed framework for applying the principles of critical theory to public policy among

U.S. critical theorists. Dryzek (1990) argued that communicative rationality and Habermas's conception of an ideal speech situation can serve as useful counter-factuals (situations that, even though they do not and probably cannot ever exist, can serve as standards against which to judge extant institutions and practices). A discursive democracy rests on a discourse that is oriented toward reciprocal under-standing, trust, and an undistorted consensus about what should be done. Dryzek argues that even though some progress might be made in attempts to democratize within the state, the best chance for transformation will occur through political movements in the public sphere (civic society, outside the state, between the peo-ple and formal government).

Model discursive institutions can be characterized both by what they are *not* and by their positive attributes. In a discursive design, no individuals possess authority on the basis of anything other than a good argument. Hierarchies would not exist. Thus, the primary political institutions of liberal democracies including representative government in which people elect others to represent their interests would not be allowed. Dryzek (1990, p. 41) says that discursive institutions would have no barriers to participation and there would be no externally autonomous for-mal constitution or rules. All the rules would be made by the group itself and could be changed by the group whenever it was important to do so. Meaningful partici-pation, Dryzek (1990) argued, requires communicatively competent persons, and some educative mechanisms may need to be in place to assure that all participants are communicatively competent.

There would be a system of communicative ethics such as those suggested by Fisher and Ury (1981) or Forester (1985a). The Fisher and Ury rules (Dryzek 1990, p. 41) are:

- Separation of individual egos from the problem-solving tasks at hand
- Emphasis on the interests of parties rather than on bargaining position
- Efforts to generate proposals of net benefit to all the actors involved
- A striving for criteria separate from the (particular) interests of each party

Dryzek adds a number of ethical criteria of his own. Disagreements should revolve around alternative conceptions of the *public* interest rather than strategic manipulation on behalf of *private* interests. Individuals should participate as *citi-zens,* Dryzek says, "not as representatives of the state or any other corporate and hierarchical body" (Dryzek 1990, p. 43). In his 1996 work, he defines the public sphere as a place where public, rather than private, interests dominate. There should be some educative effort to ensure that everyone who has an interest in the issue can participate effectively. Complicity in the state, or administration by the state, should be avoided. There should be no hierarchy or formal rules other than the ethics of communication. The decision rule should be consensus on what is to be done, even if consensus cannot be reached on why. Finally, the participants should be free to establish the principles and any rules that they believe are needed and to change these through the same discursive process.

Dryzek describes several incipient discursive designs, such as mediation, participatory or principled regulatory negotiation, and new social movements. He contends that these all involve a conflict of some type, disagreement over how to resolve it, facilitation by a third party who brings the groups together but does not impose or enforce agreements, prolonged face-to-face discussions governed by ethical rules, an effort to achieve agreement on what will be done, and voluntary compliance with whatever is agreed to. Discursive designs in the public sphere would serve at least as a buffer or facilitator enabling people to confront the power of formal government, and in a more optimistic scenario, might serve as a real-world example enabling far more fundamental transformation of formal government institutions.

As for strategies, Dryzek (1996) suggests social movements such as solidarity in Poland that actually enabled people to live as if they were in a far more democratic society than actually existed, and then were able to quickly move into the vacuum created by the collapse of the Communist state and economy. Deconstructive and reconstructive policy analysis has been used to influence public policy (Fischer 1992), and creation of different policy arguments, rationales, or the even deeper notion of discourses may enable cultural change to occur (Dryzek 1996; Fischer and Forrester 1993; Majone 1989).

Participatory Administration, Planning, Policy Analysis, and Research

Even though most critical theorists reject the notion that formal government can be democratized to the extent that it serves a nonrepressive society, there are some who are more optimistic and have outlined strategies for working within the state and across the boundaries between the state and the public sphere (Denhardt 1981, 1984; Fischer 1988; Fischer and Forester 1993; Forester 1985a, 1989; Kemp 1985).

Denhardt (1984, p. 171) says that a good place to begin in the application of critical theory to public organizations is with the structural limitations in communicative practices. "Specifically, a critical theory of public organizations would examine the technical basis of bureaucratic domination and the ideological justifications given for the domination" (1984, p. 171). Hierarchical communication patterns would have to be removed both within the organization and between the organization and its clientele. Management would be aimed not at control but rather at assisting individuals (members or clients) in discovering and pursuing their own developmental needs. There should be an "educative" approach that helps people see their true needs as well as understanding of the relationship between bureaucrats and clients that would show how bureaucracies exercise power over clients and how they subject clients to rigid and depersonalized procedures. This limits the contribution that clients might make to the operation of the agency. Denhardt sees critical public bureaucracies serving as a primary vehicle for societal self-reflection and critique (1974, p. 173).

Forester (1988) suggests that administrators should think of planning as an "attention-shaping" exercise, rather than a technical project of finding means to politically defined ends. Instead of the message "leave it to us [the planners]," Forester (1985a, p. 219) urges planners to:

- Cultivate community networks
- Listen to the concerns and interests of all participants
- Notify less-organized interests early in the planning process
- Educate citizens and community organizations about the issues
- Supply technical and political information to all parties
- Work to see that community and neighborhood nonprofessional organizations have access to information
- Encourage neighborhood groups to press for open hearings
- Encourage community-based independent reviews of projects and reports
- Assist community-based groups in exerting countervailing pressure against vested interests

Critical theorists carry their principles into the methodologies of social research and policy analysis, thereby fundamentally altering the relationship between researcher/analyst and those who are being studied. Positivist and Popperian methodologies emphasizing causal analysis intended to explain, predict, and eventually control natural or human processes are considered detrimental to democracy by many critical theorists. These methodologies create a new group of experts (policy analysts and researchers) thereby further limiting the role of ordinary people in decisions that affect them. Rather than a cadre of experts who gain authority through their empirical and causal studies, critical theory envisions a style of policy analysis and research that is self-reflective, participatory, and consistent with the principles of communicative ethics.

Policy analysis and research should uncover the empirical and normative assumptions within the discourse about the policy issues and should, itself, be a force for fairness and justice among the various parties. The policy research should involve all the impacted groups (the "stakeholders" or "constituencies") in a dialogue designed to reach agreement on the efficacy of various arguments that have been presented. Fischer (1985, p. 23) says that a critical evaluation study "is one that explicates (for the purposes of discourse) the full range of empirical and normative assumptions that contribute to a particular judgment, from manifest to latent, from concrete to abstract."

Critical theory does not necessarily imply that empirical methodologies—even causal analysis—should be replaced with phenomenological (interpretive) or philosophical (normative), but offers a strategy to integrate different kinds of knowledge (Fischer 1985, 1995; White 1986). Society relies on several types of knowledge as does public policy. Policy debates virtually always include discussions about "facts" (e.g., how many murders were there last year in the metropolitan area?), the interpretation of those facts (e.g., is this better or worse than before?

How frightened are people about this? What kinds of events and behavior were included in the definition of "murder"?), normative and philosophical arguments (Are all murders wrong? Are all kinds equally wrong and therefore appropriately punished in the same way?), and causal questions (e.g., why are there so many murders? Who commits murder? Will severe punishment deter murder?).

Critical methodologies generally assume there is no answer that should be considered "true" for all times and all places, but that through discourse a more limited and contingent type of "truth" may emerge. One of the goals of the research is to facilitate discussions that may result in consensus and agreement about what constitutes the relevant "facts" in the situation, which values or norms are important to take into account, and how much validity there is to competing interpretations and competing causal logics. Research, then, does not establish an objective or universal truth, but by facilitating informed discussions, consensus may be reached on facts, interpretations, norms to be applied, or causal logics, and these serve as "objective" or "true" within the context because people have agreed to them (Jennings 1987).

Assessment of Critical Theory

Critical theory has much to offer the study of public policy. It takes a broader view of politics and policy, weaving both into the web of social and economic relationships. The standards of communicative rationality are an important addition to the more traditional values used in assessing public policy. Critical theory calls attention to justice as a central standard that should be considered in policy analysis. Within critical theory, democracy is a way of life, not simply a process of selecting political leaders. Critical perspectives on the normative underpinnings of society provide the basis for a more active, empathic understanding of citizenship. Also important for our purposes is the emphasis critical theory places on how the social construction of reality constrains and limits human potential.

Critical theorists tend to be their own best (worst) critics. A central concern regarding critical theory and public policy is whether critical theory has lost its practical intent. Leonard (1990, p. 50) says:

> Neither the Frankfurt School nor Habermas succeed in giving critical theory a grounding that would preserve its practical intentions. It would appear then, that the idea of a critical theory remains just that—an idea. . . . Without a practical dimension, critical theory cannot achieve its own stated aim of helping those who suffer from domination and unfreedom to understand the sources of their oppression, and emancipate themselves from that oppression.

In response, however, critical theorists can point to many recent efforts to correct this problem, to make their work more accessible, and to infuse the principles of critical theory widely into the practice of social science research and theory. This is exemplified by the plethora of alternative research strategies: "action" research, "advocacy" research, "participatory" research, critical policy analysis, and critical planning methodologies. The increased number of critical policy studies previously cited emphasizes the applicability of a critical analysis of contemporary public policy.

A second concern is whether critical theory is applicable in any meaningful way to contemporary society. It seems to require people to be remarkably free of self-interest and competitiveness and to live in small-scale, self-governing communities where considerable time and effort can be devoted to civic life. How can critical theory deal effectively with conflict, polarization, and deeply entrenched opposing systems of belief? The ideal speech situation seldom exists in practice, and discussions seldom meet the standards set for true communicative rationality unless the group involved has excluded parties with different points of view, thereby undermining one of its principles of including all potentially impacted parties. There seems to be inadequate provision for irreconcilable differences and no means to resolve conflicts when consensus cannot be reached. Enormous power is granted to only a few persons—the holdouts—when consensus is required before action can be taken. Permitting a few recalcitrants to block agreement and subsequent action is hardly consistent with the notion that the only form of power should be the best argument. On the other hand, the solutions to this problem advanced by the other perspectives also can be criticized.

Pluralism recognizes the legitimacy of rules that govern actions and are applied consistently across many different institutions, such as plurality, majority, or super majority voting, definitions of eligibility for voting, rules governing the terms of debate, rules about giving proper notice, rules concerning basic rights that cannot be altered without extensive "rounds" of voting by different bodies, and so forth. These rules permit those who are more numerous or more organized to exercise power over others, even though there may not have been an adequate airing of the various points of view, and some may not have had the opportunity to participate at all. On the other hand, they permit decisions to be made that will alter the status quo even when some want to protect it. Policy science theory typically assumes there is a "best" choice and that it can be found by empirical studies of benefits and costs rather than by arguments and discussion among impacted parties. Both of these perspectives permit some to exercise power over others, against their will, without being compensated in any way, and therefore an argument can be made that they are not necessarily superior choices to the consensus envisioned by communicative rationality. Nevertheless, the critical theories grounded in communicative rationality probably do not deal with conflict as well as they should, and in practice would need to adopt many of the procedural rules and practices of liberal pluralism to avoid permitting small minorities of people to be able to protect the status quo against change, no matter how unjust the status quo happens to be.

Another concern is that communicative rationality and the ideal speech situation may only substitute some types of power for others, rather than achieving true equality among all people. What would it mean to replace the traditional types of pluralist political power (e.g., the size of the group, intensity of preferences, their ability to mobilize) by the power of persuasion, charisma, personal relationships, and logical arguments? Does communicative rationality displace the power of economics and politics into a personal and intellectual arena in which those who are well educated, charismatic, or popular have a much expanded role? The power of persuasion and charisma has at times been used in oppressive ways against women, racial and ethnic groups, and religious groups; thus policy-making processes that move toward the discursive model held out by critical theory need to be attentive to these possibilities. In spite of these issues, communicative rationality and communicative ethics have much to be said in their favor when compared with the self-interest–dominated pluralist processes or the expert-dominated scientific processes.

There is also a question about how helpful critical theory is in identifying oppression and whether it is helpful to those who are oppressed. Fay (1987, p. 28) said that critical social scientists must enlighten those who are oppressed by offering a theory "which explains why these people are frustrated and unsatisfied, why they are doomed to continue in this condition, given their conception of themselves and their social order, and why it is that they have these conceptions."

Fraser (1987), however, has questioned whether the critical theory of Habermas is helpful in identifying and analyzing male dominance over women. She contends that the categories he uses inadvertently perpetuate certain stereotypes and systems of privilege that men have enjoyed over women for centuries. There is no question that Marxism and neo-Marxism brought to public attention the repressive characteristics of capitalism; and the original Frankfurt School of Marcuse, Horkheimer, and Adorno made clear the oppressiveness of ideology, science, and technology. Yet these same theories may contain hidden assumptions that work to the disadvantage of other oppressed groups.

Finally, there is the continuing question of how fundamental change might occur. Where is the impulse for critique and reform to come from if the powerless cannot speak for themselves and the powerful have no incentive? It seems fair to say, however, that critical theorists are always working on these issues and searching for ways (such as through action or participatory research) to enable oppressed people to find a voice and avenue. Critical theory is open to a variety of sites for change including change through the cultural transformation of values, through fundamental change in the economic system, or through fundamental democratization of the state. Still, critical theories are much better at critique then they are at forging a vision or practical plan of how to get from the current political and economic systems, with their powerful resistance to fundamental change, to a more desired future.

In spite of the dilemmas of critical theory, it fills important gaps left by the other theories and we draw on critical ideas extensively in the sections that follow. One contribution is that policy should serve justice, including distributive justice as well as the elimination of oppression. Another is that policy should facilitate a new form of active, involved, empathetic citizenship. Pluralism, policy science, and public choice all have a too-narrow understanding of justice and a limited view of citizenship. The failure to examine the role of public policy in creating a just society and enabling an active citizenship has resulted in these values being largely ignored. Policy is not being held to a very high standard when issues of justice and citizenship are considered outside the range of its responsibilities.

Communicative rationality and communicative ethics could have central roles to play in a policy-making process that rejects some of the overly competitive, self-interested, and strategic features of pluralism and replaces them with a revised institutional culture in which the "rules of the game" emphasize cooperation, the collective good, and are more discursive, open, and fair to all impacted parties.

Critical theory also has called to our attention the idea that public policy is most dangerous when it succeeds in placating the public, disguises the inequalities that are tolerated and exacerbated by government, yet appears to be produced through a process that is open, competitive, and accessible. The power of media, the state, the economic arrangements, and other institutions to socially construct reality so that people believe they are living in a fair and just society is a fundamentally important insight that has not been integrated adequately into theories of public policy. We draw heavily on this insight in our theory of design. Critical and participatory democratic perspectives also are important because they argue that the transformation of society will require that people become educated about their latent interests, that the privileges held by advantaged segments of society are unmasked, that the ways in which policy serves advantaged groups and perpetuates their privileges be exposed, and that social science research should be redirected toward these ends. Even though many critical theorists are not optimistic that public policy will be used for any of these ends but likely will remain a tool of powerful economic interests, we believe the insights from critical theory will make significant contributions to an improved theory of public policy.

4
Foundations, Elements, and Consequences of Design

The thesis of this book is that policy designs have significant consequences for democracy. Designs are strongly implicated in the public policy failures so apparent over the past decades and in the declining citizen involvement in politics and lack of respect for governing institutions. Theories of public policy should be helpful in explaining how and why policy designs so commonly fail to serve democratic ends; yet as we have documented in the previous two chapters, the pluralist theory of democratic policy making has not done so, and even though the alternatives contain worthy ideas, each has significant shortcomings.

Pluralism has much to offer in its model of policy making, including its emphasis on the ways in which political power and political institutions interact to exert influence on policy makers, and the idea of an "invisible hand" that guides the system toward self-corrections when policy does not meet public expectations. Our observations, however, are that the policy-making process seldom works that way. The pluralist description of how the system "actually" works is much closer to a vision of how it "might" work—and undoubtedly there are examples of policy making that have resembled the pluralist model. The shortcomings of pluralist theory, however, are severe. Its premise that political power is widespread and that political institutions grant relatively equal access to all citizens is seldom observed in practice. Pluralism does not pay sufficient attention to the hidden and subtle forms of power (the "second" and "third" face of power) through which issues and societal conditions are socially constructed. Pluralism has not offered a sufficient set of concepts to describe policy designs and at least partly for this reason has failed to incorporate the insights from policy science and critical theory regarding the role of science and professionalism in shaping design choices and the pervasive influence of social constructions on policy choices. The values posed by pluralism—particularly those of responsiveness and accountability—are central to any theory linking policy to democracy, however, as are many of the institutions of pluralist democracy. The problem with pluralism as Dryzek (1996a) has said is that it offers a true democratic experience to only a few citizens, holds out the promise of democracy to others, and offers only the illusion of democracy to the remainder.

Policy science insights are important not only because they call our attention to the role of scientific theories and professionalized bureaucracies in policy design, but also because they emphasize that policy should be logical and should be able to solve collective problems. Policy science injects a much more optimistic view of the possibilities for government and holds out the hope that society will identify collective goals to be pursued and will choose efficient mechanisms to reach them. Public choice, in its standard form, has some similarities in its emphasis on efficiency of government, but it is far more pessimistic about the role of public policy in society and argues that governments usually are inefficient. Public choice feeds cynicism about government in much the way that pluralism has undermined more optimistic views of what democracy might achieve. Policy science and public choice also are deficient because efficiency is not the only value served by public policy. Furthermore, neither has offered a persuasive theory of how the policy-making process works and what its effects are on democracy.

Critical theory is difficult to apply, and its prescriptions for policy making that rely on communicative rationality and communicative ethics seem impossibly utopian. Nevertheless, critical theory's insights about the social construction of reality and how social constructions control people's beliefs and values need to be incorporated into public policy theory. Its ethical and normative standards for the process of communication are important corrections not only to the overly rationalistic view of the policy sciences and public choice, but also to the overly strategic and cynical processes permitted by pluralism. Justice, understood broadly, needs to be incorporated into the standards against which policy is judged.

In its own way, each of these theories has important insights and contributions; yet they do not speak to one another and have not integrated their perspectives into a more comprehensive theory of public policy. Each of these theories operates from a narrow value perspective and posits only one or two important roles for public policy in a democracy. Policy designs that pursue only one value almost always work to the disadvantage of other values. An integrated theory is needed that can posit multiple values for policy to serve in a democracy. None of these theories has developed an adequate conceptual framework to describe the characteristics of policy designs along dimensions that are important in understanding how policy affects citizens and other aspects of democracy within the society. The lack of a well-developed set of concepts to describe and compare policy designs, we believe, also is a primary reason these theories have overlooked some critically important independent variables that are as influential as political power and institutions in shaping the types of designs that exist. Specifically, analysis of policy designs reveals that the social construction of target populations and the social construction of knowledge (science and facts) are embedded within designs themselves and therefore the processes that produce these constructions must be important causal determinants of policy design. Policy theory and research also are not likely to make much progress in relating designs (as independent variables) to conditions of democracy until those aspects of policy design that impart meaning and shape beliefs of citizens are identified.

Others before us have recognized the importance of policy design and wrestled with the issues we have raised. In the next section of this chapter we will examine previous work on policy design to glean the insights they have offered. Following this brief review, the chapter sets forth the broad framework for a causal theory of policy design showing how policy designs are dynamically produced by their context and how they dynamically impact context. We then advance a more detailed and comprehensive framework for describing policy design elements emphasizing the material and symbolic dimensions that have the most important implications for democratic values.

EVOLUTION OF POLICY DESIGN THEORY

Even though the systematic study of design is relatively new within the social sciences, the idea that social relationships, policies, and institutions are designed by human decision rather than preordained by a divine or natural law is a fundamental tenet of liberal democratic thought and is deeply ingrained into American political culture. That democracy means an opportunity for people to make choices was clear to the designers of the Constitution. Federalist paper number one, for example, defines the major challenge facing the United States as:

> whether societies of men are really capable or not of establishing good government from reflection and choice, or whether they are forever destined to depend for their political constitutions on accidents and forces. (Alexander Hamilton, *Federalist I,* New York: Mentor Books, 1962, p. 33)

Legislation, guidelines, pronouncements, court rulings, programs, and practices of formal governments and private associations have designs as do constitutions. All these designs were created through dynamic processes involving characteristics of the context, human decision making, and human agency. These designs have effects, most recognizably on the alleviation of problems and the attainment of purposes, but also on many other characteristics of the society.

Herbert Simon was an early pioneer in an interdisciplinary field that has come to be known as design science, which is concerned not with the necessary, but with the contingent and not with how things are but how things might be made to be (1981). This notion of design by intentional choice is very close to the conception of the democratic exercise of general will or self-government.

Although the design perspective emphasizes the intentional and purposeful actions of human beings, it does not assume people are self-interested utility maximizers. Simon issued one of the earliest challenges to the notion that self-interest utility maximizing behavior reflects human reason and rationality. He argued that people are more likely to "satisfice" than to "maximize." Scholars who focus on the *processes* through which human action occurs find that people are multifaceted and do not follow any single rule of behavior, such as self-interest. Instead, they are intentional, purposeful, spontaneous, intuitive, self-reflective, creative, aesthetic, emotional, spiritual, self-interested, and altruistic, among other characteristics. The process leading to decisions and action is one of framing (defining the situation), searching for ideas, crafting possibilities, simulated testing of the ideas, re(framing), and so forth—a highly iterative process rather than a closely prescribed selection from among two predefined alternatives.

Another contribution from the design perspective is that context is probably the single most important predictor of what type of design will result. Designs created by people are always crafted within a context and tailored to fit some conception of the situation. Designs created for one context cannot easily be transported to another. Because contexts almost always contain multiple and sometimes conflicting values, good designs must be able to accommodate multiple points of view and perspectives. Contexts contain long historical memories that influence beliefs and shape how people will interpret various design choices.

These fundamental principles from the design perspective are important in the study of policy design: Policy designs are intentional and purposeful creations, they reflect commitment toward action, are highly complex, variable, and often unique. Designs emerge from a context and have consequences for that context, sometimes over a long period of time (Boborow and Dryzek 1987; Linder and Peters 1988; Miller 1991)

The explicit integration of a design perspective into public policy theories began in the 1950s with the work of Dahl and Lindblom who noted that during the postwar years there had been a remarkable proliferation of design forms through which governments seek to achieve policy purposes. Dahl and Lindblom (1953, p. 8) referred to the rapid invention of new policy techniques as "perhaps the greatest political revolution of our times." In the early years of the Cold War, when many people thought that societies would have to choose between socialism and capitalism, planning and the free market, regulation or laissez-faire economics, Dahl and Lindblom argued that the creation of innovative policy instruments could avoid these kinds of grand, yet simplistic dichotomies.

> Actual choices [are] neither so simple nor so grand. Not so simple because knotty problems can only be solved by painstaking attention to technical details—how else, for example, can inflation be controlled? Nor so grand because . . . most of the people neither can nor wish to experiment with the whole pattern of socioeconomic organization to attain goals more easily won. If, for example, taxation will serve the purpose, why "abolish the wages system" [as argued by socialists and communists] to ameliorate income inequality? (1953, p. 3)

Dahl and Lindblom asserted that people do not make selections between mythical grand alternatives; they decide among particular social techniques embodied in ordinary legislation. Examples of policy instruments they cited included: unemployment compensation, food stamps, cost accounting, zoning, lend-lease, cooperatives, scientific management, points rationing, slum clearance, old age pensions, disability benefits, and collective bargaining (1953, p. 7). The effects of such policy choices, cumulatively, over time, are profound.

The insight of Dahl and Lindblom that creativity and innovation in policy designs grant government the flexibility to deflect choices between grand ideologies is as important today as during the Cold War. Their criteria for evaluating policy design reflected a preoccupation with democracy. The values they proposed, against which the various "politico-economic techniques" could be judged, included freedom, rationality (including efficiency), democracy (defined as political equality), and subjective equality (1953, p. xi).

Although many scholars have included some characteristic of policy design in their studies, most have characterized policy along a single dimension. As noted in Chapters 2 and 3, pluralists tend to focus on who benefits from the policy. Public choice theorists are concerned about what type of good is being delivered (public, private, toll good, or common pool resource) and whether the policy has the incentive structure needed to ensure that self-interest will lead to desired results. Critical theorists search for the hidden assumptions, symbols, and oppressive or discriminatory characteristics in policy and interpret these against normative standards. Policy scientists are interested mainly in the implicit or explicit theories within the policy.

Lowi (1964) is widely acclaimed for being the first to offer a theoretically useful typology of policy designs and for teaching the scholarly community that public policy is not just a consequence of a political process, but also a cause of politics. This aspect of Lowi's work is especially relevant here because he offers an explanation of how different types of policy designs impact citizen participation and facilitate (or thwart) the self-correcting assumptions contained in pluralist democratic theory (Lowi 1964, 1972). He believes there are characteristics of policy that encourage affected people or groups to mobilize, make their preferences clear, and create pluralist competition. Without these characteristics, elites will dominate. Lowi's typology is based on two dimensions: whether the probability of coercion is high (costs are being distributed) or low (benefits/subsidies are being distributed); and whether the policy identifies specific targets or consists of general rules that affect the environment of groups. From these dimensions, he posits four types of policy: *distributive, regulatory, redistributive,* and *constituent.* Regulatory policy, which involves the imposition of costs in the environment, will produce pluralist competition, according to Lowi's theory. Redistributive policy will create competition among elites who lead major segments of society (political, business, and labor) acting to ensure the stability of society. Distributive policy in Lowi's framework is classic pork barrel policy and is inherently elitist, as its constituent policy, which refers to policies that direct government action and administration.

Lowi's theory prompted considerable debate, applications, and modifications (see McCool 1995 for a review). Empirical scholars have a very difficult time with the typology because they cannot fit actually existing policies into it (Greenberg et al. 1977). Without the capacity to determine where a policy fits within the typology, it is not possible to examine whether Lowi's theory connecting policy types to citizen mobilization patterns is correct. Steinberger (1980) made a very important but largely overlooked contribution when he argued that the effects of policies depend on the *meanings* and *interpretations* attached to the policy by citizens, interest groups, media, and others. Even though the policy exists and has actual consequences, such as the actual allocation of resources, the policy becomes redistributive, or regulatory, or distributive through the construction of its meaning by the public. Our work builds specifically from this same perspective in understanding both the causes and the consequences of policy designs: The social construction of reality shapes the characteristics of designs and through the meanings and interpretations attached to policy, effects on democratic values are realized.

Wilson (1979) has proposed quite a different typology for public policies, but his theory, like Lowi's, offers an explanation of how different kinds of policies produce different patterns of democratic participation. He begins with the public choice contention that goods and services have certain inherent qualities that determine the efficiencies of alternative methods of production. When policies allocate benefits over a large number of people (such as national defense) and costs are distributed widely across all taxpayers, then all people will have about the same incentive to take this issue into account in their participation patterns, and *majoritarian politics* will ensue. In majoritarian politics, elected officials (who are assumed to be motivated by a desire for re-election) are expected to pay careful attention to what the majority wants. When benefits are concentrated on only a few groups and costs also are distributed among only a few (such as regulation that favors workers at the expense of business), both will mobilize and compete with each other, in *interest group politics*. When benefits are concentrated on a few (such as "corporate" welfare), but costs are distributed widely (among all taxpayers), then there is little incentive for those who bear the costs to pay attention to what government does, but considerable advantage to the potential beneficiaries and large political payoffs for such policies. These types of situations produce a *clientist* style of politics in which elected leaders distribute expensive favors to their "clients" while the apathetic taxpayers acquiesce. *Entrepreneurial* politics occurs when small portions of society pay the costs (such as taxing the rich) to benefit large segments of society (such as educational programs). Entrepreneurial politics results in virtually uncontrolled growth, Wilson argues, because of the strong political payoffs for distributing so many benefits at the expense of so few people. Since most policies, according to Wilson, fall into either the entrepreneurial or the client types, government grows until it is inefficient and is producing more goods and services than anyone wants, at a cost much greater than what people would be willing to pay if they could purchase the goods and services on the open market. Wilson's theory has not received as much attention as Lowi's, except as an argument against "big" government, at least partly because counterexamples are so immediately apparent.

Although several others have proposed policy typologies (Eulau 1969; Froman 1967) difficulties with typologies undermine their value. The first is that actual policies are extremely complex and therefore seldom fit within any of the typologies. Even with Wilson's theory, which seems quite clear-cut, most actual policies confer different kinds of benefits to different people, some of whom are concentrated and others dispersed. In his framework, costs refer to taxation, yet policies confer other kinds of costs (through regulation or control). Lowi's typology contains the same problem as almost all actual policies contain redistributive, distributive, and even regulatory and constitutive characteristics. A second problem is that the theoretically interesting relationships Lowi and Wilson proposed between policy types and politics or democracy have seldom been verified with empirical work.

A different approach to characterizing policy design has been taken by those who, instead of trying to fit designs into a typology, have sought to characterize the elements or tools within designs and assess their implications for implementation, agency behavior, and citizen compliance (Bardach 1977; Cowen and Kamieniecki 1991; Gormley 1990; Linder and Peters 1985, 1987, 1988, 1992; May 1991; Sabatier 1987; Schneider and Ingram 1990a). The advantages and disadvantages of different kinds of designs also have been the subject of considerable research (Boborow and Dryzek 1987; Doern and Aucoin 1979; Linder and Peters 1985; Salamon 1989; Wildavsky 1979; Woodside 1986). Several scholars have pushed forward the relationship between selected aspects of policy design and democratic aspirations. Trudi Miller, for instance, has portrayed designs as containing explicit conceptions of justice (1989, 1992). John Dryzek envisions policy designs as democratic discourses (1990). Several scholars have sought to address the impact of public policy design upon citizenship (Ingram and Schneider 1993; Ingram and Smith 1993; Lipsky and Smith 1989; Stone 1988). Unfortunately, this research has not contributed much to the development of a theory of policy design, however, at least partly because there is no overarching framework to guide the studies or to absorb their lessons. The dilemma is that policy design theory needs a coherent framework to describe and compare designs, yet the complexity of designs ensures that no simplistic policy typology will work very well, because actually existing policies will defy classification. Yet, efforts to characterize the elements and dimensions of policy designs have either been too unidimensional (with much of the focus on tools or motivating devices), or have involved such unique aspects of designs that it has not been possible to relate the studies to one another or to a broader theory of policy design.

Our approach to overcoming these difficulties is, first, to situate the concept of policy design within a causal model that emphasizes the political processes through which designs are created as well as the translating processes through which effects on democracy are realized. This places policy design in a central location for studies of politics and democracy. We then propose a more comprehensive set of empirical *elements* that are found in all public policy designs and whose *dimensions* reflect theoretically interesting characteristics of designs— dimensions that we believe are important in understanding how and why policy designs affect multiple democratic values.

POLICY DESIGN, POLICY CONTEXTS, AND DYNAMIC PROCESSES

Figure 4.1 depicts the causal relationships through which issue contexts produce designs and designs, in turn, have consequences for society. The box at the left indicates that designs emerge from an *issue context* which, in turn, emerges from the broader *societal context* through a process of *framing dynamics*. The societal context encompasses all aspects of the physical, social, psychological, political, and historical world. This is the primeval soup in which all the ingredients of public life simmer and swirl and combine in constantly evolving ways. Issue contexts are the narrower, more specific (socially constructed) understandings that emerge from the societal context. Societal conditions are socially constructed into a set of beliefs, perceptions, images, and stereotypes people hold that give meaning and interpretation to the way they live. The many ingredients of issue contexts are not all equally important to an analysis of policy design, however. We believe that social constructions, political power, and institutional cultures are the most meaningful. The process of socially constructing an issue leaves within the issue definition itself an image and set of beliefs that people accept as "real." Among the many social constructions that might be important, we focus on two that are fundamental to the kinds of designs that will ensue: the social construction of potential or actual target populations and the social construction of knowledge.

Social construction refers to world making or the varying ways in which realities of the world are shaped. The idea of social construction has its origin in the subfield of sociology of knowledge (Berger and Luckmann 1967; Holzner 1968). Social constructions reflect the way in which objects present themselves according to differences in social settings, mental structures, and historical circumstances (Babst 1996; Fischer and Forester 1993; Rochefort and Cobb 1994). We live in a world of constructs that simply "are" to most ways of thinking. Social constructions are often generalized, intersubjective, and so much a part of our way of life that it is not easy to observe them as constructs. However, social constructions are not always hegemonic and instead may be the subject of contention. Different realities based on different beliefs, expectations, and interpretations may exist among different people and groups. There are many participants in the process of socially constructing the realities relevant to public policy, including elected officials, media, members of social groups, powerful and influential people, interest groups, and political parties. There is a continuing struggle to gain acceptance of a particular

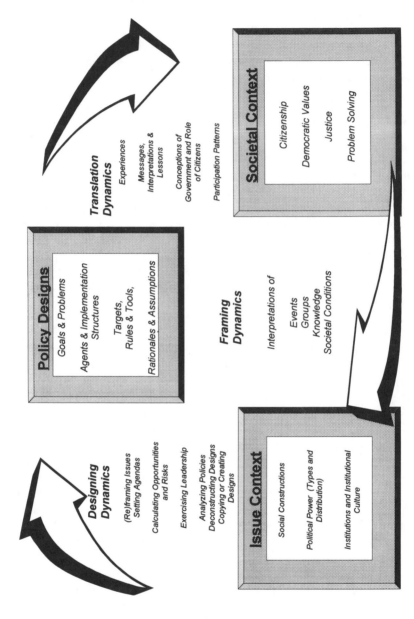

Figure 4.1. Causal portrayal of how characteristics of the policy context become embedded in policy designs and subsequently have effects on democratic values that reproduce or transform the context.

construction of events, people, history, and contemporary conditions that will become widespread and accepted.

The social construction of potential target populations refers to the images, stereotypes, and beliefs that confer identities on people and connect them with others as a social group who are possible candidates for receiving beneficial or burdensome policy. Social constructions of social groups are created by politics, culture, socialization, history, the media, literature, religion and the like. The social construction of knowledge refers to the way facts, experiences, beliefs, and events are constructed and certified as "true." Issue contexts in which scientific and professionalized knowledge has been socially constructed as true and relevant produce distinctive design patterns that differ fundamentally from those in which the knowledge orientation is focused on political knowledge, such as who has power and who is deserving or undeserving of beneficial public policy.

Recognizing political power as a key contextual characteristic for the production of policy design requires little justification or discussion as almost all theories of public policy recognize that various types of power, mediated through institutions, are primary causal factors in explaining public policy. As explained in Chapter 2, power is a complex concept and often has been described as having three faces: the power to make policy decisions and therefore decide issues directly; the power to influence through indirect means such as by determining the policy agenda or shaping the rules and norms of institutions; and the most subtle form of power which is to influence the perceptions, wants, and needs of others (Bachrach and Baratz 1961; Gaventa 1980). Power resources that enhance influence over decisions, such as votes, mobilization, and access to interest groups and elected officials, are especially important for the first face of power, but less central in the second and third. Economic power and the ability to wield expertise, control information, promulgate a public ideology, and socially construct reality are significantly important for the second and third types.

The first face of power is defined as the capacity of one person (A) to force or coerce another (B) to do something that (B) otherwise would not have done. This form of power is relatively obvious to everyone. The second and third types include persuasion, ideology, and subtle manipulation of images and clearly are more problematic because these forms may not be recognized by those who are adversely impacted by power relationships. The power of a business to determine the size of its workforce, disregarding the number of unemployed persons in the community, for example, is not usually recognized as a form of power at all. Several scholars have noted that the political/business nexus is such that direct power scarcely needs to be exercised by business leaders (Lindblom 1977; Stone 1989). Stone (1989), for example, has demonstrated that elected leaders and businesses are often able to retain power in cities because they have a common interest in functional city governance that keeps them participating, negotiating, and reaching agreements in the formulation of policy. Reform coalitions tend not to have any long-term, functional interests, however, and therefore disintegrate over time.

Ordinary citizens, then, are largely unaware of the extent to which existing power relationships may disadvantage them.

Power relationships are central to policy design because power determines which actions constitute political opportunities and which ones are political risks. Opportunities and risks, in turn, influence policy makers' perceptions of what is feasible in terms of policy action. In this sense, power constrains political leaders to focus on opportunities and discourages them from acting in the realm of risks. Power can be used for good or ill, however, and can be augmented or decreased through policy-relevant action.

Institutions are another fundamental contextual characteristic with significant importance in understanding what kinds of designs will emerge (Lieberman, Ingram, and Schneider 1995). Institutions are defined as persistent patterns of relationships and interactions including legislatures, courts, administrative agencies, nongovernmental organizations, and the like. Public policy always is produced within one or more institutional settings and the characteristics of these institutions become imprinted in the policy itself. The formal and informal rules, procedures, beliefs, and practices are important. Stimulated by the work of Kenneth Arrow (1983), who concluded that under most circumstances no mechanisms for preference aggregation could yield stable majorities, students of institutions have recognized that what appear to be majority preferences actually may be dependent on the operative structural arrangements, rules, power relationships, and cultural norms that define acceptable and unacceptable forms of argument. Much attention has been directed to the institutional biases built into legislatures and agencies, and comparative studies of policy making in different countries have found that agencies make enormous autonomous contributions in shaping the timing and content of state initiatives (Skocpol 1992). Agencies' actions regularly reinforce state authority, political longevity, and social control.

Institutions are not just collections of rules and structures that impact design. Institutions have values, norms, and ways of operating that define an institutional culture. The dynamic processes of policy design ensure that these characteristics are reflected in policy. Although institutions produce policy designs, they also are created, limited, or influenced in other ways by public policy. Once created, institutions tend to take on a life of their own through institutional cultures and routines. Their methods of recruiting, indoctrinating, and rewarding members inculcate and perpetuate institutional values. These values in turn affect institutional policy recommendations. The existence and strength of particular organizational structures are critical to state capacity to take action (Skocpol 1985). "New institutionalists," such as Gary Mucciaroni, have argued that in the United States the institutional context is more important than public preferences or issue context in determining policy designs (1985). Policy-making institutions often have distinctive cultures that direct the people within the institution toward various styles of decision making and toward particular ideas about what kind of behavior (and what kind of policy) are appropriate. As the new institutionalists have noted, the behavior within an institution may be more oriented toward doing what is appropriate within the cultural milieu of the organization than maximizing utility. In our framework, the patterns of interaction and communication within policy-making institutions, along with the ethical and normative standards that define what is acceptable and what is not, are especially important in understanding the kinds of designs that result.

Context is linked to policy designs through *designing dynamics* that involve an interaction of contextual characteristics and design possibilities with human ingenuity. This aspect of our theory draws from the work of Herbert Simon (1981), who emphasized the importance of human agency and intentionality in design, but recognized that people who engage in design activities are surrounded by a highly complex environment from which many possible choices emerge. There are many different design possibilities that interact with several possible ways of socially constructing the issue so that one or another design will appear to be the only feasible one. Persons with a stake in the policy design process may become actively involved in the framing dynamics through which the issue itself is defined. Attempts to (re)frame the issue may occur at any time. Because social construction takes place at all levels, it may be possible for designers to (re)construct the current societal conditions in such a way that the issue looks quite different than it would have otherwise, and the kinds of policy that might seem appropriate may change accordingly. As Kingdon (1984) has argued, policy entrepreneurs may take a pre-existing policy solution and construct an issue so that the solution appears to be the most logical one.

Our causal model emphasizes the dynamic processes because so much of the policy arguments focus on a socially constructed set of facts and people. Social construction is an ongoing process subject to influence by a wide range of people and societal phenomena. Thus, the issue context and the societal conditions are both subject to change during the process of design itself.

Calculations of opportunities and risks by elected officials, interest groups, potential targets, and many other participants have important influences on policy designs. The pluralist portrayal of a process of competition and bargaining among interest groups sometimes occurs and sometimes does not, but elected leaders are always attentive to whether an issue presents political opportunities or risks. Elected leaders are eager to associate themselves with policy ideas that gain them credit and avoid blame. They not only scrutinize issues as they emerge, but are continually searching for ways to create opportunities for political gain by identifying potential policy designs that will seem to be responsive to one or more real or imagined needs among various constituencies. The creation of needs and issues, through social constructions of social groups and events, plays a central role in the extent to which elected leaders can use public policy as a tool for increasing or maintaining power, or achieving other ends.

Policy entrepreneurship on the part of individual actors also plays an important role (Schneider and Teske 1995). The ability of policy entrepreneurs to frame issues in such a way that they strike a resonant cord with elected leaders or with powerful interest groups is a critical starting point for moving issues onto the political agenda. Agencies also seek to connect the target populations under their jurisdiction with issues that offer opportunities to elected officials, thereby increasing the centrality of their agency to important national concerns. Agencies can gain legitimacy and centrality by socially constructing their own constituencies so that they offer political opportunities, or so that they seem to fit logically between policy and results, thereby offering a rationale for selection.

Policy analysts and advisers influence designs by conducting studies showing the expected effectiveness of various policy design options, or by shaping the kind of knowledge and information that is considered to be important in the policy-making situation. The extent to which a policy making environment, for example, is dominated by scientific thinking instead of by political strategies is influenced by the ability of the scientific community to link policy design ideas to accepted scientific theories.

Designs are as much a matter of borrowing as they are of invention. The multiple actors in the multitude of settings that are involved in design often "pinch" ideas from other policies and other jurisdictions (Schneider and Ingram 1988). The designing process involves human behavior and its various limitations. Research on how people actually arrive at decisions and judgments indicates that the process is not necessarily linear and is governed by a number of heuristics that constrain thought process to that which is familiar. Designers rely heavily on previous experience; many times the designing dynamic involves little more than tinkering. More often than suspected, however, both the philosophy and practice of previous designs are replaced with new ideas and new strategies (Baumgartner and Jones 1993). An important role for policy analysis is enlarging the frames of reference and the alternative design possibilities beyond those more limited options that might otherwise emerge. Because the choice of policy design features has the potential to transform future contexts in ways that may or may not be advantageous to democracy, the policy analyst can be much more socially significant than simply a technician.

Policy designs constitute the next major link in the causal chain. As we have emphasized repeatedly, previous efforts to describe designs in such a way that they can be analyzed and compared have not been very successful. This lack of an adequate conceptual framework has contributed significantly to the inability of existing theories of public policy to provide adequate explanations for how and why certain kinds of designs are created or what their consequences will be. In the second part of this chapter we present the elements of design that are found in all public policies and illustrate their relationships to democratic values. Our own research has led us to focus on two common themes or "families" of characteristics: scientific professional characteristics that reflect the value orientation of science, and degenerative political characteristics embedded in designs through the strategic use of power and manipulation of social constructions. Each of these "families," however, contains numerous variations around the common theme, which we explore in Chapters 5 and 6.

Translation dynamics connects the characteristics of policy designs as independent variables to societal conditions and subsequent constructions of the issue. This translation occurs through citizens, as the designs transmit to citizens information and experiences that influence their behavior, values, and participation. Translation dynamics may be the intentional results of policy designs or may be quite accidental and fall into that large category of unintended policy effects—both negative and positive. While much of policy analysis has focused on the ways in which policies either help or hinder the achievement of stated goals, the more indirect and subtle effects on democracy also deserve attention. The most common encounters citizens have with government are not in the voting booth, nor in contributing to and contacting legislators, even though these have been the main subjects of political science research. Instead, people confront government in the hundreds of ways affecting their daily lives, including everything from paying taxes to applying for driver's licenses. Depending on the choice of policy design elements and the way they fit together, government can appear fair or unfair, logical and straightforward or illogical with hidden agendas, helpful or antagonistic, an important aspect of life or irrelevant. People can come away from encounters with government feeling informed and empowered or helpless, ignorant, and impotent. Further, even without direct experience with policy, the language and symbols contained in policy send messages about what kind of people count as important, whose interests are likely to be taken seriously, and whose problems will probably be ignored. Policies are lessons in democracy. They may establish forums and public spaces that encourage discursive dialogue among citizens, or they may separate citizens from one another and isolate and marginalize some. Policies feed the sense of entitlement of some and acquiescence to deprivation of others.

Policy designs have actual consequences, but the meanings and interpretations of the policy shape the resulting participation patterns. Whether policies result in compliance, resistance, or withdrawal depends not so much on what the policy actually does, but on how people socially construct the meaning of the policy and what they believe are appropriate and correct actions for citizens to take.

Societal context is the third anchor point of the causal model. Not all aspects of the societal context are relevant to public policy, and not all are relevant to our theory of design. We believe, however, that public policy should be evaluated along multiple dimensions, even though those dimensions may at times conflict with one another. We have concentrated our attention on the effect of policy designs on four aspects of society: democratic institutions, justice, problem solving, and citizenship—each of which is acknowledged as important by one or more of the theories previously reviewed.

A strength of pluralism is its contention that democratic political institutions and processes should deliver responsive public policies and should be accountable for actions taken. Such institutions are open, permit fair competition, provide for control of elected officials by citizens, and ensure access through numerous avenues to all citizens. Joined with this in our conception of democratic values are the concepts drawn from critical theory that institutional cultures should be characterized by discursive and ethical patterns of communication and interaction. Because public policies shape the values of citizens and influence them in ways both instrumental and symbolic, policies must be assessed in terms of whether they encourage or discourage democratic values.

The second value is problem solving. Public policies are the primary mechanism the society has for solving collective problems, and the capacity of policy to deliver on the instrumental goals is important. Policy should be effective in addressing high-priority collective problems and should not be wasteful of human or natural resources. We agree with the emphasis in policy science theory and public choice that public policy should be effective and efficient in solving collective problems, although we contend that efficiency must be more broadly understood as "not wasteful of human or natural resources" rather than as benefit cost comparisons based on market prices.

Policy also should serve justice, in the very broad sense of the term encompassing critical theory and pluralist perspectives. Almost all would agree that justice means equal treatment under the law and true equal opportunity, but beyond these, it means a society in which people are treated equally and with respect. In a just society, the human capacity for empathy is nurtured and the material goods are distributed in ways that meet a reasonable standard of fairness, such as equality, equity, need, or merit, depending on the values of the society and the context within which the distribution occurs (Deutsch 1985; Miller 1989). A just society is one that rejects the "Ordinary Vices" (Shklar 1984), such as cruelty, hatefulness, deception, hypocrisy, or actions that humiliate others.

Finally, and in many ways the most central value in our framework, is citizenship. Conceptions of citizenship and the extent to which people live up to the ideal conceptions are critical linkages to the other values we have posited. Notions of citizenship come from a variety of sources, but direct and vicarious experience with public policy and institutions are arguably the most powerful teachers and motivators. The theories of public policy taught in the public schools and ingrained in the public consciousness convey expectations about what "good citizens" believe, how much they are expected to know about politics and policy, what they should expect from public policy, and what kinds of participation are appropriate. Public policy experiences, symbols, and theories teach people what kind of behavior and ethics are permitted in politics and policy making.

Citizens are the critical linkage to responsiveness and accountability in political institutions. The self-correcting feedback mechanisms so central to pluralist theory and to Lowi's contentions regarding juridical democracy rely on citizens who pay attention to the effects of public policy and register their sentiments through the political process. Some policy designs encourage active responsible citizenship by providing arenas for participation and expectations that citizens will become involved. Other designs obfuscate and complicate, leaving the response to policy largely in the hands of lawyers, scientists, and highly skilled policy entrepreneurs.

Many designs reinforce the self-interest motivation in U.S. politics and signal that people are expected to look after their own interests (with little regard for the elusive "public interest"), and everyone is expected to cut the best deal they can for themselves. Policy so designed creates a particular culture that permeates democratic institutions and has far-reaching negative consequences for justice. A more just society depends on citizens not only expressing their own interests but empathizing with other citizens different from themselves and accepting compromise. As Landy has pointed out, good citizenship lies somewhere between self-interest and the public interest (1993). The empathetic attitudes and willingness to compromise that are so essential for a working democracy and for justice may or may not have been learned through citizen interaction with policy and citizen interpretations of the meanings of policy. Excessive emphasis on self-interest can undermine notions of the collective good and result in political arenas without sufficient ethical grounding to create trust and social capital. When trust and social capital are destroyed, democracy becomes difficult or impossible (Putnam 1993).

Citizenship also has an impact on whether policies will solve the problems toward which they are directed. Well-designed logical policy based on valid causal theories can make a difference in whether problems are solved, or at least reduced, or whether they intensify. Nevertheless, citizen response to policy is centrally important in whether policy will achieve its goals. Solving problems almost always depends on citizen cooperation and compliance with laws. Because citizens are often an integral part of making policies work, attitudes toward policies become self-fulfilling prophecies. Policies that enjoy broad-based support are more likely to achieve voluntary compliance; those that do not have support will encounter resistance and become hugely expensive (and often unsuccessful) policy experiments.

DESIGN ELEMENTS AND EFFECTS ON DEMOCRATIC VALUES

One of the greatest impediments to the development of a theory of policy design has been the absence of a conceptual framework that can capture the complexity of statutes, guidelines, programs, practices, or other empirical examples of public policies and yet remain manageable and accessible. Many researchers before us have incorporated selected aspects of policy content in their analysis and usually have linked those aspects to selected (unidimensional) policy consequences. Generally, their interest has been driven by purposes more narrowly focused than ours, such as examining implementation to see if the intent of legislation was misdirected by agencies or assessing whether instrumental goals were achieved. Policy content is much like the proverbial elephant being grappled with by blind analysts who form images of the whole on the basis of probing a part. Most researchers have used surrogates for the substance of policy, such as expenditures or the presence or absence of laws, rather than a more comprehensive portrayal of the policy. The authors of more recent public policy literature make a greater contribution to understanding the substance of policy, but usually to only one element or another.

To assess the impact of policy design on multiple values of democracy as broad as those we have selected—justice, citizenship, democratic institutions, and problem solving—requires a much more comprehensive set of concepts to portray policy design. The core empirical elements (see Figure 4.2) found in virtually all examples of policy are: goals or problems to be solved, agents, target populations, rules, tools, rationales, and assumptions (Schneider and Ingram 1990b). The analysis may begin at any point and proceed in either direction. Goals or problems signify what is to be altered or attained as a result of policy. Target populations refer to the people, groups, and/or organizations whose behavior or capacity the policy is intended to change or effect. Almost all public policies act to coerce or enable people—either directly or indirectly—to do something they otherwise would not do. These people are the targets of policy, and through them policy is supposed to achieve its intended purposes. Most policies have several targets that may or may not be connected to one another. Agent(s) refers to the institutions that are part of the formal governance structure and are responsible for the development and delivery of policy. A few policies contain no agents and are self-executing directives to targets, but most have several agents at different levels of government or in different departments within one or several levels. Agents may be established by the policy, or existing agents may be given new authority or different rules. Tools are those aspects of policy design intended to bring about the policy-relevant behavior of agents and targets. Tools provide incentives or sanctions, persuasion, education, and other means to ensure that peoples' behavior will change as a result of the policy. Rules specify the procedures for policy-relevant action and include definitions, qualifications, standards, and criteria. Rationales are the explanations and reasons given that justify, legitimate, and explain the policy. Assumptions are the implicit or explicit underlying premises that connect the elements. Policies may contain technical, behavioral, and normative assumptions.

The discussion that follows provides an introduction to each of these elements, along with examples of important theoretical dimensions and the relevance of the element for one or more of the democratic values that policy is expected to serve in a democratic society.

Goals and Problems to Be Solved

Goals or problems to be solved refer to the intentional aspects of policy designs and indicate what is to be achieved through policy. Goals are consequences of human needs, wants, and desires arising in particular contexts. Goals emerge from human perceptions of existing conditions as measured against some preferred state of affairs. The choice of goals in policy designs, therefore, reveals a great deal about conceptions of the state of democracy in a society. Policies may have one, a

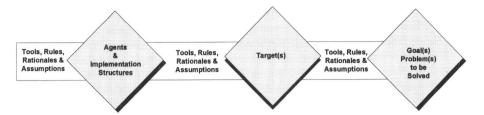

Figure 4.2. Diagram of policy design structure.

few, or many goals that may be clear or vague, realistic or unreasonable, conflict-ing or consistent. Some policies may have only one objective that is an end in itself, such as patriotism, morality, justice, or some other end state that may or may not be cultured and humane. Other designs have several goals, some or all of which are instrumental linkages to the achievement of broadly held public values such as pro-tecting the public welfare, or providing for liberty, security, and prosperity. Such linkages may or may not be viewed as credible by citizens.

Goals or problems to be solved are almost always stated in objective and tech-nical terms, yet these are social constructions of problems or desired ends. Politi-cal and normative goals are as important as technical ones, although seldom as explicitly stated (Stone 1988). The goals of policy are sometimes hidden, obscured by rationales that do not stand up to analysis of likely or actual outcomes of over-all designs. Politicians, who may be merely responding to political or ideological pressures without much interest in solving problems, must explain their actions by linking them to the resolution of some important public concern. Overt political reasons are not usually acknowledged and policy is almost always rationalized pri-marily in technical terms. A bit of probing, however, often unmasks the darker side of goal choice that relates to repaying political debts, rewarding campaign con-tributors, enlarging the jurisdiction of some agencies or portfolios of some politi-cians, or punishing those on some powerful persons' lists of enemies.

The choice of goals and identification of problems will result in benefits to some and burdens to others and therefore are linked directly to democratic con-cerns with justice, especially as conceptualized in terms of fairness, equality, or equity. Goals and problems may be broadly framed in terms of public interest or narrowly framed to affect only certain selected groups. Whether the goals selected or problems to be solved are really of concern to the citizenry is important to the responsiveness of democratic institutions. Very often problems as stated in statutes relate very poorly with what the public actually cares about. For instance, most people's perception of clean water has to do with clarity and the absence of unsightly floating objects. Water pollution legislation, in contrast, contains goal statements that are driven by numerical chemical parameters that have little or no relationship with whether water appears any cleaner. Similarly, the problem to which juvenile justice policy ostensibly is linked is the control of violent juvenile offenders. Yet, the definitions of violent juvenile crime in policy range from that which almost anyone would think is violent, such as drive-by shootings, to mischievous pranks, such as school yard fights resulting in the injury of one party with the other accused of aggravated felony assault.

Goals may also be mainly hortatory and symbolic rather than be the actual objectives of policy. The policy preambles that undergird some statutes were never intended, even by their authors, to be taken literally. The 1949 Housing Act, for example, said it was the right of every American to have a clean, safe, and sanitary dwelling unit. This goal served to rationalize profound federal government involvement in the housing industry although such an outcome has never begun to be achieved. The choice of ambitious goals that may be beyond current knowledge or organizational capacity may cause more rapid action than would take place with modest goals (Schulman 1975; Wildavsky 1979). Goals that overreach what can reasonably be expected to occur through public policy can also lead to disappointment and cynicism as citizens come to feel politicians make false promises.

Goals may change incrementally over a long period of policy development or relatively rapidly (Baumgarten and Jones 1993). Policies with long histories often contain anomalous vestiges of former goal statements that no longer bear much resemblance to the current problems or strategies. The food stamp program goal statement still highlights the reduction of agricultural surpluses rather than feeding hungry people.

Policy designs best serve democracy when the goals reflect a balance among democratic values, or when they focus on one or more aspects of democracy that are noticeably deficient in the societal context. Policies should pursue goals and problems that transcend short-term political strategies. Policy designs should be structured credibly, so that there is a strong likelihood the policy will render future problems less severe and more tractable. The goals of policy should be broad based and reflect public rather than private interests.

Target Populations

Target populations play a critical role in all the purposes policy serves in a democracy. Target populations are crucial to policy effectiveness because targets must coproduce; that is, behave in ways needed to achieve policy goals or solve problems (Schneider 1987). They are crucial to the notion of limited government in a democracy as limited government relies extensively on the voluntary compliance of targets with policy prescriptions, which greatly reduces the extent of enforcement activity. Target groups are central to the pluralist notions of justice in that their selection for benefits or burdens should reflect the legitimate political power and preferences of groups within the society. In pluralist contexts, targets sometimes are chosen with a view to mobilizing political support, and their selection may reflect coalition-building strategies of elected and administrative officials. It is not uncommon for different target groups receiving benefits to be strung together until the policy achieves a favorable balance of political support.

Targets and their choice are also central to the way citizens construct their role and that of government. Targets may be chosen on the basis of need, merit, equality, fairness, political power, wealth, image, or other principles that send messages about the values of the society and its leaders. Policy educates about the conditions of agreement and the "rules of the game." People's experiences as targets of policy shape their attitudes and orientations toward government as much, or more than, campaigns and elections. Thus, the way targets are treated by policy is central to justice, citizenship, support for democratic institutions, and democratic problem solving. Policy can either reinforce or undermine government legitimacy and sense of civic duty.

Policy designers usually have a choice among different target populations, any one of which can be logically linked to the solution of a particular problem. Who is selected and whether they are slated for benefits or burdens has obvious implications for democracy. Strategies for reducing drunk driving, for example, can focus on prohibition of drinking by persons under the age of twenty-one. They can make bartenders responsible for damages of accidents if they have served too many drinks. They can focus on repeat offenders and impose increasingly severe sanctions, or on first offenders with treatment programs. They can increase funding to drug and alcohol treatment centers, which can then serve more clients or serve them better. Public relations campaigns can attempt to change public tolerance for drunk driving, thereby making the public at large the target population. They can target the liquor industry and increase the taxes, which therefore effects the price the industry must charge to ensure a profit. Higher prices of liquor products, in turn, may cause a shift in beverage consumption. Or, they can also target recreational business such as bars and restaurants and prohibit such businesses from locating along public highways. Which target is chosen from among these many potential targets sends a message about who matters and who does not, who is assumed to be well motivated and whose behavior will damage society unless closely controlled.

Designs vary in the extent of control target populations have over their own selection and in the kinds of relationships that will exist between targets and agents. In some designs, target eligibility is determined entirely in the statute or by the caseworker; in others, the targets have some say over their eligibility. Obviously these differences are important to the degree of freedom given to targets and their sense of efficacy. Designs also differ in whether the agencies reach out to targets and ensure that they know about programs that will benefit them or whether they leave it entirely to target groups to inform themselves and come as supplicants to the agency.

Designs differ in terms of whether the targets chosen are consistent with already existing group identities, such as ethnic groups or regional ties, and whether or not such congruity reinforces negative stereotypes or creates a sense of entitlement. Regional development legislation passed by Congress in the 1960s specifically targeted Appalachia for aid and investment, for example. Affirmative action legislation is directed toward women and racial minorities. Many welfare policies are means tested; that is, a line is drawn among income categories, carving out a group of poor people to receive benefits. Policy designs may create group identities that did not previously exist. For instance, many analysts believe that Social Security encouraged the rise of powerful and self-conscious interest groups representing the elderly.

Designs differ in the kinds of values they allocate to targets. Some targets receive only benefits while others are burdened; or, targets may receive both benefits and burdens. Over time, the pattern of distributing benefits and burdens to targets may change. These changes may be because design changes actually allocate differently, or because targets interpret what they receive differently.

When policy designs include more than one target as they often do, variation in the ordering of target groups in the policy chain may be important. A group may be a proximate, first-order receptor of policy, or it may receive policy effects further down the policy chain. A fairly typical policy chain is depicted in Figure 4.3.

In this example, the agency (the Federal Reserve Board) wishes to stimulate economic recovery through new housing construction. The board reduces its interest rate to member regional banks, Target 1, who in turn lend money to local lending institutions, Target 2, at lower interest. The reduced cost of money means that real estate builders, Target 3, are able to get capital at reasonable terms and can hire additional workers and buy materials to construct housing. Further, home buyers, Target 4, will be attracted into the market because mortgage rates will be lower and there will be fewer incentives to save money, because interest rates on savings accounts will be lower. While all these targets are intended to receive some benefits, the implementation literature has taught us that there is a clear advantage to being the proximate target as the certainty of receiving the advantages decreases with the length of the policy chain (Pressman and Wildavsky 1973). It should be no surprise to anyone that, while mortgage rates were the lowest in many decades in the beginning of the 1990s, the reduction was less than the decline of interest rates paid to savings accounts. Further, to builders and home buyers the cost of borrowing remained considerably above the interest on savings accounts. Lending institutions were the primary beneficiaries because they were the proximate targets.

Policy structures the relationship between targets, between agencies, and between targets and agents that have significant implications for democracy (O'Toole 1987). In some policy designs, remote or intermediate targets are treated as catalysts or facilitators who are given authority or incentives to influence other targets as a means of automatic accountability monitoring (Gormley 1990). The Clean Air Act, for example, gives citizens' groups the right to sue agencies for failure to enforce the law against industrial, municipal, and other polluters. This is intended to be an empowering role for citizens who have an opportunity to have a real role in enforcement, as well as a mechanism of control over lower-level agencies. Increasing the liability of polluters for damages associated with their actions was embodied in the design of Superfund legislation, which anticipated that the

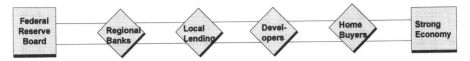

Figure 4.3. Policy chain with multiple targets.

threat of lawsuits for damages brought by other targets for damages would alter polluter behavior. Requiring industries to carry insurance against expenses for pollution cleanup involves insurance companies as a catalytic target, which is expected to protect itself from potential losses by putting conditions on those companies it insures. Private actors are forced to act as agents of the state and their experiences as such affect democratic values. The longer the policy chain is among the targets, the greater the likelihood that policy intention will become distorted or lost (Pressman and Wildavsky 1973). Moreover, it becomes more difficult to identify who is to blame for failure.

The ways target groups are defined and differentiated from other similar groups may impact their sense of justice or injustice. When targets whose characteristics and behavior objectively differ very little from one another and yet are treated very differently by public policy, an impression that government is unfair is created. Some target definitions have broad, all-encompassing criteria for eligibility whereas others are fine grained, even directing different amounts of positive or negative benefits at different targets within the same program or statute. Over time, policies may subdivide targets into finer and finer distinctions. Some may be targeted for more benefits (or more punishments). The history of juvenile justice policy, for example, is a history of successive efforts to separate more serious crimes, whose perpetrators will be punished, from less serious ones (Bortner 1988). Juveniles were first separated from adults so they could be spared the harsher treatment. In more recent times, status offenders have been separated and targeted for assistance, whereas delinquents may be punished. Violent offenders are treated like adults with more serious sanctions.

There also is variance in how targets experience policy even when it appears they are being treated alike. There may be differences in implementation, such as the way caseworkers interact with targets. Or, different cultural norms may be held by targets. There may be differences in experience among different social groups such as social classes, gender, race, region, and the like.

Target groups may be quite differentially represented on the policy agenda and in beneficial (or burdensome) policy results. For some groups, the eligibility rules may provide for everyone to receive approximately the same treatment from policy, given approximately the same level of need, whereas others may be systematically oversubscribed (more are eligible than needed to achieve goals) or undersubscribed (fewer are eligible than needed to achieve goals). Further, the extent of oversubscription or undersubscription may vary over time. For instance, policies may begin with the appropriately sized target groups, but over time the number receiving benefits may grow.

The extent to which certain social groups are consistently chosen as targets for policies and the extent to which the treatment of such targets are invariably benefits or burdens is quite significant to the inculcation of democratic values. Consider one particular target group, the eighteen years and under age group, and the number of different agencies and policies directed toward it. Teenagers are highly regulated by a large number of agencies and policies. These persons are required by school officials to attend school. In many cities they are required by police who enforce municipal statutes to be at home by 10 P.M. and to not wear the colors associated with gangs; at age eighteen, they are required by the Selective Service to register for possible draft. Marriage license bureaus and automobile driver bureaus must require that minors provide written parental consent. In some states, liquor control agencies require youthful appearing customers at bars to display their identification to barkeepers, and agencies suspend the licenses of any establishment serving drinkers under twenty-one years of age. Under the rubric of antigang ordinances, young people are denied the right to assemble or pass through public thoroughfares. As we will explore at greater length in the next chapter, the implications for this target group of being the receptors of so many policies that exert control over behavior are fairly clear. Minors are treated as dependents whose lives are more controlled than others. Young people are socialized to think of government as a coercive force. The lesson would be very different if minors were on the receiving end of many capacity-building or positive-incentive policies. While young people might feel dependent on government, they would undoubtedly be more likely to conceive of government as a positive force.

Targets receive very different symbolic messages about their worth and deservedness according to the specifics of policy design. Congress, for instance, has justified increased work requirements for jobless welfare recipients on the basis of fairness and deservedness, making comparisons to the working poor who contribute economically but receive little support from government. Citizen empowerment and the reinforcement of a sense of community can be values that drive target choices. The national service program for students and the tax deductions for college tuition championed by President Clinton are aimed at empowering and increasing the sense of citizen duty among a group who are generally apolitical, apathetic, and often alienated.

The role of public policy in encouraging an active, engaged citizenship and its role in ensuring that political institutions are democratic are closely related. People who consistently find themselves selected for burdens and ignored when beneficial policy might be provided are likely to become alienated from public life and lose legitimacy in the eyes of others. In contrast, persons who consistently find themselves selected for benefits and spared the burdens of public policy are likely to overestimate the importance and legitimacy of their own claims on government. Political participation patterns among various social groups in the United States are vastly unequal, and differential treatment by public policy is one of the major contributors to these inequalities. Good citizenship is not promoted by policies that send messages to some by encouraging them to seek privileges for themselves and others like them, but yet tell other groups that their problems are not important enough to be considered by government. Policies that perpetuate the belief that groups should seek their self-interests through government, without consideration of the impacts on others, do not promote the kind of citizenship essential in a democratic society.

Agents and Implementation Structures

Agents are means for delivering policy to target populations. Agents have the power or influence to act to achieve policy results under mandates they receive from statutes or on the basis of directives received from other agencies. Agents apply the tools, rules, and rationales developed at earlier (or higher) points in the policy chain, but they also create new tools, rules, assumptions, and rationales for themselves as well as agents below them in the chain of implementation and outcomes. Agents may have discretion to identify appropriate lower-level agents and targets, depending on whether the policy mandates or permits them to do so. The relationship among agents and the connections to targets constitute the implementation structure. Implementation structure almost disappears in policies in which there is a voluntary agreement among a collectivity and each participant is both target and self-directing agent. In slightly more complex designs there may be only one agent. In the most complicated designs there will be multiple agents at various levels of government.

In the design framework developed here, implementation is defined as the *value added to design.* The value added by agents refers to how discretion has been used to change, delete, or add to the basic blueprint or structural logic of policy. Any change in the tools, rules, rationales, target populations, agency designations, relationships among agencies, goals, or problems all constitute added values. Added values can refer to changes in the intended design or in the policy as it operates in practice. Because policy designs contain an architecture or blueprint of the policy content as it is received or produced by any actor in the system, policy implementation can be measured by the difference between the design received and the one produced by a particular actor in the system. This includes changes in the rationales, goals, tools, rules, or any other aspect of the design.

A large policy literature has developed since the 1970s that has focused on the causes of implementation success or failure, but has only incidentally discussed implications for democracy (Pressman and Wildavsky 1973; Sabatier 1987; Mazmanian and Sabatier 1983; see Ingram 1990 and O'Toole 1987 for a literature review). Some have argued that "strong" statutes containing clear allocations of authority to agents, top-down command and control techniques, and a small number of veto points in the implementation structure will produce more effective implementation. Others contend that implementation will be more successful if the statutes permit flexibility, local innovation, learning, and local ownership of programs (Berman 1980; Elmore 1987; Hjern 1982; Ingram 1978; Ingram and Schneider 1990; Ostrom 1990; Wildavsky 1979). Pressman and Wildavsky (1973) argued that involving more than one agent escalated the chances of implementation slippage. They believed simplicity and directness in implementation structures were keys to delivering policy intent and assuring responsible government.

The allocation of discretion in the policy design is a key aspect of implementation structure. Whether value can be added at various points in the policy chain depends on the allocation of discretion by the policy design. We can identify four different patterns of allocating discretion (Ingram and Schneider 1991).

"Strong statutes" limit the discretion of implementers as much as possible. Implementers are expected to reproduce the statutory design faithfully and not add significantly to it. Goals, tools, rules, and choice of targets are clear, consistent, and specific. Statutory language leaves little ambiguity about authority and intended relationships among agencies. This pattern of allocation is favored by those who believe that considerable authority from the top will be needed to ensure proper lower-level compliance and that responsible government is more important to democracy than is responsiveness (Mazmanian and Sabatier 1983; Sabatier 1987).

"Wilsonian" patterns are the same as strong statutes in relation to the specificity to goals, but wide latitude is given to implementing agencies on other matters including selection of subsequent agents in the policy chain along with tools, rules, and rationales. This pattern of discretion fits with Woodrow Wilson's philosophy that policy could be separated from administration while preserving democracy and improving responsibility. Politicians should establish the general objectives and goals; professional administrators should use their skills for determining how to reach objectives. This is also the pattern for allocation envisioned by Lowi (1979) in his notion of juridical democracy in which Congress specifies exactly what agencies are to accomplish and establishes clear rules of law within the statute, leaving to agencies and the courts implementation and enforcement responsibilities but few opportunities to alter policy intentions.

"Grassroots" designs allocate discretion of most of the critical aspects to the lowest-level agents within the formal governing structure. Objectives may be left vague, such as to search for a solution to a particular problem. Higher-level agents may have little role except to funnel resources to lower-level agents, often utilizing formula-driven decision models. A number of policies, especially in the health care area, follow this pattern and higher-level agencies are no more than service providers to lower-level agencies that make the important operational decisions. The pattern of allocation is heavily favored by the proponents of bottom-up implementation who believe that persons closest to the problem should have considerable discretion in policy design (Lipsky 1980; Berman 1980).

"Consensus-building" or "support-building" designs are intended to provide a forum for participation and discussion that will enable lower-level agents or target populations to determine what should be done. Statutes usually allocate discretion to lower-level agents or even target populations, but the statute spells out in detail the rules pertaining to participation and decision processes. Agencies may, for instance, be required to follow exacting administrative procedures, including giving notice, allowing comment, holding hearings, publishing findings, allowing for appeals, and so forth. This type of allocation is termed consensus building because the design is fashioned to facilitate a process of deliberation or coming to agreement. There are a variety of mixed patterns, including some in which the middle-level agent, often the state agency, is given authority.

"Privatized" implementation designs have become increasingly popular during the past decade and involve a configuration in which some of the actual service delivery is contracted to private-sector organizations, often nonprofits. Privatization, in some instances, is mandated by a federal statute or "encouraged" or "permitted," while in others this design is chosen by local governments. There are several types of privatization, including the complete withdrawal of government activity in a particular policy arena, but the more common practice is for government to continue providing resources for the services but to contract with the private sector for the actual operations, rather than hiring in-house staff to carry out the operational tasks.

Implementation designs also contain an identifiable pattern of resource allocation that may differ from the allocation of discretion, and such inconsistencies send messages that in our democracy political credit may count for more than effectiveness. In some policy arenas, Congress imposes strict regulations on states and locales, but provides no funding for them to meet the federal requirements, which leads to a serious problem of underfunding. In other cases, the political gain from dramatic expressions of federal effort may result in overfunding, which leads to policy designs that allocate more resources to agents and/or target groups than are needed. In the early 1970s, for example, the federal government allocated more than $20 million to the high-impact cities through the Law Enforcement Assistance Administration, which proved to be more than they could even spend during the allotted time period.

Implementation structures constrain how implementing agencies are able to deal with statutorily created design flaws. Allocations of discretion vary according to where control over resources and rules for resource allocation are located. Formula and block grants remove budgetary control from federal agencies, while program grants allow federal agencies to allocate funds according to their professional views of state and local needs and/or performance. Budget allocation processes structure bureaucratic incentives (Ingram and Schneider 1991). Fixed budgets with too few funds produce incentives for agencies to engage in "creaming" (selecting only those clients who most closely fit the professional interests of the agency) or retrenchment, where the agency restricts services or reduces quality. If the statutory authorities attempt to tighten criteria for choice of targets, agencies may engage in "relabeling." Relabeling can involve reinterpreting the characteristics of target groups so that they fit into the statutory criteria meant to exclude them or reinterpreting the characteristics to exclude those the statute intended for inclusion. If the agency is paid for each client served, they may engage in "net widening" (expanding the definition of need to serve more of the target group than intended) or relabeling persons whom the statute intended to exclude in such a way that they become eligible. The manner by which resources are distributed through the policy chain interacts with other institutional incentives and may drive policy designs in ways that have little relationship to technical considerations of efficiency and effectiveness, fairness and justice, or other democratic values.

The relationship between the type of implementation structure and the conditions of democracy is contingent and interactive. The effects of any specific implementation plan depend on the conditions within which the policy is implemented. The same implementation structure may produce quite different effects under different circumstances. Consider the case of effective problem solving. In some conditions, strong statutes will control agency shirking and gamesmanship, thereby enhancing the probability that policy will solve the problems toward which it is aimed. In other conditions, however, the lower-level agents may be much more familiar with the context in which the policy will take effect and will achieve greater effectiveness if given wide discretion to tailor the policy to fit their circumstances.

Similar interaction occurs if justice is taken as the standard. Civil rights policies intended to ensure greater equality among race and ethnic groups in the United States may have been well served by strong, top-down implementation structures and heavy penalties during the 1960s and 1970s at least partly because intransigence at the local level thwarted compliance with constitutional and statutory authority. This does not mean, however, that strong statutes also would serve racial and gender justice during a historical period when federal officials are giving lower priority to race and gender justice than are local officials. Contextual conditions also are important in understanding whether open and accessible implementation structures are advantageous to the powerful or the disadvantaged. Implementation structures that specify openness and ease of access in some circumstances may help ensure that the less powerful can participate effectively, but these same designs in other conditions give the powerful and mobilized groups even more points at which they can twist a design to their liking or resist the regulation that the design was intended to impose.

In terms of encouraging citizenship, a grassroots design that acknowledges the sense of place and the relevance of different cultures, histories, and experiences would seem to best engage the interests of citizens. Further, their loyalty to their own towns or regions may foster a willingness to set aside individual interests in favor of the welfare of the entire locality or region. However, in some regions of this country there has been a long tradition of practicing discrimination on the basis of race. Literacy tests, poll taxes, and other devices were used to limit the participation of some citizens. Embracing the rights of different places to play out their own destiny and culture has grave implications when it comes to the American South and the context of race. This does not mean that the effects of implication cannot be explained, but only that all aspects of design have to be studied *within context.*

Policy Tools

Policy tools are the elements in policy design that cause agents or targets to do something they would not otherwise do with the intention of modifying behavior to solve public problems or attain policy goals. Tools have important democratic implications in public policy designs because they direct the ways in which targets and agents are treated: They may be treated coercively or noncoercively, as smart or stupid, and as clients deserving of service or mere objects to be manipulated for government's purposes. While there have been a great many excellent studies of policy tools, most scholars have examined implications other than those affecting democratic messages and values (Anderson 1984; Bardach 1977; Elmore 1987; Gormley 1990; Hood 1986; Ripley 1966; Salamon 1989).

Our own previous work on policy tools (Schneider and Ingram 1990a) focused on how the choice of tools reflects underlying theories of individual decision and action as well as on the causes and consequences of different choices of policy tools. From a behavioral perspective, the choice of tools reflects assumptions and biases about how different people behave. Tools attempt to change behavior through several distinct mechanisms, each of which carries significant symbolic and instrumental connotations. Tools can be classified as reliance on authority, inducements or sanctions, capacity-building, hortatory, or persuasive proclamations to influence values, or learning that will enhance recognition of problems and reduce uncertainty.

Authority tools rely exclusively on authority, without the explicit or even implicit threat of other sanctions. Tools that rely heavily on authority assume that lower-level agents and targets are motivated by a desire to follow orders, or that they recognize the wisdom and expertise of those higher in the policy hierarchy and are therefore voluntarily willing to take the action needed. These tools may assume people are motivated for the common good, and will recognize that the policy needs them to behave in a particular way to achieve a common goal. Grants of authority are simply statements backed by the legitimacy of government to make laws and the expectation that they will be obeyed. From the perspective of democracy, it is important to note that authority tools reflect a philosophy that government need not give reasons or justify consequences. Authority tools signify that those at the top of a hierarchy have more information, or are wiser, than those below them. The choice of such tools reflects an underlying preference for hierarchy and a compliant society. Not only do such tools often not work, thus undercutting the democratically important role of policy design in solving problems, they sometimes teach uncivic lessons. When authority tools fail to regulate behavior as expected, some take advantage whereas those who are law-abiding feel misled and exploited.

Inducements and sanctions encourage "quasi-voluntary or quasi-coerced" actions based on tangible payoffs. These tools assume that agents and targets are rational actors motivated primarily by self-interest. Tools that use positive or negative incentives assume that people will not be motivated to take policy-relevant action unless there is something to gain or lose. Although inducements and sanctions are both types of incentives, they differ from one another in important ways. Inducements are optimistic and assume that targets and agents are good shoppers who will choose the higher-valued course of action. Inducements, particularly relatively open resource allocations, imply respect for the target population and portray a positive valence on the behavior that is desired.

User fees, rates, and charges also are used as incentives, but these do not carry as much positive valence as inducements. Regulations often are associated with charges that accrue for use of a resource above some prescribed limit. Charges are often graduated according to the amounts of a good used or the extent of the regulatory need. Charges can be distinguished from sanctions in that they do not intend to convey social disapproval of an activity. Indeed, the intent of setting fees and charges is to allocate costs in ways that are equitable, efficient, and fair.

Sanctions are negative incentives and go beyond user fees and charges in that the penalties are disproportionate to the social burden. The clear intent is to discourage targets or agents from engaging in certain activities damaging to policy objectives.

Force goes beyond sanctions and physically coerces people. Force is the ultimate use of government coercion and—when used against adults—denotes the maximum level of stigma and social condemnation.

Capacity-building tools provide training, technical assistance, education, and information needed to take policy-relevant actions. Capacity tools are not intended to be coercive, manipulative, or paternalistic (although they might be viewed that way if placed into an inappropriate context). Instead they are expected to enlighten, remove impediments, and empower action by the target group or agency itself. Targets and agents are neither bribed nor threatened. Training is provided, not indoctrination, and information is conveyed, rather than propaganda. Lack of information may be the impediment rather than monetary resources. Policy agents and targets may not know what action is needed or what alternatives are available to them and simply need to be provided information. In the context where they live, a particular problem may never have reached the conscious level and is not yet on the public or political agenda. The provision of information may sensitize them to the existence of the problem. The policy may provide education and training to enable targets and agents to take action when they do not know how to do what is required. Sometimes the impediment is an inability to reason through the complexities within the policy and determine the consequences and risks associated with particular activities. Driver education programs for teenagers and traffic offenders sometimes use simulation to illustrate the extent to which judgment and reaction time is crippled through abuse of drugs or alcohol. The lack of leadership and organization may be an impediment that can be addressed through capacity tools. Leadership academies have spread throughout the United States to increase citizen interest, support, and knowledge about local issues and how citizens and government need to work together to solve them

Hortatory tools consist mainly of proclamations, speeches, or public relations campaigns through which government exhorts people to take the actions needed by the policy. Designs that rely on hortatory and persuasive tools assume that people are motivated by images, symbols, and values. These tools aim either to change the values of agents or targets or to convince them that the behavior needed to achieve policy objectives is consistent with values already held. Imaging, labeling, and stigmatizing are common hortatory tools. Posters of Native Americans crying at environmental degradation appear on the sides of waste receptacles as a means of shaming litterers. Television spots associate sports figures with being drug free and thereby associate drug-free conditions with being sharp, physically fit, and admired. Language sometimes is used to transform negative images into positive ones (or vice versa) in hortatory portrayals. Persons who at various times in history have been called poor, disabled, crippled, retarded, or special are now referred to as "challenged" in an effort to avoid stigma. Behavior preferred by policy is associated with symbols carrying widespread public appeal such as military or sports heroes, while behavior detrimental to policy goals is portrayed as backward, out of the mainstream, or deviant. Excessive use of hortatory tools may be very damaging to democracy when they encourage divisiveness rather than reason, discussion, and moderation of negative attitudes toward fellow citizens.

Learning tools encourage agents and targets to act to solve problems, but leave the strategies to the agents or targets themselves. Learning tools encourage questioning and search. They require lessons to be drawn from experience, but do not try to anticipate which lessons. Agents are encouraged to anticipate problems through requirements to develop plans and to draw lessons through formal reporting requirements, evaluations, hearings, and institutional arrangements that promote interaction between agents and targets. Uncertainty and disagreement about goals and values are dealt with through such tools as surveys of attitudes, citizen advisory panels, focus groups, arbitration, and mediation. Uncertainty about means is addressed through such tools as research, brainstorming, pilot programs, and experimentation.

Learning tools are often directed toward initiating a discovery process rather than taking goal-directed action. While capacity-building and incentive tools are aimed at getting agents and targets to do something in particular, learning tools instigate doing things differently and deviation from past patterns is encouraged. Learning tools also differ from capacity building and the other approaches in that learning implies decentralization and empowerment rather than centralized authorities imposing their will. The Clean Air Act included requirements to establish a national study commission to make midcourse corrections once there had been a period of experience under new rules. These provisions signaled an openness that softened the impact of fairly draconian standards embodied in the legislation, if experience indicated that the actions required were not useful or too difficult and expensive. Rather than penalizing noncompliance with prescribed patterns as is the case with many incentive tools, learning tools minimize costs associated with behaviors that were taken in good faith but did not work out. Greater utilization of learning tools would seem to be beneficial to democratic values.

Policy tools, in close conjunction with the rules that specify what is to be done, define the kinds of experiences target populations will have with public policy and they define the way different agencies will relate to one another. For target populations, tools send clear signals about what kind of people they are, whether they deserve the benefits or burdens that have been assessed, and what their capacities are. Tools reflect the underlying motivations and send messages to the broader public about the characteristics of the target group. Within a policy arena, the signals sent by tools are especially noticeable when the policy separates targets into multiple subgroups and assigns different tools to each.

Tools also legitimate certain kinds of behavior and in many instances privilege particular behavioral styles. Tools that offer incentives or sanctions legitimate self-interested behavior, whereas hortatory tools often legitimate altruistic behavior as people are urged to take certain actions for the common good rather than for themselves. In situations in which self-interested behavior is rewarded, it becomes difficult for persons to behave altruistically, even when they wish to do so. Capacity-building and learning tools imply that people are capable of rational thinking and will take action, if they know what to do, without other incentives being necessary.

Over time, the tools within a specific policy arena may become highly varied and complex as policy designers seek ways to ensure greater compliance with the behavioral needs of the policy. To bring into compliance even the most extreme outliers (e.g., those who resist the policy in spite of extensive incentives or disincentives), policies may have to incorporate highly coercive tools or increase the value of incentives. Criminal justice policy, for example, becomes increasingly coercive with longer prison terms threatened in an attempt to ensure that even the most resistant person will be deterred. Given the extensive variability among individuals regarding the amount of punishment needed to ensure compliance, prison terms almost certainly will far exceed those needed to ensure compliance by most people and may never be severe enough to reach the most incalcitrant. Thus, criminal codes that attempt to deter all illegal behavior will become unjust in the sense that the punishment is disproportionately severe compared with the offense committed. Similarly, to ensure that all polluters stop polluting may require charges far higher than economically feasible.

Within agencies, the types of tools used to ensure compliance by lower-level agencies and caseworkers also send messages about the value and capacity of the agency as a whole, its clientele, or about the caseworkers as a group. State governments that systematically underfund education or welfare programs, preferring tax reductions and prison construction instead, for example, send clear messages about the value of children and poor people. Universities that systematically allocate fewer resources per student to social science and humanities programs are reflecting different values attached to technological and scientific programs of study compared with the "soft" disciplines. These kinds of allocations may eventually impact the self-image of agencies (or university departments) and their ability to serve as advocates for the target groups who stand to gain or lose by such allocations.

Rules

Rules are the procedural aspects of policy design and indicate who is to do what, where, and when. Rules circumscribe and channel policy-relevant behavior to serve policy-relevant goals. The importance of rules has long been acknowledged in organic acts and constitutional policy. Such policy is thought to be fundamental and to set the tone of all that is to come. For instance, state constitutions establish offices, specify the conditions of service, grant citizens protected rights, and determine duties. Elinor Ostrom has illustrated the importance of rules in the design of institutions established to resolve common pool resource problems (Ostrom 1990).

Eligibility rules define who the recipients of policy are intended to be and place boundaries around several different target populations that are made explicit within the design. Some eligibility rules are universalistic, so that almost all persons are eligible. Other eligibility rules are particularistic, so that to be included as a target requires that people meet a large number of requirements. For example, social security eligibility rules tend toward the universalistic type in that everyone over a certain age is eligible. On the other hand, Temporary Assistance to Needy Families, disabled workers' compensation, and food stamps are highly particularistic, and applicants must prove that they meet a number of specific criteria. Being automatically accepted by government as deserving, rather than undeserving unless proven otherwise, provides very different experiences for target populations. Rules can be clear or they may be vague and uncertain. The federal rules specifying which juvenile delinquents should be incarcerated and which should be placed on probation say that youth should be given the "least restrictive environment consistent with public safety." This rule sets a general tone implying the intention to balance the needs of the youth and the needs of the community. Considerable discretion, therefore, is given for local interpretations. Rules also may be flexible allowing for change as experience dictates, or they may be inflexible.

Timing rules specify when and in what sequence actions by targets and agents are to take place. Timing rules can include immediate action, staged requirements, or postponed action. Immediate action is often specified when action is easy to take or when the costs of inaction are high. Many laws postpone the time at which something needs to be done until the future or until such time as something else has taken place. Staged or postponed rules are more likely to be applied when problems are more difficult and several different sequenced steps are needed, such as policies to bring federal expenditures in line with federal revenue. Postponed action may also be specified when there is political opposition and postponement makes policy more acceptable. Taking immediate credit for the allocation of benefits and avoiding the blame for costs by postponing them is a misuse of rules from the perspective of fostering democracy.

Boundary or participation rules indicate who is to be included in decision processes established by policy designs. Such rules, for example, may specify that appointments to commissions must be bipartisan or that certain interest groups must be represented in appointments. Eligibility rules for judicial appointments are sometimes restricted to those recommended by bar associations. Participation rules may specify that public hearings must take place before certain administrative actions are taken. Location rules are like boundary rules in that they affect arenas for participation. Rules may specify that meetings or hearings must take place not just at headquarters, but in remote and outlying areas affected by policy.

Decision rules specify the level of approval and voting procedure necessary for action. Rules may require unanimity or supermajority, majority, or plurality support for action. Voting may take a variety of different forms including one person, one vote or cumulative voting in which each voter has a number of votes that can be stacked on one action or spread among several alternatives according to the voter's priorities. Decision rules also specify how decisions can be appealed or overturned and under what circumstances. Information rules may indicate what evidence can or cannot be considered in decisions and the way in which information is to be gathered and presented. Rules can be spelled out in detail by statutes or be spelled out in the course of implementation by lower-level agents.

Rules can reinforce or alter the prevailing distribution of power by granting advantages to certain segments of the population or denying participation and advantages to others. They can reinforce or undermine certain conceptions of justice. Rules that determine eligibility for admittance to universities based on the need to provide access to higher education for all racial/ethnic groups are based on a different conception of justice than admittance rules based on high school grades or scores on ACT/SAT examinations. Admittance rules that allocate a proportional share of educational places to each racial/ethnic group are based on an understanding of justice as requiring equal educational opportunity whereas rules based on achievement tests reflect an understanding of justice as merit. Rules that allocate budgets to departments within agencies in terms of their relative need reinforce a sense of cooperation and community based on egalitarian principles, whereas rules that allocate budgets based on "centrality to mission" or "productivity rankings" reinforce principles of merit, deservedness, or efficiency within the organization. Rules within policy differentiate the level of expectation for receiving the benefits of policy. Some policies confer rights on the target population, which carry important legal connotations. Other rules simply confer a desired state of affairs, but not one that can be claimed as a "right." Rules sometimes mandate that certain actions be taken without regard for policy costs whereas other rules specify that decision makers must balance costs with benefits.

How rules vary, like variations of other elements, has important implications for democracy. Whether a policy design is perceived as democratic depends very much on the open, inclusive, and flexible nature of rules. Among the reasons why inflexible, closed, and restrictive rules appear in designs is concern for fraud or cheating. It is possible that rules in governmental policy have become more strict as public confidence in the fairness and honesty of government has declined. Yet experience with overly strict rules fosters less positive experience and less favorable perceptions of government in a cycle damaging to democracy.

Rationales and Assumptions

Rationales are the explanations, justifications, or legitimations for the design itself or for some specific part of the design, such as the choice of a target population, tools, rules, goals, or implementation structure. Assumptions are the underlying logic that ties the elements together. Stated rationales are part of the public record, and decision makers invoke them in their explanations of why a policy is designed as it is and why it is expected to work. Rationales link design elements to context, making explicit claims that the design is responsive to the issue and will have positive effects. Context is what makes certain rationales credible; if the issue is constructed differently, then the design no longer seems a rational response. Majone (1989) argued that the role of the policy analyst is to discover the rationales, because inventing and explaining reasons is fundamental to policy intention. In the same way that legal reasoning undergirds the law, policy rationalization is essential to policy legitimacy. Further, inventing new reasons or reinterpreting old explanations is essential to policy change. Rationales send messages to target populations and others about the values of society and the worth of various social groups in relation to such values.

Some rationales may be exposed as deceptive and therefore damaging to democracy. For instance, it is widely believed that incarceration serves as a deterrent. Stringent mandatory sentencing is justified on the basis of such reasoning. Even though there is little evidence to suggest that longer sentences actually deter anyone, the rationale is consistent with a common construction of reality. Rationales must at least be plausible if they are to be politically viable. For example, it is relatively simple at this point in history to convince people that substance abuse may be lowered because of fear of discovery and therefore, that mandatory drug and alcohol testing of transportation workers will be related to reduction of accidents.

Effectiveness is but one of many important rationales, but because policies are supposed to solve problems and achieve goals, utilitarian reasoning is an especially attractive rationale. Economic rationality is a powerful guide to action in some policy areas. In natural resource policy, the advisability of building dams, levees, and other structures is determined by benefit/cost analysis. A favorable benefit/cost ratio is the seal of approval that determines which of a large number of possible projects actually get built. In more recent years, the finding of no adverse environmental impact after an environmental assessment has been conducted is required in natural resources projects. Formal tests performed by trained evaluators provide rationales that the public interest is being served. At the same time such expert rationales may marginalize the thought processes of average citizens as we discuss in Chapter 6.

Economic or scientific progress, the public interest, fairness, deservedness, justice, compensation for past injustice, equality, due process, ideology, and precedent are frequently resorted to as rationales. Some rationales are extremely powerful but usually serve only as long as they are unstated. It is clear that stereotypes and prejudice often govern choices of targets, tools, and other elements. For instance, traffic police may stop minority teenagers much more frequently than other teenagers, even though they would not officially acknowledge this or have any written policies specifying that minorities should be stopped more frequently. Racial stereotypes may well exist in the minds of police and others, but would not be considered a legitimate rationale by most persons at this point in our history. Unmasking such stereotypes in the course of analysis reduces their influence as a guide to action and strengthens the case for democratic designs.

Assumptions often are unstated and must be discovered through analysis of policy elements and the reasoning that is consistent with their connections. Rationales imply certain underlying assumptions, but assumptions may exist in policy designs quite independently of any stated rationales. Analysts who deconstruct policy logics may discover hidden and embedded assumptions that appear obvious once revealed. Assumptions contain a great deal of information about the issue context and the designing dynamics, including information about the social constructions of targets, social construction of knowledge, institutional culture, and power relationships.

The extent to which rationales lend credence to policy designs varies. Some rationales are characterized by easy-to-understand causal linkages grounded in well-accepted scientific theories whereas other rationales have causal connections that are considered to be quite illogical, requiring great leaps of faith to believe that the policy elements could possibly produce the intended effects. Policy logic may be subject to different interpretations depending on whether scientific, discursive, or other forms of rationality are applied. The logic of the design also contains messages that have effects on how citizens view government and their relationship to it. Some may contain messages that are clear and unambiguous; others will carry messages that are so subtle that even those directly impacted may be unaware. Well-designed policies contain credible logics that produce reliable results and contribute to democratic values.

From a democratic perspective, it is important that rationales have a close fit with actual policy goals and reasonable expectations of effects. Policies that are deceptive and dishonest undermine citizenship and confidence in democratic governance.

CONCLUSION

Policy designs should be a central component of any causal or interpretive theory of public policy. The way design elements are chosen and linked together determines whether policies help to solve problems or make them worse. Policy designs affect who wins and who loses. Over time, designs have a dramatic effect on the distribution of wealth and other resources within society. Most important, the choice of policy elements and the underlying policy logic reflect the current conditions of democracy and shape the future conditions. Policy designs signal whether politics is a game of self-interest or a process of deliberation through which broader, collective interests are served. Policy logic and elements teach lessons about the role of citizens in a democracy and what can be expected from government. Depending on the differential ways people are treated, lessons that prompt mobilization and involvement or alienation and withdrawal are learned by citizens.

It is our view that poorly designed policies are both the cause and consequence of degenerative forces at work in contemporary governance. Rather than democracy working to identify problems and improve governmental responses, designs too often reflect other agendas and foster the loss of democratic values. As democratic values are undermined, the conditions of democracy deteriorate even as they become part of the (future) historical context from which subsequent designs will be created.

The next two chapters elaborate on the theory of policy design we are advancing by focusing on the processes through which social constructions become embedded in design and how these constructions are then translated into effects on democracy. Chapter 5 sets forth a theory of degenerative policy design in which the social constructions of target populations play a central role. Chapter 6 contains our theory of scientific and professionalized designs that become possible through a complex interaction between power, social constructions, and characteristics of the scientific community.

5

Social Constructions of Target Populations: Degenerative Policy Designs

Much of the public policy in the United States is produced in policy-making systems dominated by divisive social constructions that stigmatize some potential target populations and extol the virtues of others. These constructions interact with the political power of the target groups to establish the political agenda, focus the terms of debate, and determine the characteristics of policy designs. This chapter will describe the designs of policy produced through what we call a "degenerative" policy-making process, suggest how they are created and perpetuated, and interpret their consequences for democracy.

DEGENERATIVE POLICY-MAKING CONTEXTS

Issue contexts in degenerative policy-making systems are characterized by an unequal distribution of political power, social constructions that separate the "deserving" from the "undeserving," and an institutional culture that legitimizes strategic, manipulative, and deceptive patterns of communication and uses of political power (see Figure 5.1). The social construction of potential target populations interacts with the extent of political power to form four different kinds of possible policy targets: advantaged (who are powerful and positively constructed); contenders (powerful but negatively constructed as undeserving or greedy); dependents (positively constructed as "good" people but relatively needy or helpless who have little or no political power); and deviants (who have virtually no political power and are negatively constructed as undeserving, violent, mean, and so forth). Policy entrepreneurs such as policy makers, interest group leaders, political parties, media, scientists, and others anticipate how an issue needs to be framed so that public policies advantageous to their own cause will appear to be the only rational response. If there is little likelihood of framing an issue so that it presents

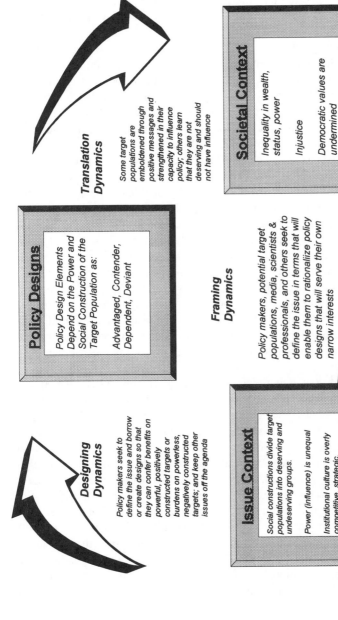

Figure 5.1. Degenerative policy-making system.

Policy Designs

Policy Design Elements Depend on the Power and Social Construction of the Target Population as:

Advantaged, Contender, Dependent, Deviant

Translation Dynamics

Some target populations are emboldened through positive messages and strengthened in their capacity to influence policy; others learn that they are not deserving and should not have influence

Societal Context

Inequality in wealth, status, power

Injustice

Democratic values are undermined

Citizenship distorted

Designing Dynamics

Policy makers seek to define the issue and borrow or create designs so that they can confer benefits on powerful, positively constructed targets or burdens on powerless, negatively constructed targets; and keep other issues off the agenda

Framing Dynamics

Policy makers, potential target populations, media, scientists & professionals, and others seek to define the issue in terms that will enable them to rationalize policy designs that will serve their own narrow interests

Issue Context

Social constructions divide target populations into deserving and undeserving groups.

Power (influence) is unequal

Institutional culture is overly competitive, strategic, manipulative, self-interested, and deceptive clear-cut political opportunities, there will be an attempt to frame it as one best addressed by the "private" sector, or by experts who will draw on scientific and professional analysis to suggest policy options.

The policy design dynamics in degenerative policy-making systems are focused on the calculation of political opportunities and risks rather than policy analysis, deconstruction of images, or discursive participation by affected groups. Political leaders actively search for issues that have been constructed in such a way that they present an opportunity to gain power, claim credit for popular policy, or increase the legitimacy and stature of the policy maker and his or her cause. Persons in policy-making positions will carefully select from among the available issues or events the ones that will enable them to confer beneficial policy on advantaged populations (powerful, well-liked groups) or punishment on deviants (politically weak, negatively constructed groups). Political leaders anticipate which issues lend themselves not only to political gain, but which also can be constructed (or reconstructed) to have a "public interest" spin and to appear to provide rational policy designs for high-priority issues even as they mainly serve a more limited purpose desired by the policy maker.

The policy designs produced by degenerative politics contain elements with quite different characteristics, depending on the type of target population. As shown in Figure 5.1, different kinds of target populations usually will be associated with particular kinds of goals, rules, tools, rationales, and assumptions. Careful analysis of policy designs will reveal the underlying assumptions and social constructions of target populations that were implicated in making a particular design politically feasible.

Policy designs contain both instrumental and symbolic messages that teach lessons about democracy, justice, citizenship, and the capacity of the society to solve collective problems. The messages and lessons are closely tied to the type of target population, however, so that persons who usually find themselves within one or another advantaged group learn quite different lessons than those who usually are treated as deviants, contenders, or dependents. In degenerative policy-making situations, each type of target group receives a rather distinctive set of messages that influences its orientation toward government and its political participation. These messages, orientations, and participation patterns are the translation dynamics that link policy to societal conditions. Degenerative policy designs exacerbate inequality in wealth, status, and power as those who already have the most tend to gain even more from public policy. Injustice across different race, gender, ethnic, and social classes is common. Democratic values are undermined and differentially reinforced. Citizenship becomes distorted and narrowed so that it mainly refers to claims of rights and the pursuit of self-interest. The effects of degenerative policy designs differ among the various types of target populations. Each group begins to take on its own distinctive expectations and conceptions of citizenship, democracy, justice, and effective problem solving. Furthermore, the instrumental consequences of policy are such that different groups live in quite different societal conditions with some experiencing a much stronger sense of citizenship, more effective problem solving, a more just society, and a richer set of democratic values than others.

Degenerative policy-making dynamics are well served (albeit unwittingly) by the idea that almost any construction of events, people, or issues is possible and can vie for legitimacy without significant constraints from ethics or from factual, empirical, or scientific evidence. Although all reality is subject to being socially constructed, it would be a mistake in politics and policy making to believe that there are no underlying material conditions or circumstances within which people live. Societal conditions are socially constructed, but these constructions are subject to deconstruction and unmasking so that differences among people can be viewed more clearly.

Institutional Culture

All types of policy-making institutions are susceptible to degenerative politics, including those of formal government (legislative, executive, and judicial) and beyond government in the workplace, professional associations, and the family. Institutions, however, differ in their vulnerability to degenerative politics. Some may have a dominant culture, often characterized in popular language as "politicized," in which almost every issue brings out strategic, manipulative, deceptive, and dishonest behavior. In degenerative ("politicized") institutional cultures, various individuals or factions use issues to further their own cause quite apart from any consideration of the actual merits of the issue itself. There may be little or no effort to find common ground or to pursue the public interest of the organization as a whole or of the constituencies it is expected to serve. Degenerative institutional cultures often contain "in" groups and "out" groups that attempt to frame issues in such a way that they can claim credit for themselves and embarrass the other side. Divisive and disrespectful language are common features of degenerative institutional cultures, and there is a marked loss of trust, civility, and collegiality. Public policy is not a means of solving problems or even resolving conflicts among competing perspectives, but is instead an instrument of power that can be used opportunistically by each faction to further its own legitimacy, popularity, or future power position. Interaction patterns are confrontational and competitive rather than discursive and cooperative. Communication styles tend to be antagonistic, deceptive, and secretive. The ethics and norms that guide cooperative interaction are largely absent. People do not have to be honest, to state real reasons, to weigh empirical evidence in terms of the nature of the problem and the probable effects of the policy, or even to treat one another with respect.

Some policy-making institutions may exhibit degenerative traits on almost every issue they consider and others may seldom show these tendencies. We expect, however, that most institutions move from one to the other *depending on the characteristics of the issue, the personalities of the participants, and the risks or opportunities offered by the various policy designs that might be devised as responses to the issue.* Issues for which failed policy may constitute a severe threat to the survival of the institution itself may bring out a less degenerative form of politics—but even here there is no guarantee. If some persons or factions are so bitterly opposed to others or alienated from the institution itself, they may politicize even the most threatening issues in an effort to actually facilitate the failure of the institution. The point here is that institutional cultures and policy-making dynamics are not permanent structural features, and a particular institution may handle one issue differently than another. The U.S. Congress, for example, often is able to consider serious foreign policy issues in a "nonpartisan" manner in which everyone seems focused on doing what is best for the country, whereas domestic social policy is much more susceptible to degenerative politics.

Participants within an institutional setting have the capacity to help direct policy making toward or away from degenerative styles. Leadership can shape the culture and standard operating procedures of an institution and attempt to construct issues so that they will be considered through a more cooperative, discursive policy-making process; or they can "politicize" issues and use them to their own advantage. Events from within or outside can create sudden "shocks" that unmask the dysfunctional characteristics of degenerative interaction patterns and grant participants and leaders the opportunity to bring about significant change. Nevertheless, the power of institutions to adhere to historical patterns of interaction that shape the beliefs and behavior of members should not be underestimated. Institutions have powerful effects on their members and newly inducted members are more likely to take on the culture of the institution than to challenge it effectively.

Social Constructions

Perhaps the single most distinctive characteristic of degenerative policy making is the focus on social constructions of potential target populations and the way social constructions interact with political power to create opportunities or risks for policy makers. The policy designs produced in these settings differ significantly from scientific and professional designs, as will be shown in the next chapter, but our focus here is on the important differences in the designs produced *within* degenerative contexts and how these systematically damage democracy.

The social construction process is one through which values and meaning become attached to events, people, patterns of action, or any other phenomena. These values and meanings enable interpretation and provide rationales for action. The process of socially constructing reality produces "social constructions" that refer to the values and meanings associated with events, persons, groups, regions, countries, or any other objective or subjective situation. The social constructions of people or events sometimes are so ingrained that most people accept them as real and as the only interpretation they can imagine. Nevertheless, constructions are not immutable, but are subject to change and manipulation through the constant interaction of events, people, media, politics, religion, science, literature, music, and others involved in the ongoing process of socially constructing the world. Constructions emerge from many stimuli including the imaginations and critique of journalists, politicians, writers, and social scientists. Individuals, however, bring their own personal experiences, observations, intuitions, and values to the socially constructed world in which they live and are able to unmask and "see through" constructions that have wandered too far from their own observations and experiences. The theory of social constructions that we embrace in this book is not one of strict constructionism in which there are no underlying material conditions; but is more of a contextual constructionism that recognizes that there are constraints and limits on the social constructions.

Institutions and societies differ not only in how specific groups or events are constructed, but in the kinds of constructions that are legitimate. In degenerative policy-making systems, the construction of persons or groups often revolves around divisive concepts such as "deserving" or "undeserving," "intelligent" or "stupid," "kind" or "mean," "loyal" or "disloyal," "violent" or "peaceful," and other value-laden terms that divide people and serve as guides for the allocation of respect, privilege, and status. In less degenerative situations, ethical constraints, empathy, or respect may make such divisive and negative constructions unlikely. When policy making is not subject to degenerative tendencies, various identities may take on distinctive constructions, but all are accorded respect that is associated with their differences.

Social constructions become central to the strategies of public officials, especially those who are in elected or highly visible positions where they are expected to pay attention to public preferences, because people care intensely not only about what they receive from government, but what others are receiving as well, and why. In degenerative policy-making systems there is a great deal to be gained politically by providing beneficial policy to "deserving" or "good" people. Those who are direct recipients will be pleased, and those who are not will view the allocation as fair. There is also much to be gained by disciplining "undeserving" people who are "lazy" or "immoral," or punishing those constructed as "criminals" or "drug kingpins."

Social constructions of actual or potential target populations vary along several dimensions: positive to negative, strongly constructed to hardly any construction at all, long-standing to those that are new or rapidly changing, those that are internally homogeneous to those that are heterogeneous, and those that are virtually consensual throughout the society to those that are heatedly debated. Poor people, for example, have been defined by public policy as those who fall below the official poverty level (or who are some specified percentage below the official poverty level). The social constructions could portray them as disadvantaged people whose poverty is not their fault or as lazy persons who are benefiting from other peoples' hard work. This group does not have a homogeneous construction, however, but is comprised of many different subgroups, each of whom may carry a different social construction and be treated differently by public policy. Disabled persons with income below the poverty level, for example, carry a more positive construction than "welfare queens" even though they both have about the same income and both receive welfare benefits. Not all target populations even have a well-defined social construction. Left-handed people have no strong construction at this point in history and have virtually no public policy directed toward them.

Types of (Potential) Target Populations

Social constructions of social groups interact with the political power of those groups to create different types of actual and potential target populations. Figure 5.2 shows how a hypothetical policy maker might array some of the groups that commonly become involved in policy designs. The horizontal dimension shows the valence attached to their social constructions. Those whose constructions are more positive are closer to the left and those with less positive constructions are closer to the right-hand side. Intermediate points reflect groups arrayed along this continua. The vertical dimension represents political power, conceptualized mainly in terms of the first face of power—to influence. The more influential groups are closer to the top and the less powerful ones closer to the bottom. The four types of target populations have been called *advantaged, contenders, dependents,* and *deviants.*

Advantaged groups are those with considerable resources to influence policy (size, voting strength, wealth, propensity to mobilize, for example) who also carry positive social constructions. Perhaps the single most salient construction from a public policy point of view is whether the group is considered to be "meritorious" and "deserving" or considered "undeserving," "unworthy," or even "greedy." Among the groups in the United States who often are constructed positively and who also have significant political power resources are business, the middle class, veterans, farmers, scientists, and senior citizens. These groups are seen as deserving, as having earned a position of respect, and of doing good things for the country. Family farmers are viewed as embodying the traditional values of family, hard work, and morality. The military is respected for its courage. Scientists are constructed as intelligent and as those who produce new information that will contribute to the economy, to military superiority, to advancements in medicine, and to an exploration of the unknown.

Contenders have political power but carry generally negative constructions. Chief executive officers (CEOs), rich people, "big unions," and "Wall Street bankers" historically have been among the groups that are powerful but constructed as greedy, not caring about the effects of their actions, and not deserving of their exalted status. Homosexuals, minority groups, and feminists are less powerful but often constructed as not deserving, asking for too much too fast, interested only in their own well-being, receiving unfair advantages, and undermining traditional values. Gun owners increasingly are losing their positive construction as sportsmen, rugged individualists, and the like in favor of a more negative construction as irre-

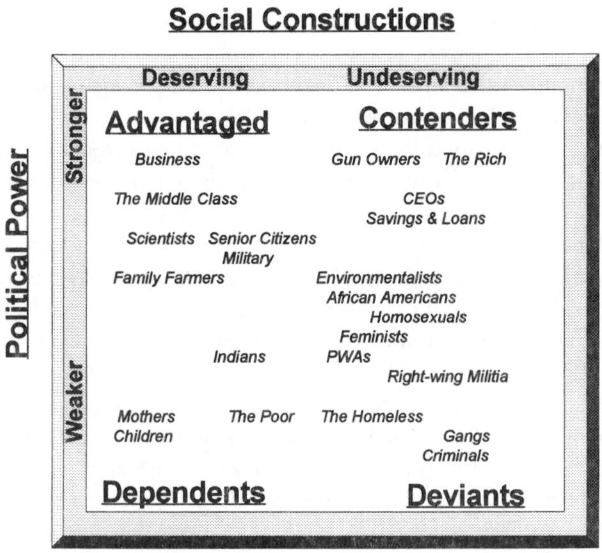

Figure 5.2. Political power resources and social construction of social groups as conceptualized by a hypothetical elected official.

sponsible and selfish people who are blocking changes needed to reduce violence or who organize into militia because of a hate for government, thereby carrying opposition to government too far.

Dependents historically have included children, mothers, the poor, and others considered to be politically weak but with positive constructions. Children are usually viewed as loving, sweet, blameless, helpless, and needing the care of others. They have almost no political power of their own, and even the advocacy groups that have emerged on their behalf tend to be far less powerful than those who work on behalf of business, senior citizens, farmers, the military, and so on. Mothers are seen as persons to be loved and admired but who have almost no political or public presence. Mothers Against Drunk Driving is one of the few examples of political mobilization. The construction of mothers assumes that their appropriate place is in the home. The most positive constructions of the poor tend to focus on their helplessness and the adversities that condemn them to their life of poverty. More negative constructions portray them as lazy, undisciplined, immoral, or as lacking intelligence. The homeless are pitied, but not viewed as entirely blameless for their plight. Teenagers do not carry constructions as positive as those of younger children, but not usually negative, either. Teens are seen as needing guidance to thwart their irresponsibility.

Deviants, such as criminals, gangs, and drug kingpins are in the worst situation as they are both politically weak and negatively constructed. Gangs, criminals, and drug kingpins are constructed as violent, dangerous, threatening, and deserving to be punished. Communists and fascists are other examples of powerless, negatively constructed groups. Communists once were constructed as evil, extremely dangerous, and threatening to American values. Their worldwide decline is gradually altering this image into one of a defeated political enemy.

Some social constructions are quite unstable and subject to rapid change. Elected officials, advocates, and members of social groups do not simply respond in passive ways to the social constructions established by society or the media. Groups and their advocates struggle to obtain a more positive construction. Elected leaders not only attempt to influence the construction, but are poised to take quick advantage of opportunities for changes in social constructions that may have political payoffs for themselves or their political party. Other social constructions may remain constant over a long period of time, as have the prevailing constructions of criminals or communists, but others are subject to continual debate, manipulation, and incremental or sudden change. Persons living with AIDS (PWAs) were initially constructed primarily as deviants—gay men or drug users who are being punished by God for their sins and who deserve to die young. When research identified hemophiliacs, children, and heterosexuals as victims, however, the media began portraying such persons as "undeserving victims," and a far more differentiated group of constructions became possible. The revelations that admired Americans such as Rock Hudson and others suffered from the disease have helped reduce the stigma. Social constructions are created through politics, media portrayals, religion, movies, literature, education, and social science researchers. Events, such as the Oklahoma City bombing, may have sudden and long-lasting effects on the social constructions of groups such as the "right wing militia."

Political power also is not a static phenomenon, as the context of the situation may have much to do with the power of an individual or group; and the power (or perception of power) can be changed and manipulated. The pluralists and public choice scholars have made an important contribution when they point out that even relatively small groups can be powerful if they succeed in convincing public officials that they are the critical swing votes in a closely contested election and will cast their support on the basis of a single issue. The ability of carefully crafted media messages and the skill of political public relations firms have fundamentally altered the ability of a group to make itself appear to be politically powerful. Groups may become more powerful by mobilizing for political action; by manipulating their own construction toward one that will be received more favorably by the public; or by portraying their opponents in negative ways (privileged, greedy, untrustworthy).

A social group that is a potential target population may not fit into only one category of social construction, but may have members arrayed across the four types. The American Indian population, for example, might be perceived as having a very small number of persons in the advantaged quadrant as there may be a few who have both power and positive social constructions, a slightly larger number who have political power but who do not have positive constructions (such as the American Indian Movement), a larger number who are viewed as dependents (good people, but lacking power and generally less capable), and a smaller number who are viewed as deviants.

Most people do not identify just with one group, however, and individuals may find themselves associated with many groups that have different social constructions. These individuals will have a variety of experiences with public policy. Others, however, may identify with or be affiliated only with groups that fall primarily into one of the social constructions. Consider a divorced woman president of a large bank with two teenage children and who is an activist in various feminist movements. As a bank president, she will often be treated as a member of an advantaged population. When she is called by the police to obtain the release of one of her children who has been arrested for having an open container in the vehicle, she will be treated as a part of the dependent or deviant population. In her extracurricular feminist political activities lobbying for various feminist issues she will experience politics as a member of the contender group—quite a different type of political interaction than she generally would experience as a bank president. Young black men, in contrast, may experience life as a member of the negatively constructed deviant population, even if such constructions are not warranted. Some middle-aged white men may have generally consistent experiences as members of the advantaged population, whereas others may find themselves in situations where they are viewed as having more power and privilege than they deserve, and experience the kinds of contempt directed at contenders.

Designing and Framing Dynamics: Calculation of Political Opportunities and Risks

The behavior of public officials is strongly influenced by the political power and the social constructions of potential target populations. The direct political power of constituency groups can have immediate implications, but the social constructions of groups targeted by policy may have profound effects stemming from the way the media and other constituency groups view the appropriateness of the policies. In addition to power and social constructions, however, public officials must pay some attention to producing public policies that are addressed to major public problems and that are effective (Arnold 1990; Kelman 1987; Quade 1982). In spite of the erosion of democratic forms and processes, Americans have maintained a sense of democratic values and have not accepted as legitimate the highly politicized characteristics of modern democracy. Public officials are expected to explain and justify their policy positions to the electorate by articulating a vision of the public interest and then showing how a proposed policy is logically connected to these widely shared public values (Arnold 1990; Habermas 1975; Offe 1985). To maintain credible arguments about policy effectiveness, they need to have a believable causal logic connecting the various aspects of the policy design to desired outcomes. Thus, public officials have to pay attention to the logical connection between the target groups and the goals that might be achieved. They also must take into account the tendency of the American public to believe in fairness and justice. Government should not give anyone more than they deserve, nor should government contribute to unfairness or injustice. These pressures yield countervailing tendencies and place policy makers in situations of conflicting values.

Public policy can confer either benefits or burdens (or both) to each of the four types of potential target populations, producing eight different policy arenas, each of which produces its own distinctive array of political opportunities and risks. Figure 5.3 shows the opportunities and risks for distributing benefits and burdens within each of the eight policy arenas. Beneficial policy includes such things as subsidies, rules that grant advantages to the group in their economic or social pursuits, tax breaks, policy tools that grant the group control, rationales that provide positive constructions for the group, or other government actions that enable the group to gain values that it prefers. Burdens are the negative side of these same concepts: taxation, rules that confer disadvantages, tools that constrict control or liberty, or other actions that confer negative values on a group.

It is important to notice that only two segments of the policy box offer clearcut political opportunities (see Figure 5.4). One is to provide beneficial policy to powerful, positively constructed groups. The second area of opportunity is found at the back of the box: to provide punishment policies to negatively constructed, powerless groups. All the other policy arenas are characterized mainly by risks or possibly negative results.

The different types of potential or actual target populations are centrally important in understanding public policy because, in degenerative contexts, many of the differences found in policy designs can be traced to the type of target groups. Differences in the characteristics of target populations are systematically associated with differences in allocation of benefits and burdens, choice of policy rules and tools, the implementation systems, and the rationales. These distinctions in policy design lead to differences in the messages (meanings) found in public policy that, in turn, produce different understandings of citizenship and democracy among target populations.

In the discussion that follows, we develop a theory linking each of the elements of design (as dependent variables) to the different types of target populations (as independent variables) and offer possible explanations of the dynamic processes through which the linkage occurs.

CHOOSING TARGETS FOR BENEFITS AND BURDENS

In degenerative policy-making systems target populations are often identified first, sometimes even before problems to be solved and goals established. Potential issues are closely scrutinized in terms of who the possible target populations might be and whether these offer risks or opportunities for political leaders. Most of the other design elements depend on who the targets are, including the critical decision of whether benefits or burdens will be prescribed. As we noted in Chapter 4,

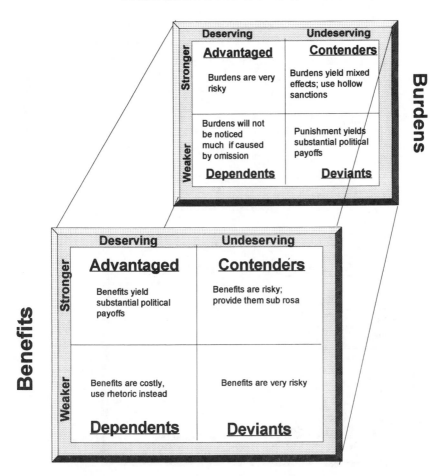

Figure 5.3. Policy design characteristics depend on power and social constructions of target populations and whether benefits or burdens are being distributed.

even when goals or problems to be solved are selected first, targets tend to be highly substitutable. In degenerative situations, the substitutability becomes exceptionally broad due to the ability and willingness of policy makers to manipulate information and facts thereby making almost any policy design seem to be a logical approach to the problem. The result is a distinctive pattern in the allocation of benefits and burdens.

Advantaged Populations

In degenerative policy-making systems target populations that are defined as both powerful and positive (the advantaged) are selected whenever possible for beneficial

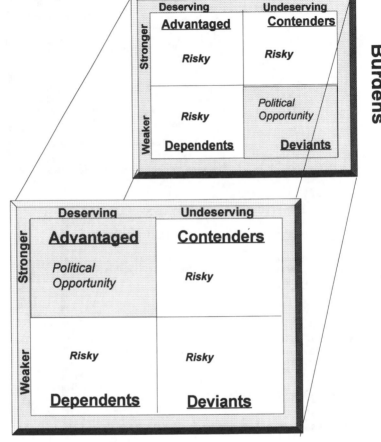

Figure 5.4. Only two arenas offer clear-cut political opportunities: providing benefits to advantaged groups and burdens to target groups constructed as deviants. All other areas are politically risky.

policy and are seldom chosen for policies that allocate costs. Distributive policies that contain only benefits usually go to advantaged populations and arouse little opposition. The lack of contention can be attributed not only to the lack of visible costs to others, but also to the positive image of the group and the ability of legislators to mask and hide the policies from public view. Even when the policies become known, it is unlikely that a public can be mobilized against policy that helps strong and well-regarded people. Advantaged populations will find it easier than other groups to get their issues on legislative agendas, for they offer attractive policy opportunities that public officials can use to generate the appearance of enlightened leadership. Advantaged groups have the resources and capacity to shape their own constructions and to combat attempts that would portray them negatively. They are much better able to protect themselves from budget cuts than are people constructed as dependents, contenders, or deviants.

One of the best and most long-standing examples in the United States is the use of tax breaks and subsidies by state and local governments to attract powerful, positively constructed business and industry from other states. To entice Toyota to build an assembly plant in their state, for example, Kentucky officials offered an estimated $140 million in incentives (Dionne 1993). In Illinois, the state and local officials eager to keep the headquarters of Sears, Roebuck and Company offered to put up $61 million to build highways and improve the prospective site (Dionne 1993). Voters in Maricopa County, Arizona, approved a special sales tax earmarked to build a baseball stadium for a major league expansion team that subsequently was recruited to the area.

At the national level, science and technology policy intended to strengthen the military and economic competitiveness was estimated in 1995 at more than $70 billion dollars each year. The Star Wars initiative cost more than $30 billion before it was shut down. Agriculture subsidies are granted to strengthen the family farm and ensure the competitiveness of American agriculture abroad. Attempts to limit entitlements to senior citizens were repeatedly derailed in the 1980s and 1990s by the intense political power and positive image of this group. Projects considered to be "pork barrel" are far more likely to be directed at advantaged populations within the congressional district than toward contenders, deviants, or dependents. There are enormous expenditures on "middle-class" or "corporate" welfare, estimated by Robert Reich, secretary of labor in the Clinton administration, at $250 billion. Examples include tax write-offs for interest paid on home mortgages that benefit homeowners and federal subsidies for international advertising to firms.

The easiest problems for elected officials to address will be those for which advantaged segments of the population receive benefits that can be logically connected with public interest goals. In degenerative policy systems, however, these groups may receive beneficial policy even if the causal linkages to some ostensibly common or public purpose lack credibility or are entirely absent. The advantaged groups often will be chosen as first-order (proximate) targets even when others would be more logical or efficient. For instance, in the name of alleviating poverty, money is first distributed not to the poor, but to advantaged groups who populate local government and nonprofit agencies. Employment policy selects industrial employers as a first-order (proximate) target rather than the jobless. Housing policy allocates money to home builders and housing investors as a means of ultimately benefiting the homeless. The proximate position of the advantaged as targets in the policy chain is important because there is greater certainty of actually receiving the benefits if one is a more proximate target.

Advantaged groups are not often selected as targets for policies that allocate costs. Because of the ability of advantaged groups to wield political power and to mobilize others, policies unfavorable to advantaged groups are infeasible, or even repellent (Arnold 1990). Such policies are highly contentious, and public officials will go to great lengths to keep such issues off the agenda. For example, it is difficult to generate support for burdensome regulations of positively viewed businesses because the proximate target groups will oppose the policies vigorously and argue that the chain of effects is not likely to produce the desired results anyway. Or, they may argue that other groups are more logical and if chosen as targets would have a greater impact. The secondary or remote target groups who presumably will benefit from the regulations may not provide as much support as expected, because of the uncertainty that the cause and effect logic within the policy is correct (Arnold 1990).

In most instances where burdensome policy is directed to advantaged groups as proximate targets, other advantaged target groups are also intended as beneficiaries. The policy chain often is such that one target group must take action so that others can benefit, and it is possible to portray the burden as a fair or equitable share or an unavoidable condition of accomplishing a desired end. Regulatory policy such as the Clean Air Act has been justified as necessary to protect health. During periods of droughts, rationing policy that limits water use in urban areas is politically most acceptable if it applies to all categories of users and is voluntary.

The risks for politicians who direct burdens toward advantaged groups are obvious. Advantaged groups have sufficient power to generate and support a viable opponent in subsequent elections; but perhaps even more important, the groups often have sufficient power to not comply with the legislation at all and to challenge it at every step in its implementation. There are also some risks or constraints even when providing beneficial policy to advantaged groups. The political attractiveness of these policies may entice public officials into providing far more favors from government than are necessary to achieve policy that is effective, fair, or representative of public preferences. The results may be increasingly ineffective policy, producing the need for public officials to engage in media campaigns intended to convince the public that policies are working and to mask the true effects. The public may begin to see allocation of benefits as unfair and may shift their perception of advantaged groups from deserving to greedy or privileged, thereby undercutting their popular support. This too is costly to public officials, because it is quite difficult to gain political advantages by designing public policy for contenders (powerful groups that are constructed as greedy or undeserving).

One of the effects of this dynamic in sophisticated political institutions is that political leaders will take care not to appear to give special privileges but will emphasize purportedly universalistic application of rules that appear to treat everyone equally. The highly specific elaboration of presumably universalistic rules in legislation sometimes masks the myriad ways that the policy will produce outcomes mainly for advantaged groups.

Benefits and Burdens for Contenders

The ideals of U.S. democracy are such that too much power and privilege will eventually draw resentment and suspicion. Privileged and elite groups that appear to be abusing power are vulnerable to being cast in a negative light. Corporations, Wall Street bankers, the rich, defense contractors, gun owners, and even savings and loan associations have been portrayed as special interests who have too much power, enjoy too many privileges, and have gotten more than they deserve.

Tax policies offer insight into the ways in which powerful but negatively constructed groups were able to gain substantial benefits for themselves, largely hidden from public view. Since 1977, federal tax burdens have steadily been shifted from the rich to the middle and working class. Between 1977 and 1990, Congress enacted seven major tax bills that resulted in a 36 percent reduction in the tax burden of the richest 1 percent of the population. Middle-class families realized a 7 percent increase (Greider 1992). How was this done? Greider (1992) says: "In order to accomplish such distorted outcomes, the governing elites and monetary interests are required to create a series of elaborate screens around the subject of taxes—a moving tableau of convincing illusions that distracts the public from the real content and gives politicians a place to hide."

The types of deception described by Greider (1992) included collusion between the political parties in agreeing on the need for tax cuts on the wealthy and increases on others when appearing to be in disagreement over this matter. Policy studies and blue ribbon commissions issued reports contending that tax reductions on upper-income people were needed to spur investments that would create jobs. Economic development was linked to capital creation, and thereby to the wealthy, rather than to incomes and employment. Pressure to deal effectively with the huge national deficit was deflated by increasing Social Security payroll taxes, one of the most regressive of all taxes, thereby creating a huge surplus in this fund that counts against the actual size of the national debt. Social Security has a fixed ceiling, such that all income above a certain level is exempt. In 1997, persons making millions a year paid the same in Social Security taxes as those making $65,400. This tax was raised ostensibly to protect the "pay as you go" financing for Social Security.

Powerful but negatively viewed groups present almost no political opportunities and numerous risks for policy designers. Contenders are only occasionally the recipients of directly beneficial policy, because to serve their interests too blatantly is to risk countervailing mobilization and resistance from the general public. When policy directed toward contenders places them in proximate positions as direct recipients of beneficial policy, the policies are likely to be opaque and deceptive as they contain benefits noticed only by members of the target groups and largely hidden from everyone else. Beneficial policy can be provided, however, if both parties find it in their interests to do so and the media attention can be directed elsewhere, as exemplified by the tax cuts for the rich during the 1980s and 1990s and the favorable regulatory policies (and lack of regulatory restrictions) for Wall Street bankers. There is no question that public opinion supported higher tax rates for high-income groups, not lower ones, and continued regulation to prevent failure of the nation's financial institutions. Nevertheless, the complexity of the issues, the tacit agreement between the parties, and the failure of the media to educate the public about these issues shut them out of this debate.

Contenders are more likely to be positioned as remote targets for whom positive effects will be more difficult to trace because they are only one of a number of beneficiaries, some of whom are more popular and better regarded. The extension of federal deposit insurance to $100,000 in 1993 (up from $40,000) appeared to grant added protection to substantial portions of the middle class. In fact, however, this provision defused the potential outrage of the middle class when savings and loan associations were being shut down for insolvency. The federal government eschewed proposals to cover the shortfall through special taxes on depositors or levies on the institutions themselves (both of which would have risked substantial mobilization of negative public opinion), and instead covered the defaults from the general fund, passing the costs (estimated at $200 billion) to the general public through increased deficits.

Another example is the agriculture export subsidy. This program began a decade ago to bolster crop exports that would help beleaguered farmers. Instead, the $40 billion program has enriched a small group of multinational corporations while doing little to expand the American share of the world's agricultural markets (*New York Times,* Oct. 10, 1993). From 1986 to 1989, one program involving $1.38 billion paid out more than half of its funds to four multinational corporations, two of them actually based in Europe. In this example, a positively constructed group (family farmers) is used as the apparent target population; but most of the money goes to multinational corporations whose officers and shareholders are far removed from the fields and lifestyles of family farmers.

In degenerative situations public officials prefer policies that the public and media believe inflict burdens on powerful, negative groups, but that actually have few if any negative effects. Policies pertaining to defense contractors offer a useful example. Defense contractors are often accused of cost overruns, inefficiency, and fraud. These companies may be fined what appear to be large amounts. Teledyne Industries paid $17.5 million in fines in 1992; General Electric paid $70 million for conspiring to defraud the U.S. military; Northrop was fined $17 million in 1990 for falsifying records; Sundstrand settled for a fine of $115 million in 1988 (*Tribune Newspapers* 1993). All these companies could have been banned permanently from competing for future government contracts, but they were not. For example, GE was banned for five days and then reinstated. The others were not banned at all. All receive far more in government contracts than they pay in fines.

Contenders usually have sufficient control to blunt the imposition of burdens, but not enough power to gain much in terms of visible benefits unless they are able to disguise, obfuscate, and mislead the media and the public. Statutes directed toward these contending groups are likely to be complex, vague, and deceptive. It may be difficult to discern from the statute who the policy favors or hinders because discretion and responsibility often will be passed on to lower-level agencies and governments.

For contenders, the public generally will oppose beneficial policy because these groups are viewed as undeserving or greedy, but the groups themselves are powerful enough to inflict considerable political damage if they are denied benefits or if they are assigned burdens. Thus, much of the policy in this quadrant will be sub rosa and carry mixed messages. The public portrayal will be that these groups are not being favored by government but are being restricted in their actions. The private messages, however, will reassure the groups that policies will be helpful to them and restrictions are largely meaningless. Benefits will tend to be hidden from public views; burdens (costs) will tend to be widely publicized but hollow and unenforceable.

Emergent Contending Groups

Special consideration needs to be given to the cluster of target populations whose power lies mainly in their legal, ethical, and moral claims for equality and justice, rather than in their economic position. These groups tend to be those moving toward contender status from either the deviant or dependent, due to an increase in their political power. Examples include environmentalists, African Americans, American Indians, feminists, gays and lesbians, persons living with AIDS (PWAs), and right-wing militia, among others. Emergent groups are distinguished from other contenders and advantaged groups in that they have traditionally been disliked and discriminated against. They have never had access to the kinds of political power wielded by elites. Their power lies partially in their legal and moral claims, almost always emerging as a result of court rulings. Political power also lies in their emergence as a financial player on the political scene (through PACs), increased mobilization, and increased cohesion. Their power, however, in no way rivals that of the rich, defense contractors, gun owners, and so forth.

Their social constructions are decidedly mixed but tend to be more negative than positive. The emergent groups that are left of center have been attacked by the "political correctness" movement, which has attempted to de-legitimize them by claiming that they are dictating a new set of values and practices that grant special advantages to them at the expense of values and practices defined by traditional Western society. The groups themselves argue that those traditional values established systems of privilege that discriminated against them, and that public policy too often reflects these same kinds of biases. Sexual harassment policies offer a useful example. Federal guidelines seemingly promise considerable protection for women against hostile environments or "chilly" climates that make it more difficult for women to do their job. University guidelines usually offer such protection, but counter these by ensuring that first amendment rights of free speech and press will not be abridged. Thus, "hate speech" that creates distinctly chilly climates, hostile environments, and isolation of women making it extremely difficult for them to do their jobs is protected. The courts have virtually required that women must be able to prove that they were not able to cope with the hostility in the environment. It is not enough to prove the environment is hostile; women have been required to prove that they were "victims" of the environment and unable to overcome its effects. Those who were able to overcome the effects have no claim to sexual harassment. The policy here is one that seems to promise redress for historical disadvantages inflicted through a combination of policy and economic circumstances; yet, the policy almost never offers any actual redress of grievances for those it was intended to protect.

President Clinton's attempt to end military exclusion of homosexuals is an example of the extraordinary difficulty created when beneficial policy is directed toward an emergent contender group. The military, with strong congressional backing, developed literally dozens of reasons why homosexuals should not serve, ranging from the need for male bonding to the possibility that homosexuals should be excluded for their own protection. The policy situation became a maze of confusion. For a time homosexuals were still forbidden to serve in the military and subject to dishonorable discharge, but the military had the option of not enforcing this policy by substituting the principle of "don't ask, don't tell, don't pursue."

Some emergent groups, such as the "right-wing militia," and some militant leftist organizations attempt to be recognized as political movements rather than "common criminals." Timothy McVeigh, accused in the Oklahoma City bombing ("terrorist") attack, reportedly said that he was a prisoner of war. Even though the media at times seem to acknowledge the avowedly political nature of these movements, policy responses have been almost exclusively the same as those used against "ordinary criminals" accused of illegal activities.

Benefits, Burdens, and Deviant Groups

Targeting people for punishment is much more prevalent in public policy than is often acknowledged. Particularly during periods of economic hardship, the political system will find it difficult to sustain itself through the distribution of benefits to advantaged groups without risking national bankruptcy. Thus, governments are especially likely to shift toward a politics of punishment as a means for displacing blame onto others and creating opportunities for political gain. Political leaders have much to gain from punishing those who lack power and who are constructed as deviant.

Some powerless groups offer easy scapegoats for societal problems, and policies directing punishment at such groups offer straightforward evidence of government control and power. Legislators in the United States have come to anticipate an outpouring of public support by punishing negatively constructed targets. Providing punishments to persons constructed as deviants yields little or no resistance as these groups have essentially no political power, and the actions are generally applauded by the broader public because they believe deviants deserve to be punished.

The political opportunities offered by powerless people with negative images who are constructed as deviants are surprisingly similar to those of advantaged groups, except that deviants receive punishment whereas advantaged people receive subsidies and favorable regulations. Such policies will be high on the legislative agenda, especially during election campaigns. The highly predictable popularity of tough criminal justice statutes is a vivid illustration of the political attractiveness of punishment directed at powerless, negatively viewed groups.

The political attractiveness of punishment policy results in extraordinarily dishonest policy processes and designs that can be observed at both the federal and local levels. Federal criminal justice policy in the United States has expanded over the past century to cover a wide range of offenses, especially drug offenses, justifying an enormous increase in federal expenditures for law enforcement. Federal mandatory sentencing has resulted in sentences so harsh that virtually all federal and state judges are opposed to them (American Bar Association 1993). The American Bar Association has criticized the criminal justice system's mandatory sentencing policies for directing so much attention to drug offenses and putting away so many low-level drug offenders for long terms that overcrowded prisons are forced to prematurely release murderers, rapists, kidnappers, and armed robbers (American Bar Association 1993). In an ABA-sponsored Gallup poll, over 90 percent of federal judges said that mandatory minimum sentences for federal narcotics violations were a bad idea. Forty percent acknowledged that mandatory minimums had a disproportionate impact on minorities, and 56 percent said they had worked poorly. Eighty-eight percent of federal judges said that too many crimes once handled in state courts have been made federal offenses (American Bar Association 1993, pp. 78–79).

State and local policy also has expanded to cover a much broader array of incidents—many of them previously considered civil actions or simply "accidents" to be handled by the parties involved. The United States has one of the highest crime rates and the highest rate of incarceration among the industrialized nations of the world.

In spite of the attractiveness of punishment policy to federal officials, only about 5 percent of all offenses committed each year are violations of federal law. The crimes that most Americans fear the most (rape, robbery, murder, burglary) are the responsibility of state and local governments. The amount of money Congress expends on punishment has soared in the 1990s as it increased from about $750 million a year in 1993 to more than $20 billion in 1995. The federal politics of crime are extraordinarily deceptive in the sense that enormous credit is claimed by federal officials for policy that has almost no effects on crime. During the 1990s it has become almost an annual ritual for Congress to debate (and usually pass) a "get tough on crime" bill with more mandatory sentences, more death penalties, and expanded federal jurisdiction over new offenses. One prominent senator proposed making it a violation of federal law to join or recruit others to join a gang that engages in illegal activities. Federal authority has extended the death penalty to over fifty-two offenses, including "car jacking" if a death occurs, and the death of postal workers.

Another aspect of the dishonesty in punishment policy is found in the continued political and media hype regarding dramatic increases in violent crime. Virtually all ordinary citizens believe that there has been a dramatic increase; yet victimization surveys taken since 1973 show gradual declines in the rate of murder, rape, aggravated assault, burglary, and robbery (Bortner et al. 1993). Even the Uniform Crime Reports, the FBI's report on incidents known to law enforcement, show declines between 1973 and 1995 in all these categories of crime except aggravated assault. As it has become increasingly difficult to sustain credibility regarding the "rapid increase in violence," attention has shifted to the fact that violence by young men is increasing rapidly. The manipulation of discourse about crime and punishment has prevented a meaningful discussion and thwarted the development of sensible policies.

Negatively constructed powerless groups will usually be proximate targets of punishment policy, and the extent of burdens will be greater than needed to actually achieve effective results. The negative social constructions make it likely that these groups often will receive burdens even when it is illogical from the perspective of policy effectiveness.

Targets regarded as deviants rarely receive beneficial policy, and then only as secondary (or remote) beneficiaries. Direct beneficial policy often is the result of court decisions grounded in constitutional rights. The critical legal studies movement has argued (and demonstrated) that courts often reproduce prevailing societal values in such a way that class, race, and gender biases are found in court outcomes. Nevertheless, it also is apparent that beneficial policy for deviant populations is far more likely to originate in the courts than in the halls of state or national legislatures. For example, it is extremely difficult to pass policies to construct prisons, even when the courts find overcrowding to be inhumane and experts testify that the conditions in jails perpetuate criminality. Even when support comes, it is usually indirect and deviants are at best remote targets. Thus one of the advantages to policy makers of privatizing prisons is that private firms rather than departments of correction can be identified as beneficiaries of prison construction funds.

Constraints and risks exist in directing punishment policy at deviants. One risk is that this group will be expanded beyond the bounds of popular morality so that too many people are being punished, thereby generating disrespect for the law and rejection of the deviant social construction because it obviously does not apply to such a large number of persons. This is what happened in the early part of the twentieth century with prohibition: An increasing number of people were being labeled as "criminals" who did not accept this construction of themselves. They eventually succeeded in overturning prohibition laws, but only after drinking became an accepted middle-class social habit. A similar phenomenon may be occurring with drug use in the 1990s, as an increasing number of middle-class persons and popular heroes in sports and other entertainment fields are known users of addictive drugs. Discretionary application of the law that directs enforcement mainly at persons who carry negative constructions due to their race or class, however, has thwarted more organized efforts to decriminalize or legalize drugs.

A second risk is that political leaders do not like to spend money on negatively constructed groups; hence efforts will be made to devise policies that political leaders can take credit for but without the expenditure of public funds. A common example is to increase the severity of punishment for classes of offenses that are extremely rare. The actual costs of such a policy are almost zero, because few people are ever arrested for these offenses; but the political payoff to public officials is believed to be quite high.

Benefits, Burdens, and Dependent Populations

Dependent targets have less political power than advantaged groups and are more positively constructed than deviants. Their constructions, however, usually emphasize their helplessness and neediness. The fragmentation of dependent populations, lack of organization, low rates of participation, and lack of material resources contribute to their powerlessness. There may be structural barriers to participation: Children under age 18, for example, cannot vote. Native Americans on reservations are clustered into only a few state legislative districts. Other groups are gerrymandered, resulting in even less representation. Dependent targets tend to have very little economic power or position. These groups may share common interests, but they seldom mobilize for effective action.

Dependents are viewed as incapable, by themselves, of changing their powerless situation or solving their own problems. They are perceived to lack the capacity, skills, character, discipline, and will to manage their own destiny. Some persons constructed as dependents have less physical power, which then is accompanied by lack of access to arenas where physical power is not even important, such as in economic productivity in an advanced society. These people are often the wards of others: Parents make decisions for their children; in much of society, married men make decisions for their families; Native Americans are under the trust responsibility of the federal government; and disabled people are reliant on others for assistance in their daily routines.

Dependents have a positive construction, but not one that is highly valued in the modern society. Dependents are viewed as deserving of assistance because their problems are not their fault in the sense that they themselves cannot solve them. They have no choice but to be dependent. However, these are not bad people and they have not done anything to deserve punishment.

Dependent populations are the recipients of beneficial policies, but less so than one would expect, given the magnitude of their problems. This is partly because their situation is seen as a "natural" product of their lack of capability and productivity. Also, their problems are viewed as the proper prerogative of private-sector groups, such as churches, local volunteers, organizations, philanthropists, and nonprofits.

Public officials want to be aligned with their interests, but their lack of political power means that directing resources toward their interests will result in few political advantages. Instead, rhetorical policies are often used since these permit elected leaders to show great concern through widespread public announcements, but relieve them of the need to allocate resources. Policies in this area tend to be left to lower levels of government or to the private sector. When dependents are targeted for benefits, the benefits commonly are passed through other agents, and dependents have little control over the design of the policies. Deception will also be common in this arena as elected officials will attempt to show that dependents are receiving adequate benefits from the government even though their problems are primarily the responsibility of the private and volunteer sectors of society.

Social welfare policy offers one of the best examples of beneficial policy directed toward a dependent population (the poor). In 1995, the federal government spent more than $50 billion a year on various types of welfare support including food stamps, Aid to Families with Dependent Children (AFDC), and Social Security benefits for the disabled (supplemental security income, SSI). Ordinary Social Security is not considered to be "welfare," because it is constructed as a policy in which those who have paid are simply reaping the rewards of their own investments. Most of the criticism was directed at the AFDC program. Conservatives deplored it because it rewarded dependency, illegitimacy, and granted a "free ride" to too many nonworking adults. Liberals claim that it stigmatized the poor, did not treat them with respect or offer genuine opportunities for personal advancement, and failed to even bring them to the poverty level in terms of income.

Policies of this type tend to be avoided by the federal government if at all possible, with responsibility shifted to states and locales. It is not surprising that the federal government in 1996 replaced AFDC with TANF (Temporary Assistance to Needy Families), ended the federal cash guarantee, and shifted responsibility for welfare to the states. It also is not surprising, as Hecht (1996) has shown, that federal and state policies have become increasingly negative, along with increasingly negative constructions of the target groups as undisciplined persons unwilling to work or immoral mothers who have illegitimate children to garner the increase in their welfare checks. When dependent populations who have not done anything overtly deviant are, nevertheless, socially constructed in a negative manner, public officials want to enjoy the political benefits of appearing to be tough while avoiding the pitfalls of seeming to be mean. Much of the dynamics of policy design for dependent people hinges on separating the deserving from the undeserving. Skocpol (1992) argues that Social Security, which was a targeted program but universal beyond the age qualification, has been successful because it could engender widespread support whereas the means-tested AFDC program was aimed only at "needy" populations.

The Juvenile Justice and Delinquency Prevention Act of 1974 is an example of the creative statutory styles that may be used to direct beneficial policy toward dependent populations who are vulnerable to being negatively constructed. The prelude to the act noted that "more than half" of the serious crime in the nation was committed by juveniles (Juvenile Justice and Delinquency Prevention Act of 1974). It went on to point out that the juvenile justice systems (which are state and local systems) did not have the resources or expertise to deal with the problem. It specified a developmental theory of delinquency: "present juvenile courts . . . are inadequate to meet the needs of the countless abandoned and dependent children, who, because of [these] failures to provide effective services may become delinquent" (Juvenile Justice and Delinquency Prevention Act of 1974, p. 1109).

The statute contains a creative logic that enables Congress to provide beneficial policy to the "countless abandoned and dependent children" (who obviously are deserving of help and who have committed no crimes) and simultaneously decrease serious delinquency, thereby addressing the problem of serious crime in the United States. By assuming that status offenders who do not receive necessary services will progress to serious delinquency, Congress has been able to have it both ways. The direct recipients of federal funds are not juvenile delinquents or status offenders but are agencies of state government and nonprofits.

Warner's (1996) study of the youth service bills in the U.S. Congress over the past thirty years offers an interesting example of how attempts to help the most disadvantaged youth consistently were derailed through negative constructions of the youth (as lazy, draft dodgers, druggies, dropouts). Only after a concerted attempt by policy entrepreneurs to change the social construction of the youth, and to alter the rationale of the policy from one of "helping" disadvantaged youth to one of offering all youth an opportunity to provide service to their country, was it possible for the legislation to be passed.

Common Design Characteristics in the Choice of Targets

Table 5.1 summarizes design characteristics and flaws that are traceable to the choice of target populations. Several concepts are important. Representation, subscription, and funding levels vary from very low to very high. Representation in policy design refers to how often the target group finds that its high priority issues are on the policy agenda and its preferences reflected in policy designs.

Subscription refers to how many of the potential target population are specified as eligible. Subscription may be universal, meaning that all of the group are eligible without burdensome qualification rules, or it may be particularistic, meaning that there are screening rules, means-testing, or other mechanisms ensuring that only a fraction of those who actually could benefit will be included. Oversubscription refers to a situation in which more of the target group are eligible than needed to accomplish the instrumental goals of the policy; undersubscription means that fewer are eligible than needed to achieve instrumentally defined goals. The level of funding refers to the extent of government-appropriated resources for the target population.

As noted in Table 5.1, policy-making processes in degenerative pluralist situations are expected to be associated with different types of designs, depending on the power and social constructions of targets. Advantaged populations tend to have high levels of representation in policy designs that allocate benefits to them; the eligibility rules usually include everyone, and extensive funding is provided. These

Table 5.1. Common Design Characteristics in Choice of Targets Populations

	Advantaged	Traditional Contenders	Emerging Contenders	Dependents	Deviants
CHOOSING TARGETS FOR BENEFICIAL POLICY					
Agenda representation	Strongly represented	Weakly represented	Weakly represented	Weakly represented	Almost no representation
Target eligibility Funding	Universalistic Very high funding	Particularistic Low funding	Particularistic Low funding	Particularistic Low funding	Very particularistic Very Low funding
CHOOSING TARGETS FOR BURDENSOME POLICY					
Agenda representation	Very little representation	Strong representation	Strong representation	Some representation	Very strong representation
Target eligibility Funding	Very particularistic Very low funding	Very particularistic Very low funding	Particularistic Very low funding	Particularistic Low funding	Universalistic Significant funding
TYPES OF STATUTES					
For delivering benefits	Suboptimal linkage to goals Strong statutes Some deception	Confusing Subrosa Very deceptive	Illogical Hollow Deceptive	More logical Hollow Deceptive	Logical Hollow Deceptive
For delivering burdens	More logical Hollow Very deceptive	Confusing Hollow Very deceptive	Illogical Mixed Deceptive	Illogical Strong Deceptive	Illogical Strong Deceptive

policies often are illogical, as public officials choose target populations to whom they want to provide beneficial policy even if these targets are not the most appropriate ones, given the goals of the program. Similarly, goals may be chosen not because of their national importance, but because they permit beneficial policy to be given to advantaged groups. We also contend that these policies are often deceptive although this is not as much of a problem as for the other types of targets. Nevertheless, historical assessments indicate deception even in this most popular area of policy design. For example, the decades of beneficial policy provided to military contractors in the name of anti-Communism may have appeared to be open, honest, and perfectly logical at the time. Yet, in retrospect, it is obvious that the threat was greatly overstated at least for the past several decades if not before. The deception, then, often lies in the creation of hegemonic discourses not subject to refutation. These discourses, themselves, should be viewed as deceptive. As they unravel, policy becomes increasingly dishonest because public officials go to even greater deceptions to maintain the illusion that provision of beneficial policy to these groups serves a vital national interest.

Advantaged groups, on the other hand, tend to have lower levels of representation, subscription, and funding when burdensome policy is being considered. Statutes and guidelines inflicting burdensome regulations on advantaged groups are more likely to be hollow, weak, easy to circumvent, or left to local levels for implementation and enforcement.

Punishment policies for deviants have many of the same characteristics as beneficial policy for advantaged groups. Punishment policies are frequently on the political agenda because of their political appeal. The ever-widening net of the criminal justice system speaks to the oversubscription of punishment, especially as it is inflicted on groups that already suffer from negative constructions, such as minority men. These policies have significant funding, in comparison with some of the other target groups, but not as much as allocated to the provision of benefits to advantaged populations. Even though there is great political attractiveness to punishing those who have been constructed as deviant, there is a negative payoff for having to spend money on any "undeserving" group. On the other hand, the political opportunities inherent in punishment are so much greater than those in some alternative policies, such as early prevention and intervention, that punishment policies usually are much better funded than the alternative strategies.

The political attractiveness of punishment suggests that such policies will be used in situations in which they are illogical, leading to ineffective policy. As with advantaged populations, punishment policies for persons constructed as deviants require a near-hegemonic discourse to maintain the official legitimacy of policies. Over time, the political attractiveness of these policies expands the net ever wider until it is more likely that uniform application would reveal these policies as political ploys. At that point, however, policies are likely to become increasingly deceptive.

The war on drugs is an excellent example, as enforcement of drug policy has consistently targeted minority males whose arrest rates for drug use are several times greater than that for whites even though survey research indicates that there are no differences in the actual use of drugs among these populations (Meier 1994). Additional evidence is found in the difference in penalties for crack cocaine compared with regular cocaine. Crack cocaine is the drug of choice among minority and poor populations whereas regular cocaine is used mainly by upper-class white professionals. Under the federal mandatory sentencing laws, possessing 5.1 grams of crack draws a federally mandated sentence of 5 years without parole whereas 5.1 grams of regular cocaine draws probation. The U.S. sentencing commission noted that blacks make up 91.5 percent of those sentenced in 1992 under federal law for crimes involving crack. In cases involving powdered cocaine, however, 32 percent were white, 40 percent were Hispanic, and 27 percent were black (*Arizona Republic,* Feb. 27, 1996, p. A5). Data from the federal bureau of prisons show that 60 percent of the federal inmates are serving time for drug crimes (*Arizona Republic,* Dec. 4, 1995, p. 1).

Beneficial policies for deviants tend to have low levels of representation, subscription, and funding. They also are deceptive. In degenerative policy-making situations it simply does not make sense to waste resources on people who seldom vote and who are so unpopular that helping them reverberates into negative assessments from the broader public. When benefits are provided through the legislative process, they often are attributed to court actions or are concealed in some way. In some states, for example, the terminology for nonincarcerative sanctions for criminals is "community punishment."

The most deceptive policies are expected to be found when the target population is contenders. Regardless of whether benefits or burdens are being distributed, the contentiousness and political risks of providing policy to traditional contenders (i.e., the powerful but disliked groups) are extraordinary. Benefits are likely to be distributed through sub rosa and deceptive means. Burdens will be given considerable attention (and often take the form of policy that is hollow or rhetorical).

For contenders, however, we have not been able to propose any general tendencies for policies in terms of levels of representation, subscription, or funding. The distribution of benefits and burdens to contenders depends on the skills and strategies of the groups, the vigilance of the press, and the values of the political leaders. In degenerative policy-making systems political leaders would like to keep issues involving contenders off the agenda, but the political power of these groups is very high and not entirely neutralized by their negative constructions. The extent of media attention is critical in understanding why and when beneficial policies for contenders will be feasible. Almost always, these need to be offset by policies that can be touted as burdensome, even if few burdens will actually ever be inflicted.

Policies for emergent contenders are similarly contentious, but the historical lack of power and construction as dependents or deviants make a difference in policy design. Some emergent contenders in the 1980s and 1990s have been constructed as "liberals," who, in turn, are associated with negative values in the popular political lexicon. It is unlikely that beneficial policy will be overrepresented or overfunded because these groups do not have sufficient power to gain substantial advantages. On the other hand, they may have sufficient legal claims or moral/ethical claims to avoid the serious underrepresentation, undersubscription, and underfunding found among deviants and dependents. Benefits are likely to be hollow and deceptive. Burdens will tend to be hidden or masked.

Dependents offer few political opportunities and tend to be largely ignored. When it is possible to do something for this group and pass the cost on to lower levels of government or the private sector, however, political leaders will quickly rally behind such actions. As with deviants, action by legislatures may be prompted mainly by court decisions requiring due process protection or equal rights. Many of the problems and issues that dependents need to have addressed will be labeled as outside the purview of government. Policy often is rhetorical. In terms of benefits, dependents will generally have low levels of representation, subscription, and funding, but not as low as deviants. Burdens will be more common than might be expected, given the largely positive "blameless" image of dependent groups, due to the unwillingness to spend money on such groups; but policy designs and political rhetoric will attempt to mask or hide the burdens from the broader public to avoid the appearance of being mean or uncaring.

TOOLS, RULES, AND RATIONALES

The tools, rules, and rationales found in policy designs differ for many reasons, including the history of the policy arena and the current knowledge paradigms driving policy specialists. Degenerative pluralist contexts, however, tend to produce designs with distinctive patterns of tools, rules, and rationales that vary systematically with the power and social constructions of the target populations (Table 5.2).

Rules and Tools

For advantaged groups who are constructed as deserving, intelligent, and public-spirited, the policy tools tend to emphasize subsidies that build capacity or provide inducements for actions to be taken. When delivering beneficial policy to the advantaged groups, certain types of capacity-building tools are commonly used, especially provision of free information, training, and technical assistance. The political payoffs for providing beneficial policy to these groups is such that outreach programs will be common, in which the agencies seek out all eligible persons and encourage them to utilize the policy opportunities that have been made available (Ingram and Schneider 1991). Evaluations to determine the actual effectiveness of providing beneficial policy to advantaged groups are almost never stipulated in the federal legislation. Advantaged groups usually will have rules that permit them considerable organizational autonomy.

Table 5.2. Tools, Rules, Rationales for Different Types of Target Groups

	Advantaged	Contenders	Dependents	Deviants
TOOLS				
For delivering benefits	Capacity building Subsidies Entitlements Free information Outreach programs	Mixed, unpredictable	Income-tested subsidies Authority Persuasion Free information Client must establish eligibility	Authority with threat of punishment
For delivering burdens	Self-regulation and learning Inducements (positive) Standards and charges (sometimes sanctions)	Single out one high-profile group for heavy sanctions	Authority, sanctions	Sanctions, force, death
RULES				
For delivering benefits	Inclusive	Delegated to lower level agencies	Exclusionary, mandatory evaluations	Exclusionary, require evaluations
For delivering burdens	Set deadlines far into the future	Delegate to lower level	Strict, complex eligibility requirements	Strict, complex eligibility
RATIONALES				
For delivering benefits	Important national interests are being served, such as national defense or economic competitiveness Efficient/effective means to the goal	Understated: necessary to achieve economic or defense goals	Justice: equal opportunity, need, fairness	Justice: equality, rights, fairness
For delivering burdens	They must sacrifice for the good of the country's economic or defense needs The burden is in their own interests over the long term	Overstated: a correction for their greediness; the country is "not ready" for them to be treated better; they have made "errors" in their political strategies	Adherence to universalistic principles unfortunately disadvantages them Other priorities must be met, leaving not enough resources for everyone Rules are for "their own good"	They deserve to be punished; the public must be protected from them

When burdens, rather than benefits, are directed at the advantaged groups, the rules and tools will be less predictable and more likely to change, but self-regulation that entrusts the group to learn from its own behavior and voluntarily take actions to achieve policy goals will be preferred, along with positive inducements. When these are not effective in inducing the desired behavior, policies may shift toward "standards and charges" that do not stigmatize the organization for its activities, but simply attempt to discourage certain actions (such as pollution) by charging for it. Sanctions and force are less likely to be used in connection with powerful, positively viewed groups, and when such penalties are specified, these often are emasculated in the implementation process. When advantaged groups are faced with stiff regulatory action or reductions in subsidies or entitlements, policy makers often place the effective date of such actions far into the future, providing the target groups with ample time to contest, delay, or overturn the policy.

Policy tools and rules for dependent groups (such as mothers or children) are expected to be somewhat different. Subsidies will be given, but eligibility requirements often involve labeling and stigmatizing recipients. Subsidies to farmers do not require income tests, for example, but college students must prove that they are needy and without resources. Outreach programs will be less common than they are with more powerful groups, and many programs will require clients to present themselves to the agency to receive benefits. Subsidy programs for dependents, such as college students, the disabled, the poor, or the unemployed, usually do not seek out eligible persons but rely on those who are eligible to make their case to the agency itself.

Hortatory tools (that focus on persuasion and exhortation) will commonly be used for dependent groups, even when the pervasiveness of the problem would suggest that more direct intervention is needed. Groups in the dependent category will not usually be encouraged or given support to devise their own solutions to problems, but will have to rely on agencies to help them. For example, battered women still must rely mainly on the police for assistance rather than having self-help organizations that are eligible as direct recipients for government funds. Another policy tool, the use of authority, will be more common than with the powerful positively viewed groups because dependents are not considered as self-reliant. The so-called gag rule imposed by the Bush administration that prohibited family planning clinic personnel from providing information about abortions even when asked directly was an example of the more paternalistic attributes of policy directed at dependent populations. Information tools are likely to be used, even when direct·resources are needed (such as in AIDS prevention programs). Public officials in generative contexts simply do not like to spend money on powerless groups and will use other tools whenever possible.

The dominant tools for deviants are expected to be more coercive and often involve sanctions, force, and even death. In contrast with the kinds of regulations used when advantaged populations are burdened, groups constructed as deviants will at worst be incarcerated or executed, and at best will be left free but denied information, discouraged from organizing, and subjected to the authority of others, including experts, rather than helped to form their own self-regulatory organizations. For example, youth gangs are more likely to be punished for congregating than they are to be encouraged to direct their energy toward constructive activities.

When beneficial policies are directed at deviant groups, such as rehabilitation programs, they ordinarily attempt to change the person through authoritarian means, rather than attack the structural problems that are the basis of the problem itself. Drug diversion programs, for example, usually will require attendance, drug testing, and threaten participants with heavy penalties for failure to comply with the rules.

Rationales

Rationales are important elements of policy design because they serve to legitimate designs and fit them into the value paradigm of the citizenry. The disparity between democratic values held by American citizens and the actual conditions of life in the American democracy produces a serious problem of governmental legitimacy. Policy proposals have to be explained and justified in value terms acceptable to the public. Policy designers try to explain how policies, in spite of appearances, serve common rather than special interests. Rationales are provided for the extraordinary inequalities that exist in a society presumably offering equal opportunity to all citizens. Rationales are used to justify the agenda, the policy goals, the selection of target populations, and the specific rules and tools that are used.

The rationales differ, however, dependent on the power and social construction of the target population, and can be used to either perpetuate or change dominant values and existing social constructions. When policy makers allocate benefits to well-off and powerful groups, they stress the close instrumental links to some social good, such as national defense or economic competitiveness. Helping "good" people is not favoritism; it is serving the public interest. From the 1940s until well into the 1980s, national defense was the primary national goal. In the 1990s, with the demise of the communist world, economic competitiveness has to some extent replaced the goal of national defense. In either case, the same groups (business, military, science, for example) are usually viewed as the key players in achieving these national goals. Justice-oriented rationales, such as equality, equity, need, harmony, rights, and so forth, are *not* commonly used to justify the provision of beneficial public policy to advantaged groups. Efficiency often is emphasized as the reason for the selection of particular target groups and particular tools. For example, federal science and technology policy is justified on the grounds of national defense and/or economic competitiveness. The groups chosen are said to be an efficient mechanism for ensuring the United States maintains its technological edge vis-à-vis other countries.

Similar rationales are used even when burdens are being distributed to advantaged groups. The close association of the welfare of advantaged groups with the public interest is not challenged. Instead, groups may be told that they are not being made relatively worse off, compared with their competitors, and that all will gain in the long run. Policies to control common pool resource problems, such as water and air, usually claim that it will protect the resource for everyone, and that the regulations will prevent a single firm within their group from gaining advantages and depleting the resource. In those cases where it is impossible to construe a burden as a benefit, then the rationale may claim that it is technically unavoidable if the common-interest goals (such as national defense) are to be served. The burden impacts everyone, and it is not practical to make an exception for the advantaged groups. The advantaged are not being singled out, and they are sacrificing for the public good.

For traditional contending groups that have substantial power but are negatively constructed as "greedy" or "corrupt," the rationale is sharply different depending on whether they are receiving benefits or burdens. When powerful unions or large corporations are allocated burdensome regulations designed to curb their privileges, the public rationale will overstate the magnitude of the burden and will construe it as a correction for their greed or excessive power. On the other hand, private communications may suggest that the burden is not excessive or will have little impact. When the regulations are likely to have an impact, the rationales may emphasize that the "climate" is not conducive to any other policy options, and that corrections are needed because of their excessive unpopularity.

When traditional contending groups receive benefits, the rationales will understate the magnitude of the gain, which is made easier because the gains often are cloaked as procedures that enable the group to have privileged access to lower-level agencies or governments where the elected officials will not be held accountable for the groups' gains. When the benefits are obvious and can credibly be linked to instrumental goals, such as international global competitiveness, arguments will be made that it would not be possible to achieve the goal without also benefiting the group.

Emergent contending groups are moving from positions of dependency or deviancy to a more powerful political presence, and the rationales differ accordingly. Beneficial policy often is the direct result of court decisions that have forced legislative action and the policy rationales are grounded in statements about rights, provision of equal opportunities, due process of law, and the like. Rationales seldom reflect positively on the groups themselves or their linkages to important national instrumental interests such as economic competitiveness or national defense. For example, rulings by the Clinton administration to permit homosexuals to serve in the armed forces and the Federal Bureau of Investigation are rationalized mainly in terms of the rights of such persons to serve, rather than in statements about the unique strengths that they bring to the military or to the FBI. Their service is defended on the grounds that there are no just reasons to exclude them, rather than the ways in which they would increase the effectiveness of the military or the Federal Bureau of Investigation.

When emergent contending groups are the recipients of burdensome policy, they may be led to believe that they made errors in their political strategies, or that the public simply is "not ready" for such drastic action so rapidly. Policy actions may be delayed because of difficulties in determining what the "problem" actually is or how a solution might be devised without disadvantaging powerful groups in society. When so-called universalistic principles continue to exclude women and minorities from the upper echelons in higher education and corporations, for example, the problem sometimes is traced to the attitudes and preparation of the women and minorities themselves. Delayed representation can then be blamed on the "pipeline" problem—that it takes many years for people to gain the education and experiences needed for these lofty positions. Decades of continued exclusion may occur before the putatively universalistic principles are recognized as containing hidden biases that systematically continue to disadvantage women and minorities.

Rationales for powerless groups also seem to emphasize justice-oriented legitimations rather than instrumental ones. There is no inherent logic to this; rather, the values of modern American society simply seem to be favor instrumental goals over justice-oriented goals even though it could be argued that they must go hand in hand or that justice is inherently more important. It may be the case that instrumental goals are preferred because this permits policy to continue distributing benefits to those who are more powerful. Similarly, elected officials may not want to use instrumental justifications for policies that benefit less powerful people, even when it would be perfectly logical to do so, as this would then require larger expenditures on such groups. Education is a good example. In spite of strenuous efforts by educators to claim that education is the fundamental basis for economic viability (and in spite of the logic of this position), political leaders tend to ignore this justification because to acknowledge it would require massive shifts of expenditures. On the other hand, if education is justified in terms of providing equal opportunities, then there is less pressure from the public to insist on improvements in the quality of education. Justice-oriented goals, if pursued with the same intensity as instrumental ones, would result in radically different patterns of value allocations.

Benefits conferred on negatively viewed powerless groups, such as "criminals," frequently are argued as unavoidable in order to protect important constitutional principles that confer rights on everyone. Sometimes claims will be made, however, that beneficial policies (such as rehabilitation for criminals) are efficient mechanisms for achieving public safety. This argument usually is difficult to sustain. Significant segments of the public believe that these people deserve to be punished and that rehabilitation policies will not work to reduce crime. Part of the social construction of these groups is that they respond mainly to punishment.

Burdens for powerless groups who are positively constructed, such as "children," may be justified as an efficient mechanism to protect the individual from harm or to achieve public purposes. For powerful groups, choices are limited only when there is no other way to achieve certain goals. Persons in the powerful groups are constructed as "intelligent," and "able to make good choices." Powerless groups are not usually constructed this way, but are viewed as needing direction. "For her own good" is a common reason given for incarcerating girls who have run away from home or who are living with a boyfriend. Child labor laws that removed choices from children and their families were done to protect the children.

IMPLEMENTATION AND TARGET POPULATIONS

Differences in the implementation structures for the four different types of target populations are summarized in Table 5.3.

Advantaged Populations

When distributing benefits to advantaged groups, the implementation may follow a version of the strong statute model in which the specific target populations are chosen by the legislative body and written into the statute. Elected officials like to take credit for providing benefits to powerful, positively viewed groups, and there is enormous pressure for them to continue expanding such programs as long as the resources cannot be traced to any particular tax or tax increase. In these types of designs, there is likely to be very poor connections between the choice of the target population and the public interest rationales that are given. Administrators are likely to be confronted with the task of creating logical rationales and achieving public interest goals, but will not have the discretion to shift resources to other target populations who might be more closely linked to the goals. Water projects, for example, are typically selected by Congress leaving to the agency the task of showing that such policies have actually reduced flood losses.

Different types of implementation problems will be encountered when the pressures to allocate funds result in continued expansion of promises and eligibility, but without expansion of the resource base. In these situations, the policy area will become oversubscribed in relation to its resources. Elected officials will prefer not to have to choose from among the eligible who will receive and who will be left out. Instead, they will give discretion to the agency to determine eligibility. The heightened expectations, combined with the scarcity of resources, produces serious implementation problems as the eligibility rules will become the target of intense debate between the agency and the target groups and perhaps among the target groups themselves. Regardless of the rules developed by the agency, target groups that are left out will bring pressure to change the eligibility criteria or will seek alternative ways to receive the benefits and will raise complaints with elected officials. These groups press their claims aggressively because they believe in the legitimacy of their interests. In turn, the elected officials will accuse the agency of inefficiency, wasting resources, or developing unnecessarily restrictive rules. In oversubscribed situations, oversight will be more sporadic as the elected officials may intervene at any time on behalf of a particular constituent who was left out or to alter the selection criteria the agency has developed.

Table 5.3. Characteristics of Implementation

	Advantaged	Contenders	Dependents	Deviants
For delivering benefits	Strong statutes but with fuzzy or misleading rationales When oversubscription occurs, agencies or targets will be given discretion to determine eligibility rules	Decentralized with agency discretion over most elements	Decentralized for program design, but specific eligibility rules mandated at higher levels Strong oversight Agency "creaming" and "relabeling"	Decentralized for program design; statute may provide specific eligibility rules Legislative intervention common Agency "relabeling"
For delivering burdens	Consensus-building models with long "softening up" period followed by Wilsonian designs Frequent legislative intervention to make exceptions	Narrowly drawn strong statutes with fine-grained distinctions among target subgroups singling out a few for heavy regulation	Decentralized with agency discretion often accompanied by agency "relabeling" or stonewalling to minimize harm	Strong statutes In oversubscribed situations, agencies will have discretion to set priorities among different targets

The allocation of federal research funds to universities is an example of allocations to an advantaged population that becomes oversubscribed compared to its resource allocations. Discretion over allocation decisions has been granted to the agencies, and most of them have established peer review systems that permit members of the target population itself to determine the actual allocations. The criteria are grounded in merit: the quality of the work and its importance to knowledge or society. The message sent by these policies is that those who receive federal grants are important and deserving of their grants. They contribute to the national interest and deserve the exalted prestige that accompanies grant awards.

Within universities, the increasing prestige and priority given to the natural sciences, as compared with the humanities, arts, and social sciences, may be traced at least partly to their advantaged position within the federal grant process. The prestige of universities is measured by the Carnegie Foundations's "Research I" ratings, which rate universities in terms of the total amount of federal funding. Pressure from target populations who have not received what they consider to be a fair share of the federal research largesse has led to complaints, and Congress has intervened to alter the allocations. The National Science Foundation, for example, was pressured into developing a grant program that had as its explicit purpose the allocation of research funds to states that have been underrepresented in NSF funding. Also, between 1990 and 1995 there was a substantial increase in the number of special "pork barrel" projects that are funded (line item) by Congress to universities.

When burdens are being distributed to advantaged groups, there may be a lengthy softening-up process characterized by designs that solicit local-level input and encourage target populations to take voluntary actions themselves that might allay the need for more directive policies. After specific regulations are chosen, the implementation usually will give wide discretion to agencies to choose the eligible target populations, thereby shielding elected leaders from specific blame. Congress, for example, usually will pass along this design responsibility, but also will introduce numerous procedural protection in the statute. These procedural devices enable the advantaged populations to access other arenas through which they may avoid or defeat the regulations. When agencies attempt to enforce the rules, they may be portrayed as attempting to interfere unnecessarily with the target population, as if the agency wishes to take away the legitimate rights of those who are being regulated.

Even when elected officials confer burdens on advantaged groups, they are inclined to intervene later and make exceptions or place certain types of actions off-limits to the agency, making it difficult for the agency to achieve the goals of the program. The list of federal policies that have been watered down or completely emasculated through this process is very long (see, for example, Greider 1992).

Implementation is invariably difficult because the target populations have come to associate their interests with the national interest. They have power, and they believe they are deserving. As Greider says, "corporate interests, on the whole, still do not accept that they must comply with the new regulatory controls enacted during the last twenty-five years. . . . That's real political power—choosing whether to honor a law or resist it" (p. 110).

Policies restricting the behavior or resources of advantaged populations will be underfunded and undersubscribed, but they probably will be more rational and logical in the sense of achieving instrumental goals, or more efficacious in terms of increasing fairness. There are almost no reasons, otherwise, to incur the wrath of powerful, positively viewed target populations.

Contenders

For contenders, the implementation structure will differ depending on whether benefits or burdens are being distributed. When benefits are allocated they may grant considerable discretion to agencies or state and local governments to avoid accusations of pork barrel politics for undeserving publics. When burdens are allocated, the legislation may select one of the worst cases and make an example of it with very specific and draconian penalties, as was done with the banning of assault weapons and the double indemnity penalty for purposeful polluters in the Superfund legislation. The legislation may provide tools that sound tough, such as the $10,000 per car penalty for violation of the clean air act, but that are difficult if not impossible to use. To have imposed this penalty on the automobile manufacturers would have pushed them into bankruptcy. In relation to contenders, public officials will try to divide the target population to isolate a few of the worst cases and focus attention on them, permitting the others to shift into the deserving (advantaged) groups.

Implementation will always be difficult. Agencies will have to deal with the confusing and complex problems created by the statute itself, by the mixed messages, by frequent interventions and changes in rationales offered by elected officials, and by chronic shortages in resources.

Dependent Target Populations

For dependents, elected officials will grant considerable discretion to agencies to choose from among the eligible populations those who are to receive benefits, but eligibility rules will be tightly written into the statute to prevent those who are not "deserving" from receiving the benefits. Federal officials during the past several years have increasingly written statutes or regulations that extend health, welfare, or unemployment benefits to "deserving" segments of disadvantaged populations, but have passed the costs of these regulations to state or local governments and to agencies who are expected to provide additional services without additional resources.

Implementation problems will be different than for the advantaged or contenders. There will be consistent pressure to ensure that the "deserving" have been separated from the "undeserving" and that ineligible persons (e.g., "nondeserving ones") are not receiving the benefits. The food stamp program, for example, has been plagued since its inception with congressional charges that ineligible persons are receiving the benefits. Similar concern has not usually been shown by Congress over whether federal research grants have gone to incompetent researchers, or whether military bases are located in the strategically most appropriate places, or whether there are cost overruns in defense contracts.

Agency personnel, especially caseworkers, will find their work frustrating as they continually seek to extend the services to the full number of persons who they believe need them. If agencies follow their professional models and try to help the disadvantaged populations, the advantaged groups may accuse them of being leftists or liberals, or of simply trying to build up their own agency at the expense of other, more legitimate, needs. If agencies believe that more resources may be available in the future, they may extend services (net-widening) to as many as possible in the hope that documentation of the need will result in more resources. If resources are not forthcoming, however, the agency will find itself overextended and confronted with the problem of either reducing quality or turning away clients who could benefit from their programs. Universities often find themselves in this situation. Elected officials then may intervene and bring pressure on the agency to become more efficient and to serve more of those who could benefit. Quality of service may become quite unimportant to elected officials, or they may attempt to tie budgets to specific service unit costs.

It becomes risky for agencies to make resource claims or to press the need for expanded services because such claims may only lead to additional efforts to control the "shirking" tendency of the agency and to increase its "efficiency." Agencies may resort to creaming and take only the clients who are easiest to handle, or who have the best fit with the professional aspirations of the caseworkers in the agency.

Burdensome policy for dependents differs fundamentally from that for advantaged groups. Dependent populations seldom are found in businesses or professions that are impacted by the types of regulations discussed for advantaged groups. Instead, dependents are especially impacted by regulations that reduce access to services or opportunities for children, women, minorities, or disadvantaged populations. Such regulations often apply only to the public sector, thereby permitting those with more resources to seek services privately. Health care rules that preclude public funds for abortions are an example, as was the "gag" rule regarding abortion that applied only to clinics receiving federal funds. Youth are the target of many regulations that do not apply to adults, including the prohibition on alcohol for the 18- to 21-year-old population, and the increasing criminalization of many relatively normal activities of the young.

Dependents also are disadvantaged by regressive taxation policies and by the extent to which government depends on business to provide social services such as health care. Agencies often find themselves at odds with burdensome policies for dependent groups, as it may be much clearer to professionals that burdens are unfair, detrimental to the achievement of policy goals, and oppressive. Agencies may stonewall implementation, as it is often hard to detect what actually transpires between clients and caseworkers. Or agencies may engage in relabeling, where they use professional diagnosis to place clients in categories that will make them eligible for benefits (even if the statute intended to exclude them), or will exclude them from burdens (even when the statute intended for them to be included).

Deviant Populations

Strong statutes with clear, specific, and detailed instructions are commonly found when delivering punishment to deviant populations. The political attractiveness of punishment, however, tends to result in oversubscription and the implementation strategies change to Wilsonian patterns in which the elected leaders set broad goals, leaving details to lower-level agencies. The oversubscription problem in criminal justice typically has been handled by granting discretion at the police, prosecutorial, judicial, and correction decision points. If judicial sentences are mandated, for example, more discretion will be exercised by prosecutors, police, and correctional release officials. In states where statutes have sought to remove almost all discretion, prison overcrowding has pushed expenses to all-time high levels and resulted in court interventions requiring the reduction in double and triple celling.

Decentralized implementation is more likely when providing politically risky benefits to deviant groups. Beneficial policy will be underfunded and undersubscribed. Federal policy may mandate extensive policy analysis or evaluation (or both) to ensure that the programs are effective. Broad discretion is likely to be given to the agencies to avoid legislative responsibility for the programs. Agencies may have a much larger role in policy design for these groups. Rehabilitation programs, welfare, civil rights, and affirmative action programs are some of the types of policies that benefit the powerless groups who are negatively viewed. Mandates for these have emerged from the courts in support of the due process or other clauses of the Constitution, and much of the program and policy design has been by agencies, often at the local or state level. Even though decentralized implementation is common, legislative intervention can be expected to redefine eligibility for beneficial programs by subdividing eligibles into those who are the "most deviant" and excluding them from the beneficial policies, thereby shifting them into the more punishment-oriented programs. Agencies often respond by "relabeling" their clients in an attempt to maintain eligibility for beneficial programs.

TRANSLATION DYNAMICS: IMPLICATIONS FOR JUSTICE, CITIZENSHIP, AND DEMOCRACY

The elements of policy design impart messages to target populations that inform them of their status as citizens and how they and people like themselves are likely to be treated by government. Such information becomes internalized into a conception of the meaning of citizenship that influences their orientations toward government and their participation. Policy teaches lessons about what groups people belong to, the characteristics of groups with which people identify, what they deserve from government, and what is expected of them. The messages indicate whether the problems of the target population are legitimate ones for government attention, what kind of game politics is (public-spirited or the pursuit of private interests), and who usually wins.

Citizens encounter and internalize the messages not only through observation of politics and media coverage, but also through their direct, personal experiences with public policy. These experiences tell them whether they are viewed as "clients" by government and bureaucracies or whether they are treated as "objects." Experience with policy tells people whether they are atomized individuals who must deal directly with government and bureaucracy to press their own claims, or whether they are participants in a cooperative process joining with others to solve problems collectively for the common good. Citizen orientations toward government impact their participation patterns.

The personal messages for advantaged members of society are that they are good, intelligent people (Table 5.4). When they receive benefits from government, it is not a special favor or because of their "need" but because they are contributing to public welfare. For these groups, reliance on government is not a signal that they cannot solve their own problems. Government appears easy to manipulate and therefore responsive to them and they are reinforced in their belief that their interests coincide with the public interest. Policies often involve outreach and seldom require needs tests; thus the advantaged do not see themselves as claimants or as dependent on government. Instead, they are a crucial part of the effort to achieve national goals, such as national defense or economic vitality. When they are regulated, they examine rationales closely to see whether burdens are equitably allocated and whether their sacrifice is truly necessary for a public purpose. When other groups are singled out for benefits, especially those who are less powerful or negatively constructed, they tend to believe that the government is on the wrong track. Advantaged groups are quick to sense favoritism whenever groups other than themselves receive benefits.

Advantaged groups are positively oriented toward policy and politics, so long as government continues to be favorable toward them, but they have little respect for government. Experiences with policy teach them that government is important, the political process is fundamentally sound, government can be held responsible for producing beneficial policy, and there are payoffs from mobilizing and supporting government officials. The game can be won within the rules, at least by those who know the rules well, have access to extensive legal advice, and can utilize all three branches of government at local, state, and national levels. They have little respect for any group that seeks to operate outside the system. The powerful, popular groups are active participants in traditional ways, such as voting, interest group activity, campaign contributions and so forth. When policies are ineffective, especially when there are sustained periods of economic problems, they blame government rather than themselves and they mobilize for change. When government no longer benefits them, these groups are likely to organize and devise private alternatives to public services,

Table 5.4. Messages, Citizen Orientations, and Participation

	Advantaged	Contenders	Dependents	Deviants
MESSAGES				
Personal	Good, intelligent	Controversial	Helpless, needy	Bad, dangerous
"Your" problems are...	Important public concerns	In conflict with others	The responsibility of the private sector	Your own personal responsibility
Government should treat you...	With respect	With fear or caution	With pity	With disrespect, hate
ORIENTATIONS				
Toward government	Disdainful but supportive	Suspicious, vigilant	Disinterested, passive	Angry, oppressed
Toward own interests	Coincide with the public interest	Conflictive with others	Private responsibility	Personal responsibility
Toward others' claims	Not legitimate	Competitive rivals	More important than their own	Simply privileges
Toward the political "game"	Open, winnable	Involves raw use of power, crooked	Hierarchical and elitist	Abusive use of power
PARTICIPATION				
Mobilization				
Voting, interest groups	High	Moderate	Low	Low
Disruptive (strikes, riots)	Low	Moderate	Low	Moderate
Self-governance potential (private provision)	High	Moderate	Low	Low
Citizen-agency interaction	Agency outreach	Targets subvert implementation	Client must initiate contact	Avoidance

such as private schools, security systems, mental health services, and so on. And they object even more strenuously to government regulation or to government providing benefits to others. As they increasingly provide services for themselves, they withdraw support for government provision of such services to others, thereby contributing to an ever-widening gulf in the quality of life experienced by the haves and have-nots in modern American society.

Contenders receive different messages. Policy tells them that they are powerful, but they will be treated with suspicion rather than respect. Their power is meaningful only when accompanied by a strategy that will hide the true effects from public view. Politics is highly contentious; no one will take care of them except themselves. Thus, they must use power to pursue their own interests. Contenders realize that conflict is common. They must be constantly vigilant and calculating to ensure that government serves their ends. They believe that government is not really interested in solving problems, but in wielding power. The difference between the public and private messages that government sends to these groups teaches them that government is not to be trusted. Private power is more important than public interests, and rationales are simply subterfuge rather than valid arguments justifying the distribution of benefits and costs. Politics is a corrupt game; winners have successfully used power and they may have not stayed within the rules of the game. Participation patterns tend toward the use of informal means, such as the use of influential connections and campaign contributions. Participation may disregard the rules or laws; manipulation and subterfuge are common.

The messages to dependents are that they are powerless, helpless, and needy. Their problems are their own responsibility, but they are unable to solve them by themselves. Policy teaches them that it is not in the public's interest to solve their problems, and they get attention only through the generosity of others. To be forced to depend on a "safety net" means one is not much of a player. The tools and rationales imply that government is responsive to them only when they subject themselves to government and relinquish power over their own choices. Income testing and the typical requirement that they must apply to the agency for benefits (rather than being sought out through outreach programs) require them to admit their dependency status. Even when beneficial policy is provided, it is accompanied by labeling and stigma. Policy sometimes attempts to overcome negative stereotyping by replacing one label with another, such as using "physically challenged" instead of "disabled," which was introduced as a less stigmatizing word than "handicapped," which, itself, was used as a replacement for "crippled." Unfortunately, stigma often catches up with the new label. Information programs that rely on propaganda and stereotypes for effectiveness primarily reinforce the prevailing social constructions. Efforts to reduce the spread of HIV by appealing to young black males through sports figures such as Magic Johnson may reinforce the image of young blacks as sexually promiscuous.

The messages result in orientations toward government characterized by disinterest and passivity. In contrast with the advantaged groups, the powerless—even when positively constructed—do not see their interests as coinciding with an important public goal, and instead tend to buy into the idea that their problems are individual and should be dealt with through the private sector. They may view the claims of others, especially the powerful advantaged groups, as being more legitimate than their own. The game of politics is a bureaucratic game in which they wait in line and eventually get what others want them to have. Participation is low and conventional, but their primary form of interaction with government is as applicants or claimants who are applying for services to a bureaucracy.

Persons who are both powerless and negatively constructed will have mainly negative experiences with government, but differences in design elements will lead to different messages than those received by other groups. The dominant messages are that they are "bad" people whose behavior constitutes a problem for others. They can expect to be disciplined or punished unless they change their behavior or avoid contact with the government. Accordingly, these people often fail to claim government benefits for which they are eligible. On the other hand, government often is unable to catch them for their misdeeds and commonly fails to punish even when individuals are apprehended. Thus, government appears to be arbitrary and unpredictable. The rules of law and justice have no positive connotations. Orientations will be that of angry and oppressed people who have no faith in government's fairness or effectiveness. They see themselves as alone and as individual players who have no chance of winning in a game that they view as essentially corrupt. Conventional forms of participation such as voting and running for office will be viewed as largely ineffective or irrelevant.

People labeled as deviants will find it much more difficult to organize and mobilize for protection of their interests, at least partly because of their fragmentation and distrust of one another. Studies of homelessness, prostitution, and prison inmates have documented the cultural and organizational barriers to effective political organization (Ferraro et al. 1995; Hall 1992). People will struggle, nevertheless, to organize and gain enough internal trust that they can present themselves as legitimate participants in the political system. Some will attempt to portray their behavior as an illness, thereby removing their personal responsibility for it and making it easier for them to be viewed as dependents. Alcoholics and the mentally ill have used this strategy effectively to shift their construction from deviance to dependency. Others will struggle to have their beliefs and behavior understood as political acts rather than as criminal acts, a strategy used by the Irish Republican Army (Mulcahey 1995), the right-wing militia in the United States, and by some juvenile gangs who have held national "summits" of gang leaders. Other groups may organize politically to thwart stigmatizing public policy and simultaneously to relabel their behavior from "deviant" to "natural" (such as homosexuality) thereby destigmatizing the behavior and making the continued negative social construction more difficult. If efforts at political organization are effective, deviant groups may gain sufficient political power that they move toward the contender category and come to resemble the "emerging contender" groups described earlier. If they are not effective, participation will lag and become more sporadic, disruptive, and individualized such as strikes, demonstrations, riots, and terrorist attacks. As with the contenders, the deviants are more inclined to work outside the conventional forms of participation and to break the rules.

DYNAMICS AND PATHOLOGIES

In a society where the policy design process operates with reasonable fairness, different groups within society will experience a variety of different constructions, depending on the policy arena. In truly democratic and discursive systems, virtually all social groups would carry generally positive constructions. In degenerative situations, however, advantaged groups will almost always win and believe their victory was for the good of the society, and others will almost always lose and be told that their loss was their own fault. Degenerative policy making produces designs that perpetuate or accentuate the degenerative tendencies themselves. Even though the process of specifying targets and constructing their power and deservedness is dynamic and constantly changing, the theory presented here suggests that there is no pluralist-like "invisible hand" that guides the society toward self-corrective policies. Once a policy-making system becomes addicted to the politics of social constructions and the dynamics of strategic, manipulative, and deceptive competition based on pursuit of self-interested goals through public policy, then the self-corrections of pluralism will not be operative. Instead of self-corrections through mobilization of negatively impacted groups—as pluralism expects—degenerative policy designs and processes teach dependents and deviants that mobilization is pointless. It teaches the advantaged that mobilization is their ticket to continued advantageous policy, and it teaches contenders to be deceptive. The result is an accentuation of degenerative tendencies.

Nevertheless, this is not a deterministic system. As noted previously, policy-making institutions that exhibit degenerative tendencies vis-à-vis some issues do not necessarily always engage in this style of decision making. Institutional cultures are subject to change through human agency, events that present an opportunity for new leadership to emerge, challenges from scientific and professional perspectives, deconstruction of assumed "realities" exposing hypocrisy and permitting alternative understandings, and social movements from ordinary people who are unwilling to accept their lack of power and unfavorable constructions. New information and events alter public perceptions of the causal linkages creating public problems or of the fairness of the system thereby altering perceptions of who the appropriate targets should be.

The AIDS issue provides an illustration of how degenerative politics emerges, changes, and allocates values based on social constructions. Before 1983, AIDS was presented by the media as a medical research problem, and most news stories originated in science journal articles. The only active participants perceived as involved in the issue besides medical researchers were gay men, who, as a potential target of policy, stirred little sympathetic response. As long as the likely effects of AIDS were limited to negatively constructed groups, ongoing medical research, isolation, and quarantine were viewed as appropriate policy tools. Government targeted immigrants and prisoners for mandatory drug testing. The level of funding was extremely low and even within the medical community, it was difficult to find scientists willing to devote their time or reallocate their resources to study the disease. After AIDS was found to occur in babies and among individuals who had received transfusions of infected blood, both attention to the issue and policy tools began to change. Doctors, dentists, and other medical workers also were counted among the stricken, and solely burdensome policies did not seem appropriate.

The story of Ryan White, a 13-year-old schoolboy in Indiana who was banned from his classroom, added a civil rights dimension to the story. Gay men's political activism identified more public funding of research and more adequate health care as appropriate policy tools. The cohesion and bravery displayed by the groups began to alter the previous very negative construction of gays, although the primary effect was to create greater differentiation among the various type of persons with AIDS, as was reflected in the funding allocations contained in the Ryan White Act of 1990 (Donovan 1994).

AIDS emerged as a major policy issue when potential target groups grew broader, mobilized and gained political strength, and vigorously challenged the previously negative constructions. Public support for spending on the issue increased enormously as the disease was revealed to affect heterosexuals whose behavior was no different from millions of other Americans. The announcement that basketball star Magic Johnson tested positive and the death of tennis champion Arthur Ashe demonstrated that the disease could affect practically anyone, including the famous and well liked. These changes in the image of persons with AIDS coincided with the realization by some within the scientific and medical community that AIDS offered exciting avenues of new research. This provided an important and much more advantaged ally in the political struggle and took some of the pressure away from politicians who could justify increased research on the grounds that this was recommended by the scientific community. Even these more optimistic developments, however, cannot be interpreted to mean that AIDS moved from degenerative policy making to a more democratic or more scientific/rationalized style. Some target populations (the "blameless" victims) are earmarked for considerable research and positive policy, whereas others (the "deviant" victims) continue to receive far less funding than their numbers would suggest. Also, as Donovan (1996) has shown, one of the most promising public policy approaches—the provision of sterilized needles—has repeatedly been rejected as it combines the negative social constructions of drug users and persons with AIDS. Thus, the history of AIDS policy indicates that even though there has been some progress made toward less degenerative policy designs, the struggle is ongoing and (in contrast with pluralist theory) it does not depend simply on the power and mobilization of the negatively impacted groups. The capacity to gain a more positive social construction is central to the struggle itself.

Even though we believe that the dominant tendency in degenerative policy-making systems is toward accentuation of the negative effects rather than self-correction, there are some other countervailing tendencies. Americans' commitment to fair play and democratic values often operates against always placing the same people among advantaged targets. The media, popular culture, and other carriers of social constructions respond to stimuli other than government and may begin to portray the advantaged targets as "greedy" rather than "deserving." Movies, books, columnists, and dramatic events serve as catalysts for changes in social constructions. The credibility of policies that offer benefits to advantaged groups declines when there are too many objective reasons, verifiable with personal experiences or credible scientific studies, showing that policy is ineffective in solving problems. Personal experience, policy analysis, or deconstructive logic may show that important problems are not even being addressed, or that the design of policies is illogical and not actually intended to serve the stated goals. When deceptions of various kinds are deconstructed and shown for their true colors, government loses legitimacy and its rationales are called into question. This presents an opportunity for change.

The social construction of scientists and universities, for example, is not always positive. After Texas was chosen as the site for the superconducting super collider and the coalition of physicists with other state and local areas vying for the project no longer existed, doubts were raised in Congress whether the superconducting super collider really was a high national priority. Scientists were sharply questioned about the immediate payoff from the proposed research for ordinary Americans, and doubts were expressed about whether the nation really could afford the project in light of other national needs. Cost overruns and shoddy management made it an easy target. When introduced in 1982 it was to cost $4.4 billion, but had grown to $11 billion by late 1993 before it was abruptly canceled by Congress. Scientists blamed it on the public's inability to understand science, their own lack of power, and poor connections with political leaders, but maintained that it was more important scientifically than other projects that had been spared.

Universities have been embarrassed in recent years by government audits that exposed inappropriate uses of indirect cost charges associated with federal research grants. After newspapers revealed that one university president had used such funds to buy a yacht, other universities voluntarily returned overcharges to save their reputations. A spate of books and articles have emerged criticizing universities for lobbying Congress for pork barrel research appropriations. Others criticize universities for their shabby treatment of undergraduates and neglect of their instructional responsibilities. Several states have mandated specific teaching loads in an effort to increase efficiency and improve undergraduate instruction. In 1996, Congress reduced the almost $600 million in line-item (noncompetitive) research grants to $296 million (Cordes 1997). Even though the university's "pork barrel" rose to $440 million in 1997, the amount was far below the $763 million provided in 1993 (Cordes 1997). These two examples show that it is not always possible to simply continue providing costly advantageous policy even to advantaged populations, particularly when they can be socially constructed as taking unfair advantage or getting more than they deserve.

It also is not possible to continually expand the scope of punishment to ever-larger groups. When common behaviors of large numbers of ordinary people become subject to negative stereotyping, the public does not automatically acquiesce. The 1986 immigration legislation had to give amnesty to millions of long-time undocumented residents not only because expulsion was impossible to enforce, but also because alternatives appeared to be mean-spirited. Perhaps Americans' sense of fair play places limits on punishment policy when it becomes draconian or is expanded to too many people.

When policy-making systems deviate from the common patterns of degenerative politics and provide beneficial policy to dependent or deviant groups, this may set in motion a change in the orientation and participation patterns that will help move a society toward a more inclusive democracy. The Social Security insurance program is an example. Social Security was initially supported by business and other conservative groups as a counterproposal to the more radical plans of the Townsend movement that supported guaranteed government pensions to all elderly persons. At the time of its enactment, 1935, the policy was directed toward a group that almost certainly would have been mainly constructed as dependent. The elderly who would benefit the most from the program tended to be less well-off groups of working people as well as elderly women, who outlived their husbands by about a decade. These were largely unorganized groups with low voter turnout and little or no political clout. The fact that everyone would be protected from the fear of the "poorhouse" in their old age made this a viable political opportunity for the Democratic administration, and the rationale presenting the payments simply as earnings on investments paved the way for broad support.

The popular perception that Social Security is simply earnings gained from investments still persists to this day, even though the logic was partially undermined in 1939 when the system was expanded to include dependents and survivors. At that time, the rationale could have shifted from an insurance program that simply provided a return on an investment, to a welfare program designed to protect certain segments of society from poverty. Such a construction, however, has never become widespread. Perhaps the most important single attribute of the policy design was that eligibility was universal (beyond the designated age) rather than means-tested. This granted all of the target population a construction as people who had worked hard all their life, invested their money in Social Security, and deserved to have it returned so that they could care for themselves in their old age. Social security beneficiaries have grown in numbers, wealth, political power, and have done so without losing the largely positive social construction (as hard-working, deserving people). The marked contrast here is with Aid to Dependent Children (Aid to Families with Dependent Children), which began as a means-tested program for dependent children. At its initiation, most of the recipients were young white women whose husbands had died in the war (Berkowitz 1991). As the demographics of this group changed, so did the social constructions, toward a group commonly viewed as young, minority, unwed mothers who do not want to work. This social construction—even though inaccurate in terms of empirical evidence—was instrumental in the passage of the 1996 Welfare Reform Act. One can only speculate what might have happened if the initial design had provided for family benefits that were not means-tested.

For there to be a self-correcting process within degenerative politics, there needs to be a self-correcting dynamic for social constructions. Instead, stereotypes of privilege and deservedness and stigma of deviance and culpability have settled on some groups in American society and stick with them regardless of the policy area. Social constructions are increasingly a matter of pigeonholing rather than diagnosis or creativity. There are many examples of policies for advantaged groups that surely should have been corrected long before they were (and many that have not yet been scaled back). Corporate welfare contributes far more to the national deficit than does AFDC or food stamps, yet the former is largely protected and the latter two were constantly threatened by budget cuts until the federal guarantee was ended in the Welfare Reform Act of 1996. Punishment policies have been expanded to an exceptional extent, in spite of the costs of imprisonment; and there is as yet no end in sight. These examples make it appear that degenerative policy-making systems and the designs they produce are self-perpetuating and feed on one another without any automatic or internal corrective mechanisms. Changes that break the pattern may be more commonly introduced only by external events too large and important to be ignored. One of the important areas for future research is to document the conditions and stimuli that precede change in degenerative politics.

Alternatives to Degenerative Politics

Not all policy-making systems are degenerative. The designs that emerge from degenerative politics are but one "family" of designs, and different types of policies emerge from other policy-making systems. In the next chapter we take up the question of whether scientific professionalized processes and the professionalized designs developed within them offer a viable strategy to overcome the problems with degenerative policy making.

6

Social Constructions of Knowledge: Scientific and Professional Policy Designs

Whereas degenerative politics based on political power and social constructions of target groups characterize some contemporary policy areas, others appear to reflect more objective and utilitarian influences. Scientific and professional values and perspectives have made strong inroads in a number of fields and completely dominate others. The disrepute in which politics driven by power and social constructions of target groups is held by many citizens has spurred a desire for more disinterested and unbiased policy designs (Valelly 1993). Society's high regard for science and technology has cast the scientific method of reasoning in a particularly favorable light. This chapter considers whether and under what circumstances increased emphasis on science and professionalism in policy choices can be an antidote to the negative influences of political power combined with value-laden social constructions in degenerative politics.

The relationship between science and public policy is beset with curious contradictions and nagging questions. Scientists and policy specialists claim they are able to escape the influence of social constructions by focusing on natural laws and by verifying conclusions through a scientific method that includes peer review and replication of research results. Yet, what passes as facts in science are matters of social construction, and the scientific process involves relationships between humans and among humanly constructed institutions. Further, scientists and policy specialists believe their best advice is being disregarded even as policy makers assert that choices are based on sound scientific principle. Among the bothersome questions are the following: How are social constructions of scientific findings different from social constructions of target groups? How can it be that virtually all policy actors in some areas take pains to clothe their arguments in goal-oriented, problem-solving language? If this is the case, how can scientists complain of impotence in their attempts to influence policy? Is it possible that policy designs chosen by scientists and professionals who attempt to be unbiased and dispassionate work to the advantage of status quo interests and the disadvantage of democratic deliberation?

Figure 6.1 depicts the scientific and professional policy-making system and guides the organization of the chapter. The issue context is characterized by scientific constructions of facts and institutions that have been colonized by scientists and professionals who share a common scientific approach to knowledge. Designing dynamics are driven by the risks and rewards perceived by political leaders and the extent to which science offers a degree of safety and security in politically dangerous situations. The extent of scientific and professional unity affect the calculation of risks and opportunities by policy makers. After addressing these issues, the chapter turns to the characteristics of designs that flow from scientific and professional dominance of policy making. The choices of goals, targets, tools, rules, and implementation structures tend to be technocratic and differ greatly from those described in the previous chapter. Scientific and technical designs send messages that marginalize citizens and have important implications for the openness and responsiveness of government. The societal consequences include less participatory citizens and the emergence of an elite corps of experts—both of which are destructive of democracy.

SCIENTIFIC AND PROFESSIONAL ISSUE CONTEXTS

The illusion that policy making can become more objective by diminishing the role of politics and increasing the role of experts has wellsprings at least as old as the progressive era. Many of the reforms adopted at the beginning of this century were aimed at replacing entrenched interests with objective experts. Later, the critical role played by science and technology in the victory of Allied forces in World War II convinced many that government could be more successful by putting aside political differences and providing science the resources and authority to uncover solutions to problems. The Manhattan Project provided a model of what could be accomplished through a partnership of science and government. The incredible success achieved by university scientists-turned-weaponeers was testimony that the scientific community could deliver the answers to other major problems including economic growth and full employment. In exchange, scientists could expect major funding for their research and employment for their students by government (Gilpin and Wright 1964, p. 6).

Utilitarian rationality provides the dominant value in this postwar context and the assumption is made that the public interest is always served by increasing knowledge. Problems are best approached dispassionately with as much knowledge as possible. Politics and values have a place, but should be constrained to setting priorities among broadly defined goals. All other aspects of policy should be designed by experts. Scientists and professionals should define policy issues, fashion the means to reach goals, and use the scientific method to identify preferable

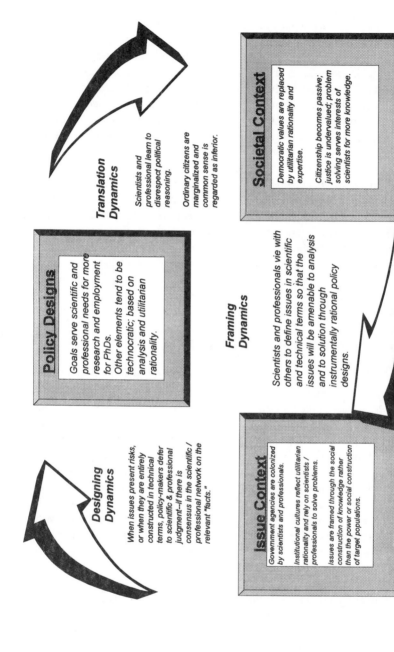

Figure 6.1. Scientific and professional policy-making system.

choices among alternatives (Quade 1982). A thorough valuative discourse does not take place (MacRae 1979). Instead, the values dear to scientists become everyone's values. Expanding databases, developing scientific theory, advancing technology, training scientists and professionals, and fostering the employment of scientists and professionals are seen as goods in themselves. Scientists portray themselves as especially endowed to bring order and sense to the political process. Effective policy making requires just what scientists have to offer: objective sifting of facts, balanced visions, thoughtful reflection, and the mobilization of the best wisdom and the highest competence (Wood 1964, p. 64).

The purpose of policy within this context is unidimensional: Policies should solve problems. The scientific and professional perspective concerning rationality is very narrow and utilitarian, rather than broadly advancing the art of good living and ethical behavior. Rationality is reduced to a mere instrument rather than an agency of moral insight (Marcuse 1964). Specialists and experts with scientific credentials aid and abet the disappearance of the public sphere. A large part of policy design is removed from public discourse. Insofar as a scientific establishment gains control of policy design, the values of ordinary citizens with common-sense wisdom are degraded. The technical solutions that scientists favor detract from building the capacity of ordinary citizens.

Institutional Culture

The institutional dimension of the issue context is one in which the science establishment plays a large role. Not only has there been an exponential rise in public research and development funds, but heavily technological missions govern many public agencies. These agencies often operate to provide grants, contracts, and attractive job offers to scientists outside the agency and look to scientists and professional constituencies for support. The linkage of science and government has been further institutionalized in agencies like the National Science Foundation and the National Academy of Sciences, and in the widespread use of science advisory committees (Ingram, Milward, and Laird 1991). As long ago as 1964, the expansion of the scientific establishment was so marked that Don K. Price wrote, "Yet the plain fact is that science has become the major establishment in the American political system: the only set of institutions for which tax funds are appropriated only on faith, and under concordats which protect the autonomy, if not the cloistered calm of the laboratory" (Price 1964, p. 20).

While the prestige of science has not been able to maintain unquestioned esteem (Ezrahi 1991; MacRae 1976), the influence of scientists and professionals has been fortified and extended through their colonization of many institutions important to policy, particularly government agencies. There is a natural affinity of science and professionals within agencies because of shared values including: belief inspecialization, division of labor, objective rationales, and employment on the basis of qualifications. Generalists trained in management and administration are replaced by specialists with substantive disciplinary training, and scientists have gained management skills that make them comfortable in agency hierarchies (Page 1992). This is a powerful combination because of the tendency of government agencies to intrude into every aspect of modern life. Layer on layer of bureaucracy has been added to government so that government is thicker than ever before and accountability within administration has become very diffuse (Light 1995). Government agencies, by adding large numbers of jobs, have come to serve as an important source of professional employment.

Max Weber's classic analysis of why political leaders lose control of bureaucracy is doubly relevant to understanding the institutional culture of government agencies now that they have become inhabited by scientists and professionals. Weber believed that bureaucracy would become dominant over its political "masters" not so much because of growing numbers, but rather because of the control of information. Weber wrote, "Bureaucracy naturally prefers a poorly informed, and hence powerless, parliament at least in so far as this ignorance is compatible with the bureaucracy's own interest" (Weber 1978, p. 991). The specialized knowledge and jargon used by scientists and professionals within agencies increases the remoteness of the agency from ordinary people and their political representatives. The prevailing language is simply impenetrable without specialized education, and citizens are regarded as supplicants or clients rather than participants in governance.

Government agencies are not the only influential institution colonized by science and professionals. Legislative committee staffs and interest groups have hired scientists and professionals largely in an effort to engage, influence, and control government agencies by meeting them on their own terms. PhDs have become as common as law degrees among actors in the legislative process, and interest groups commonly employ science in lobbying. For instance, environmental groups have come to rely as much on scientific evidence as on traditional techniques of lobbying to score points (Hays and Hays 1987). Government scientists joined hands with scientists hired by environmental groups to propel the issue of global warming onto the national agenda (Ingram, Milward, and Laird 1991). Further, a large number of Washington-based think tanks employ scientists and professionals to do science in service of an ideological bias (Greider 1992, pp. 300–301). Scientists and professionals in universities continually renew the supply of professionals and specialized information.

There has been relatively little attention given by political scientists to the role of science in politics or the politics of science (Cozzens and Woodhouse 1995). Perhaps this is because political scientists, like almost everyone else, have accepted that science is exceptional. Science is thought to be different because it is involved in the search for truth. Scientists are accepted as arbiters of facts on the basis of their professionalism, autonomy, and superior intellect. Scientific exceptionalism may also have wellsprings in the close association thought to exist between science and economic progress. A group of scholars, mainly sociologists, writing in a field called science and technology studies, has in recent years challenged whether science is so dissimilar from or superior to other kinds of knowledge and other types of institutions (Jasanoff, Markle, Peterson, Pinch 1995).

Social Construction of Knowledge

Science represents only one of a number of possible knowledge systems, and its dominance of modern life is so complete it is difficult even to conceive of a world ordered differently. Critical theory has sensitized us to the differences between the concept of reason as employed by classical theorists (as a means for achieving the good life) and objective scientific reason (as an instrument to achieve certain specific ends). Knowledge, too, can refer to very different things. Throughout human history the variation of knowledge systems and the different consequent structures for imposing order on the world are surprising to modern people who see progress coming only through science. Gothic cathedrals such as Chartes achieved the appearance of rationality, order, calculation, and uniformity but were built discontinuously, without architecture or plans through the use of templates to achieve incredibly complex structures lasting centuries. The Anasazi established themselves in the American Southwest and thrived for centuries in a very harsh environment through the use of calendars along with ritual, myth, poetry, and architecture. The Incas used a system of radial marking lines from Cusco marked at intervals with stone cairns or shrines. These shrines integrated religious and astronomical knowledge but also provided precision required by a state bureaucracy that coordinated irrigation, agriculture, trade, taxes, and warfare (Watson-Verran and Turnbull 1995).

In all cases of different ways of understanding the natural world, knowledge has had an intimate relationship with accountability, authority, and power. In the history of Western culture, the divine right of kings based on theologic concepts was replaced during the Renaissance with human attempts to impose order rationally. For instance, as theology was displaced by science, nature replaced God as the limit to human schemes; and scientists became the priests who articulated natural laws. Science was harnessed to collective action. Instrumental reason made the coercive power of the state acceptable (Ezrahi 1991).

The creation of knowledge is a human endeavor that takes place within societies, not as we sometimes suppose as scientists/explorers pioneer the natural world outside society and bring back knowledge of it. There is a process of fact construction that is parallel to the value or image construction that was the subject of the last chapter. Natural science is a kind of fact factory in which constructions occur through a process of interaction and negotiation (Cetina 1995). Sociologists studying the activity of laboratories have described them as assemblages of readers and writers who spend a majority of their time with large inscription devices. Successful laboratory scientists have developed considerable skill in pinning down elusive figures, traces, inscriptions, and in the art of persuasion. The latter skill enables them to convince others that what they are doing is important and what they say is true. They are so skillful they are able to convince others that their analysis is simply following a consistent line of interpretation of available evidence, and no persuasion is involved at all (Latour and Woolgar 1979, p. 70). Professional and institutional relationships are critical to laboratory work. Materials are taken out of their natural setting and processes are removed from their original time context. Through human arrangements, including protocols and certifications, samples and test results are trusted to be reliable even when lab work takes place in distant locations by unknown persons (Cetina 1995). Science is neither exceptional nor immune from social and political forces. It is just that the social constructions, institutions, and actors in scientific and professionalized policy-making systems are quite different from those in degenerative systems.

Empirical studies of scientific work have revealed that negotiation is fundamental to the elements, outcomes, and procedures of fact production. Scientific outcomes are frequently "undetermined" and are often opaque, murky, ambiguous, and in need of interpretation. The scientific process of "discovery" is more aptly conceptualized as contention, discourse, argumentation, creation of consensus, and (importantly) social construction (Cetina 1995). This process takes place through very strong scientific institutions of which laboratories, working group relationships, disciplines, credentials, certifications, peer review, journal publications, and science prizes among myriad other aspects of the science establishment are a part.

Designing Dynamics

We expect that science will have a stronger role in policy design when the scientific establishment has achieved a high level of cohesion in its scientific theories and has mobilized scientists into a policy network. Science moves forward through a process of certifying agreements whereby facts are taken out of dispute and are no longer active questions. Agreement or consensus, then, is very important to the creation of scientific credibility for policy arguments. Common allegiance to scientific and professional norms as well as a shared perspective and a common body of knowledge also assist in linking specialists together in policy networks (Beer 1977; Fischer 1990; Heclo 1974; Mitchell 1987). Policy decisions and designs depend on the strength of relationships within such networks that link scientists from universities, agencies, think tanks, interest groups, and corporations. Such webs of relationships founded on expertise, scientific knowledge, and allegiance vary a great deal in terms of coherence but even when coherence is low, there is general agreement on what passes for acceptable knowledge and evidence in the policy debate.

Professional networks contain both policy communities and policy complexes. In all networks there is a common agreement about the technical nature of the issue, but the extent of agreement or disagreement about specific policy design approaches can vary widely. Policy communities are the more closely knit, coherent, stable, and closed forms of networks. Policy communities exist where there is a high degree of unity and exclusivity among scientific and professional actors who have reached a consensus on existing problems, potential solutions, and desired outcomes. There is a continuity among actors extending over long periods of time. Whatever groups are adversely affected and might oppose the policy community remain unmobilized (Marsh and Rhodes 1993). Unless participants share membership in the community their knowledge is considered irrelevant. Professionally oriented government agencies dealing with the subject matter are an important part of a policy community and hold the same policy conceptions. The space and planetary science policy community is an example of a cohesive community.

At the other end of the continuum are loosely connected networks called policy complexes. Policy complexes encompass a large diversity of opinion. While all the members agree that utilitarian rationality and science should govern decisions, there is much diversity in terms of which disciplines are thought to be most relevant. Even members of the same discipline may disagree sharply about what evidence dictates in terms of policy. Further, scientists placed in different settings such as agencies, interest groups, or think tanks often are at odds with one another. Government agencies within a diverse policy network are often more constituency oriented than professionally motivated. The poverty and homelessness policy complex is, for example, quite divided about scientific findings (Kyle 1996a).

The influence of scientists and professionals depends on the consensus the network can build in favor of particular policy design choices. A policy community gains impetus for policy agreement from its unity. A complex is more likely to offer contending policy viewpoints that are treated by elected leaders as rationalizations for positions taken on other grounds. Influence also depends, however, on the strength of government agencies even when they espouse scientific and professional viewpoints. Where such institutions are strong, scientific perspectives are much more likely to prevail even in the face of powerful interests.

Exploiting Political Opportunities and Avoiding Risks

The literature that assesses the opportunity of science to influence policy is not at all consistent. Public policy and public administration scholars including Deborah Stone (1988), Frank Fischer (1990), and Edward Page (1992) have written eloquently about the negative consequences to political accountability and democracy resulting from the dominance of scientific and professional values in policy making. Other scholars, however, have written that the political controls exercised by elected officials are considerable (Fesler and Kettl 1991; Rourke 1984). Administrative rules and procedures assure openness in formulating policy. Elected officials can curb excessive professionalism through power over leadership appointments, agency jurisdictions, and budgets. Some researchers note the extent to which the modern scientific community reinforces democratic values in that it resists public controls over research questions or findings, and it is generally nonhierarchical (Smith 1992). In fact, some observers see scientists and professionals as more used and abused by government than the other way around. Sociologist

Chandra Mukerji believes that scientists are kept on tap by government to give advice that will avoid grave technical and scientific errors and to identify scientific opportunities. Their testimony is also used to bolster policy alternatives that are mainly chosen for reasons unrelated to science. She writes:

> The process of giving the voice of science to the state for its political ends is in formal terms the opposite of ventriloquism. Scientists do not send their voices out to speak through the mouths of mute government officials. Government officials extort the language of science and scientists' analytic skills to do their political jobs. Scientists are made mute except for when politicians find their voices useful. (1989, p. 198)

While Mukerji seeks solutions in fortifying the resolve and cohesion of science in the face of power, others offer very different strategies. MacRae, for instance, believes that the role of science in public policy could be improved by scientists themselves, but only if they are educated differently. Scientists need to be trained in reasonable value discourse including those values central to democracy (MacRae 1979).

We hypothesize that the influence of scientific and professional knowledge on public policy depends on whether issues are framed in such a way that they present political opportunities to elected officials, or whether they mainly present political risks. Recall from our analysis in the last chapter that political opportunities exist by distributing benefits to advantaged groups (who are powerful and positively constructed), and there are equally strong political gains from providing burdens to deviants. Contenders (who have political power but are viewed negatively) and dependents (who are politically weak but evoke sympathy) present a mixed bag of risks and opportunities and therefore are dealt with by complex and subtle policies in which scientific constructions of facts can provide useful justifications. However, the off diagonal of providing burdens to advantaged and benefits to deviants is politically risky, and it is here that professional and scientific policy designs become independently influential.

Elected officials are sensitive to political risks and opportunities that include present threats to their influence and re-election as well as anticipated dangers. Politicians are always attuned to the distribution and exercise of political power. As we set forth in Chapter 5, elected officials are also influenced by prospective threats of becoming trapped into taking stands that are at odds with prevailing social constructions. For these reasons politicians try to do good things for powerful, positively constructed targets and punish powerless, negatively constructed interests. Where clear signals about risk or opportunity are absent, or it is impossible to avoid the dangers of imposing costs on the advantaged interests or benefits to the deviants, politicians will try to avoid blame by involving science and professional expertise in policy design.

The strong cultural attachment to the scientific method and instrumental reasoning is such that politicians usually try to clothe their choices in objective technical terms even though they are otherwise motivated. It is easy for policy researchers to overestimate the influence of scientists and professionals because politicians often employ their nomenclature. The official language of public policy is to justify policy design with reference to the underlying substantive logic. Politicians wish to be viewed as well-informed and objective. Even though policy actions may be taken primarily to satisfy powerful groups or to respond to social constructions, politicians must articulate some sort of instrumental reasoning that connects policy actions to substantive results. In these cases, scientific or professional opinions are simply rationalizations that permit politicians to take advantage of opportunities or avoid risks.

Figures 6.2, 6.3, 6.4, and 6.5 portray the likely extent of scientific and professional influence on politics and policy under different issue contexts, different degrees of scientific network cohesion, and different alignments of scientific findings with policy positions that are politically expedient. The issue contexts across the four figures differ from one another by the types of political opportunities or risks that are presented. The polar positions on scientific network cohesion are reflected in contrasting influence of unified communities, where mainstream science is not challenged by scientific detractors, with that of the more loosely knit complexes where there may be a large contingent of maverick scientists challenging mainstream theory. Alignment refers to whether the preponderant scientific evidence supports the same policy position that offers political gain to elected leaders, or whether scientific evidence supports policies that are risky from a political point of view.

Figure 6.2 illustrates an issue context in which power and social constructions of target groups converge to present elected officials with clear openings to build political capital. The politically most profitable situation is the one reflected by the branch on the far left of Figure 6.2. A unified policy community exists, and the findings of mainstream science converge with the policy that offers political gain. Here there is a unified scientific community without renegade scientists. In this type of issue context, politicians do not need to worry that prestigious voices from the science community will cause them to regret their actions when they do good things for good people and provide burdens to deviants. The interesting questions are likely to be the extent to which science and professional reasoning is adopted as a main rationale, the extent to which scientists and professionals gain as beneficiaries of policy, and the extent to which science is likely to correct for policy design flaws that may occur due to the lucrative political payoffs from this policy arena. While elected leaders will wish to borrow whatever expert rationales they can find, they will be loathe to share credit for positive outcomes with scientists or professionals within government agencies. However, if scientific institutions are powerful and form a strong alliance with advantaged target groups, science may well gain large benefits and contribute to overrepresentation, oversubscription, or overfunding, all of which involve the provision of more collective action than is necessary and efficient to achieve public purposes. The scientific/industrial complex that has driven the defense establishment with its enormous and practically

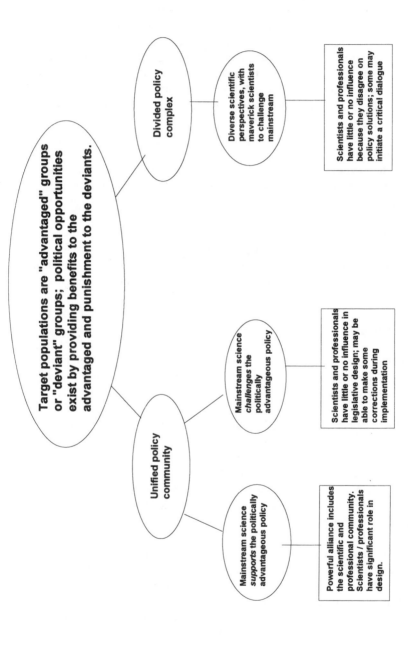

Figure 6.2. Scenario showing expected influence of scientists and professionals in situations that offer significant political opportunities (providing benefits to advantaged groups or punishment to deviants), given different levels of unity/diversity within the scientific and professional alliances and the policy position supported by mainstream scientific theory.

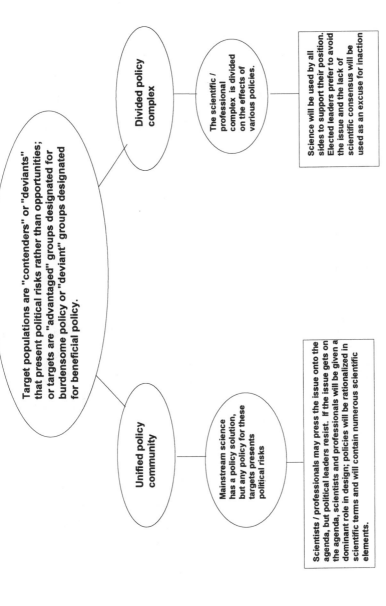

Figure 6.3. Scenario showing expected influence of scientists and professionals in situations that offer significant political risks, given whether the scientific/professional alliance is unified and has a mainstream policy position or whether it is divided and has divided perspectives of whether there are policy solutions or what these might be.

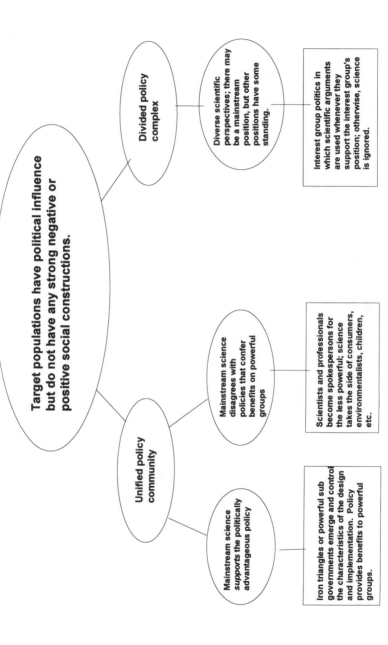

Figure 6.4. Scenario showing expected influence of scientists and professionals in situations in which the target populations have significant political influence but do not carry strong positive or negative social constructions, given whether the scientific/professional alliances are unified or divided and whether mainstream science supports of challenges the politically advantageous policy position.

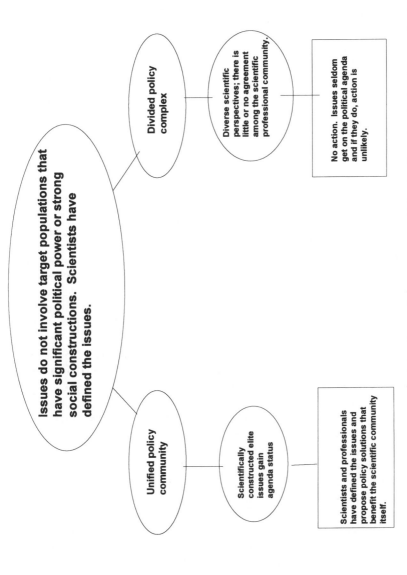

Figure 6.5. Scenario showing expected influence of scientists and professionals in situations in which scientific and professional perspectives have framed the issue. There are no target populations with significant political power or with strong positive social constructions. The policy field has been left to the scientific/professional community.

impregnable budget is an example. Another example is the National Institutes of Health that receive overly generous funding to address health problems of advantaged populations and not incidentally grant huge advantages to health scientists and professionals and drug companies.

The situation is modified somewhat when the preponderance of the scientific network takes issue with the policy directions dictated by power and social construction of target groups as is the case in the middle branch in Figure 6.2. Can science introduce some discipline when it comes to oversubscription of good things to advantaged people and burdens to bad people? Scientists and professionals may have some influence in the implementation process if they are strongly united and the agency involved is highly professionalized. There are strong reasons why a policy community will want to correct policy errors in choice of targets, tools, rules, or other elements that have resulted in oversubscription of benefits to advantaged groups or burdens to deviant groups. Agencies bolstered by a united policy community will wish to gain autonomy to make and implement policy as they see fit. Moreover, executive branch officials are accountable for the delivery of substantive results. Agencies are placed in situations in which they must construct serviceable linkages and mechanisms even though the designs contain populations who are scarcely connected to goals. The choices available to agency officials are to modify the policy design so that it is workable or to obfuscate actual effects. When the agency is part of a strong policy community, we expect it will do the former.

The imposition of professional standards by agencies in the process of implementation is more likely when the scientific basis is strong and professionals have a coherent and unified view of problems. Under such conditions, agencies will resort to a variety of strategies. Under circumstances in which the original design leads to oversubscription or to a target group that is too large to logically, efficiently, or effectively serve policy, agencies will engage in restriction, relabeling, and goal enhancement. Higher standards will be applied to target groups to reduce numbers below that intended by the elected officials who originally created the design. Whether or not the modifications to policy design made in the process of implementation will be subsequently challenged by elected officials will depend on several factors. The credibility of the instrumental reasoning and the respect garnered by scientists and professionals are important considerations. Also important are the reactions of target groups and whether they can mobilize against agency actions. In any case, scientific and professional perspectives have a better chance of prevailing in administrative arenas because legislators infrequently exercise careful and continuous oversight over the implementation processes.

In issue contexts offering significant political capital, we expect science will have very little influence when it is truly divided as is portrayed in the far right branch of Figure 6.2. Where scientists hold different positions on these kinds of issues, detractors will be ignored even by their colleagues, and political leaders probably will ignore whatever cautious voices of moderation the detractors may raise in the policy formulation phase. There is some chance, however, that dissenting scientists who seem to be voices in the wilderness can lay the foundations for a critical dialogue that ultimately may lead to policy change.

Figure 6.3 presents the issue context that contains many more risks than opportunities to elected leaders. There is no convergence of signals to elected leaders. These kinds of policy situations involve policies toward contenders and dependents. Where contenders are involved, political leaders risk offending powerful interests if they resist their policy demands, but if they provide the desired policies, they will incur the wrath of the public for catering to undeserving powerful groups. For dependents, political leaders risk appearing uncaring or immoral if they do nothing, or wasting precious legislative resources on dependents whose needs are not high national priorities. If there is a strong and united scientific community including professionalized agencies, there is some chance that elected leaders can be persuaded to put issues involving these kinds of target populations on the agenda. The kinds of policies adopted, however, tend to be rationalized in highly scientific and technical terms. Elected leaders try to present the case that the (scientifically constructed) facts of the matter gave them no choice. Further, the policy design is likely to employ technically based standards and automatic decision aids. Agency officials are likely to be given a great deal of discretion so that the inevitable blame for unpopular policies will be placed on them rather than on elected leaders.

Under such politically risky conditions, politicians are likely to write very general legislation wherein beneficiaries and losers are difficult to define. Employment of scientific and professional rationales is attractive to elected politicians under these conditions because targets are identified through objective reasoning that cuts across conventional social and economic cleavages. Groups that were, under normal conditions, likely to be constructed favorably get relabeled. For instance, regulatory water pollution policy by its very nature imposes costs on small businesses that are normally constructed as advantaged. The criteria for becoming a target of such legislation is whether a business discharges residuals into surface or groundwater. Companies that otherwise would appear to be both positive and powerful become labeled "potential polluters" through causal logic.

The imposition of costs on interests that normally would be considered powerful and positive is rationalized in technical terms and is likely to provoke technical counterarguments if there is another credible scientific position available. Affected industries have countered the Environmental Protection Agency's positions on what are considered regulatable quantities of substances in discharged sewer water through testimony from industry water chemists. The strength of agency professionalism in face of strong political pressures is important to the integrity of the design of legislation and its implementation. This proposition is consistent with the findings of Mucciarone (1995) who concluded that strong institutions (that is, organizations with high esprit de corps, excess organizational capacity, and a high degree of professionalism) were the best explanation of government's ability to impose costs on powerful interests. Where agencies are not so strong and the causal theory on which they rely is disputed, agencies are unable to hold their own ground against political opposition. Where causal linkages are subject to more than one plausible interpretation, powerful interests hurt by policies will respond with their own scientists and experts. Under these circumstances, formulating and implementing regulatory policy becomes a debate among experts within a loosely structured policy complex. While experts engaged in the complex on behalf of the regulating agency and the regulated may disagree sharply, the argument is conducted among specialists who share the same fundamental agreement about the sort of data and reasoning that is relevant.

Where there is a divided policy complex as is the case in the right branch of Figure 6.3, scientific credibility will be claimed by all sides. More than likely the lack of scientific consensus will be used as an excuse for inaction by elected leaders.

Figure 6.4 portrays a more traditional pluralistic issue context in which competition between powerful interests who do not have positive or negative social constructions determines the allocation of benefits and burdens. As is illustrated by the left branch of Figure 6.4, where science and professional perspectives are consistently in accord with those of the most powerful interests, iron triangles or subgovernments emerge (Cater 1959; Freeman 1965; McCool 1994). Policy benefits powerful constituencies that are served by agencies and legislative committees. Distributive policies that benefit powerful interests are cloaked with professional rationales such as the engineering feasibility and benefit cost analysis that has long supported the western water reclamation projects (Ingram 1990).

The middle branch of Figure 6.4 shows science playing a positive role in correcting policy errors. In this issue context, mainstream science disagrees with the policy solutions that would serve powerful interests. Science is in the position of speaking truth to power. Much of the policy science literature that portrays science and professionalism as preferred problem solvers finds its empirical examples from this issue context. Scientists concerned with the ozone hole are able to gain an international convention to ban chlorofluorocarbons even though they are manufactured by powerful international chemical corporations. Forestry scientists are able to win some battles in favor of natural fires and prescribed burning even though they are opposed by inholders and tourist industries in national parks and forests. Close examination of many of these cases suggests that the influence of science and professionals depended very much on whether they provided a margin of victory in the balance of power among contending interests. When government takes the side of powerful interest groups, science and professionals can be employed in victorious battles by environmentalists and consumer groups. Much of the credit for what appears to be a victory by science must be shared with the interest group movements that also draw on power resources other than expertise.

Where the opinions of scientists are all over the map, as they are in the right branch of Figure 6.4, then legislative logrolling will take place, blatantly ignoring what conflicting scientists see as negative policy consequences. Scientists are among the many babbling voices listened to purely on the basis of their power.

Increasingly, science is being drawn into interest group battles especially when science is not united. Contending interests hire advocacy scientists to do studies that will provide support for their points of view. The Union of Concerned Scientists in a series of advertisements in the *New York Times* in 1995 and 1996 has drawn attention to what it terms "junk science," that is, science that fails to follow many of the tenets of objectivity and disinterestedness, such as: the tobacco industry hires expert witnesses to testify that nicotine is not addictive; and the coal industry disputes the claim that there is long-term global climate change related to human-made greenhouse gasses. While such advocacy or junk science may generate grants and jobs for science, it may help to undermine the strength and credibility of scientific constructions of truth in policy making.

The final issue context is considered in Figure 6.5. These issues are scientifically constructed without clear social constructions of target groups or powerful interest group involvement. These are the scientifically constructed elite issues that gain agenda status purely because they are of interest to science and bring benefits to scientific policy communities. A number of big science projects that receive federal agency support and large congressional funding fall in this category including the human genome project, where an attempt is being made to construct a DNA map of Homo sapiens, and the earth observation system, where a space platform will collect data through remote sensing.

This issue context also includes cases in which elected politicians are uncertain about present or future political risk. In such cases, politicians are likely to recommend further study of a given policy or issue. Generating more knowledge is often perceived as politically advantageous because in our technically oriented society more knowledge is generally believed to be beneficial. In yet other circumstances, politicians face no risks unless some important function of government fails to perform adequately. Because scientists and professionals are supposed to know how to keep matters running smoothly, their choices are relied on absolutely. The degenerative influence on democracy of the kinds of policies that are represented in scientifically dominated contexts demands further consideration. Dressing social issues in scientifically constructed cloth tends to transform the way issues appear to citizens.

Scientifically and Professionally Constructed Issues

Science and professionalism are part and parcel of contemporary politics, and under some circumstances they contribute to flawed designs. Their function is especially likely to be damaging when they commandeer an issue with important social value implications and transform it into a matter of elite scientific and professional concern. In such cases they define the issue, specify the goals, supply the assumptions, and rationalize the policy element choices. Political actors perceive little opportunity or risk in such issues and play no part in issue definition and agenda setting. The major risk to public officials is to be caught at odds with the scientists and professionals who have come to be regarded by the public as having special knowledge about such issues. Public officials can profit from their involvement in these issues only by having the wisdom to defer to the experts. Issues captured by scientists are portrayed as too important or too complicated to be left to political choices in a society that denigrates politics. Such issue areas often seem best addressed by proven scientific approaches or technical solutions. Every effort is made to obscure the political aspects of design choices and to exaggerate the technical content. There is little interest by the public or elected officials in these topics, and elected officials are anxious to depoliticize the issues and remove them from the public agenda.

When issues have been constructed in scientific terms, significant policy choices often are consigned to technical decision-making bodies. Public utilities such as water, sewer, gas, and electric services are often governed by professionalized bodies staffed by experts. The choice about which military bases should be closed or remain open in the post–Cold War era has been largely vested in a bipartisan base closing commission that applies largely technical criteria in making its recommendations.

Issues that might well be more broadly cast sometimes are defined as technical issues involving a limited scientific audience. Even though there is an obvious public interest in such areas as the supply of human organs for transplant, elected officials are comfortable in legislating only certain peripheral policy aspects such as providing a publicly supported organ bank to which there is wide information access. Whether the highly desirable jobs in the military are open to women is an issue of great interest to many feminists, but Army and Marine Corps policies bar women from such jobs through nominally objective and expert definitions of ground combat risk. Important issues of democratic accountability should be raised about policy definitions that obscure the extent and nature of public interests in certain policy issues.

Restricting the criteria for decision in some issue areas to technical criteria frequently has a conservative, status quo bias. For instance, the procedure for closing military bases calls for an objective evaluation of eight indicators that collectively determine the "military value" of each base. Heavily weighted among these indicators is the current deployment of various military units—a deployment that clearly reflects past political decisions. It is entirely possible that bases are being closed today as a result of the dynamics of power politics operating decades ago. Further, the fundamental decision to close bases rather than to otherwise reap the victory in the Cold War, such as making deeper personnel cuts or forgoing upgrades in weapon technology, is not being publicly examined (Imwalle 1994).

Similar questions concerning democratic accountability can be raised about medical domination of the organ transplant issue. For instance, a medical invention—the development of the immunosuppressant cyclosporin—dramatically reduced the likelihood that donated and implanted hearts, livers, kidneys, and lungs might be rejected. The demand for human organs increased but the cost of organ transplants remained very high. It was obvious that the demand and need far exceeded the availability of organ transplants to ordinary persons. Rather than addressing the broader, obviously political, issue of how and whether public financial resources should be spent on organ transplants, the U.S. Congress opted for a narrow scientific and professional issue definition that focused only on increasing supply, but not on the equity issues involved in allocation. The National Organ Transplant Act of 1984 (PL 98507) prohibited the sale of organs and mandated the development and maintenance of a registry of organ donors and recipients, funded promotion of organ donations, and required medical professionals to ask the relevant families of critically injured patients about donations. The absolute value of transplants relative to other medical procedures or the ages, ability to pay, and other characteristics of donor recipients were not among the issues addressed. The prevailing assumption was that if the medical community wanted to perform transplants, the government should smooth the way (Duvall 1995).

While Congress has removed some of the formal barriers against women in the service and women in assignments leading to the top, other purportedly objective criteria weed out women. Women are now assigned to combat specialties in the Air Force and Navy, opening the way to commands that culminate in service leadership. Congress stopped short of opening ground combat specialties, however, which are the primary sources of Army and Marine Corps leadership. Confronted with the politically charged image of women in foxholes, legislators deferred to the services and allowed them to define, based on military expertise, different levels of risk of encountering direct ground combat where people are shooting at each other face-to-face. Women now fly aircraft that face direct air-to-air or ground-to-air fire, but assignment rules purportedly protect women from those assignments that sustain the most casualties in a conventional ground war. Ironically, this concentrates women in lightly-armed units, communications, transportation, supply, and the like, which are the most vulnerable to attacks by small units of commandos or guerrillas. Such attacks would seem to be the primary threat in what the military now calls "operations other than war," the most common use of our military today. Resistance to changes in traditionally male roles is strengthened by other nominally objective standards. Service members periodically take tests measuring general physical fitness, but the test results have been bracketed by age and gender. While age is non-controversial (a forty-year-old is not expected to run as fast as an eighteen-year-old), gender-differentiated standards excite complaints of politically motivated lowering of necessary "objective" standards. The choice of criteria, presumably intended to fairly measure individual fitness, provides ammunition for unofficial internal opposition to women, as well as fueling periodic external questioning of women's competence. Despite the obvious inability of the military to employ anywhere close to a representative number of females in the services (11 percent in military service compared with over half the population), legislators have continued to treat job descriptions and criteria as professional subjects over which the military establishment should have practical control (C. Brown 1995).

While science and professionals gain a great deal from issues they are able to construct in their own specialist terms, partnership with the state and bureaucracy involves dangers for science as well as for democracy. Science in the service of any interest other than its own makes sacrifices. It has been observed that science in the service of the state tends not to be open-ended and innovative. Few true scientific breakthroughs or unexpected and exciting results come from this sort of science (Salter 1988). That science profits in terms of research support, public acclaim, and positions open only to experts is clear.

The classic example of the dangers involved in a science and professional dominance of policy is the atomic/nuclear energy community that existed following the Second World War until the early 1970s. This policy community was created in secrecy during the Manhattan Project, which designed the atomic weapons dropped on Japan. Out of that experience, the community brought a spirit of invincibility and a burden of moral debt. Atomic scientists and engineers could accomplish any goal. Finding peaceful uses of the atom was the challenge to which the community turned. The postwar atomic/nuclear community continued to operate in exclusive secrecy that was institutionalized in special relationships with Congress. An unusual Joint Committee on Atomic Energy was authorized to conduct its operations behind closed doors. The members of the joint House and Senate committee were friends of atomic energy who accepted continued secrecy, expressed no skepticism, and exercised no real oversight. The 1946 Atomic Energy Act declared a most general and ambitious goal:

> It is hereby declared to be the policy of the people of the United States that subject at all times to the paramount objective of assuring the common defense and security, the development and utilization of atomic energy shall, so far as practicable, be directed toward improving the public welfare, increasing the standards of living, strengthening free competition in private enterprise, and promoting world peace. (1946, pp. 724, 756)

In pursuit of this goal a powerful Atomic Energy Commission was directed to conduct research and development activities with fissionable and radioactive materials for medical, biological, health, or medical purposes (U.S. Congress 1946, pp. 724, 758). Under this mandate, the commission granted permits, allowed access to classified materials, and provided resources to research institutions that conducted a variety of experiments.

More than 30 years later it was revealed that medical researchers under the aegis of the Atomic Energy Commission used citizens of the United States as "guinea pigs" without their knowledge or consent.

> Literally hundreds of individuals were exposed to radiation in experiments that provided little or no medical benefits to the subjects. The chief objectives of these experiments were to directly measure the biological effects of radioactive material; to measure doses from injected, ingested, or inhaled radioactive substances; or to measure the time it took radioactive substances to pass through the human body. American citizens thus became nuclear calibration

devices. (U.S. House of Representatives, Subcommittee on Energy Conservation and Power of the Committee on Energy and Commerce 1986, p. 1; hereafter USSECP)

The human subjects were captive audiences—prisoners, elderly, infirm, and mentally retarded—which experimenters might frighteningly have considered "expendable" (USSECP 1986, p. 1).

The narrow perspective and secrecy of the atomic/nuclear policy community allowed such experiments to be justified as serving the goals of science. To members of the atomic/nuclear community, gaining scientific knowledge—not protecting the rights of individuals—was the highest concern. In the rarified context of the laboratory, human subjects were data and not constitutionally protected citizens. Scientific investigators were given broad freedom to pursue knowledge without fetters. The ends justified the means.

The secrecy and exclusivity of the atomic/nuclear power community shielded its activities from serious questioning for decades. A series of events ultimately eroded its autonomy, including accidents at nuclear power plants, issues raised by scientists who parted company with the community, and the end of the Cold War. While this example of the damage possible when a scientific/professional policy community captures a policy area is extreme, it is not unique. Scientific communities have evidenced some of the same characteristics and potentially the same policy control in genetic research and engineering, high-energy physics in the pursuit of the Superconducting Super Collider, and geoscientists in global climate change. The near unanimity that characterizes scientists in such policy communities would seem to run counter to the independence and professionalism scientists claim for themselves. The roots of behavior that preserve agreement and exclusivity appear to be fostered by the dependence of the communities on government resources. In the case of the Superconducting Super Collider, practically every high-energy physicist in the United States appeared to be directly or indirectly helped by the project.

CHARACTERISTICS OF SCIENTIFIC/PROFESSIONAL DESIGN ELEMENTS

Goals, Problems, and Objectives

The most accurate measure of the extent to which science and professionals influence policy design in an issue area is reflected in the formulation of goals. In policy areas dominated by professional communities in partnership with professional bureaucracies, goals are often identical to professional interests: gathering information, increasing knowledge, and training and seeking employment for professionals. Such professional goals may be very different from those of ordinary people for whom knowledge and scientific advance is much less important. From the perspective of laypersons, an inordinate amount of national resources are expended to gather knowledge for which there is little public demand. In fact, government may be expending resources in certain fields like electronics and biotechnology that will lead to less technically advanced citizens losing work.

Goals strongly influenced by scientific and professional perspectives tend to be stated in broad terms, allowing professionals great leeway in interpretation. For example, the Atomic Energy Act of 1946 referred vaguely to common defense, security, and public welfare. In pursuit of this general mandate, the Atomic Energy Commission was given great flexibility.

Where science and professionalism have come to dominate, goals are utilitarian, and no distinction is made between what is good for science and professional groups and what serves the public interest. The political attractiveness to elected officials of seemingly objective goals is obvious, especially when the alternative is to run afoul of the social construction of targets. Rather than advocating good things to bad people or bad things to good people, politicians are simply supporting objective reason. For instance, Speaker of the House Newt Gingrich confronted the issue of whether Congress should be funding medical research that helps AIDS victims by suggesting that Congress should get out of the business of setting medical research priorities. Instead, a board of physicians and medical scientists should annually convene to set funding priorities based on what disease their professional community believes can be most successfully targeted for cure. The board would, for instance, identify promising breakthroughs in Parkinson's disease as justification for directing more medical research toward this fruitful area (Public Broadcasting System, July 6, 1995).

There are many other examples of how members of Congress have sidestepped public debates over values by adopting narrow, scientific definitions of problems. For instance, the National Organ Transplant Act simply assumed that facilitating organ transplants was good for society. Insofar as choices were involved, they were to be made by professionals. The act mandated a Task Force on Organ Transplantation whose main function was to study the organ procurement system and offer recommendations for improvement (Duvall 1995). Setting up independent agencies and study commissions composed of professionals and specialists is a common means through which elected leaders defer tough political choices. The Base Closing Commission and the Federal Reserve Board are classic examples.

In other cases, electoral politicians are foreclosed from value decisions because science itself has raised issues and defined them in terms that serve the interests of science including gaining more data, funding research, and training and employing professionals. The interest of science in pushing back the frontiers of cellular and genetic research has led to a heavily government-funded attempt to identify the gene structure of persons who are genetically predisposed to contract certain diseases, such as Alzheimer's disease or breast cancer. Obtaining such information is accepted as a goal even though such acquisition may not lead to any alleviation or solution and may even lead to human suffering. After all, the most immediate application of knowledge about genetic predispositions of individuals may well be by insurance companies wishing to avoid the coverage of high-risk persons. Global climate change reached the political agenda not because anyone experienced it. So far variations in weather are well within normal patterns. Instead, the problem is based on extrapolation from models. Further, it is not really possible to identify which areas of the world will be particularly affected without more research. The ability of scientists to measure minute quantities of toxic substances in air or water has tended to drive environmental regulations rather than actual incidence of environmental disease.

Political blame for setting politically controversial goals is sometimes deflected to a planning process in which the public putatively plays a large role. The one policy design element over which even scientists and professionals believe citizens' values should hold sway is the setting of goals. From this perspective it is most convenient if the public sets goals far in advance so that professionals can be about the business of establishing the means to reach specified goals without insecurity and uncertainty about the goals being suddenly changed. Legislation requiring goal setting as a part of planning processes that simulated the scientific process has been adopted in many areas, particularly in natural resources. In federal agencies such as the National Forest Service, National Park Service and the Bureau of Land Management, professionals are supposed to develop policy scenarios portraying alternative futures based on certain assumptions and reflecting different values. The public is invited to participate in the choice among futures. By framing the alternative futures, the agency involved greatly reduces the options open to the public. The assumptions on which scenarios are based are often not clear to laypersons. Usually the future chosen is some middle ground clearly preferred by the professionals. Further, the representatives of the public willing to become engaged so early, before consequences are actually understood or felt, tend to be members of the policy community who specialize in the policy area. The consequence is that actual public participation is forgone, not fostered. Should objections to agencies' actions arise, it is explained that the agency is only following policy designs previously publically adopted.

Targets

From a rational, utilitarian perspective, the proper targets of policies are those persons whose actions are most likely to deliver goals. Science and professionals have no interest in the political power or the social construction of targets. Should the social identity of targets overlap with groups objectively chosen to accomplish policy, the coincidence would be purely accidental. This objectivity breaks down when it comes to the selection of professionals and scientists as instruments of policy. When scientists and professionals themselves are targeted by policy, the preference is for beneficial, capacity-building policy that permits targets to have maximum freedom of action. Therefore, the kinds of targets identified in scientific/professional contexts depend on the extent to which professional communities influence policy design.

Where scientists and professionals are united in a policy community and there is a strong bureaucracy that shares their perspective, the major targets are the scientists and professionals. Researchers and military professionals, for example, were specified as the major actors in early atomic energy policy. Similarly, physicians and specialists are empowered to fill in the details and implement organ transfer legislation. Membership in such target groups is closely circumscribed by the scientists and professionals themselves on the basis of professional criteria including educational credentials, peer reviews, and competitive qualifying exams. Every effort is made to insulate recipients from outside "political" influences.

Under circumstances in which scientists and professionals carry less influence and are used to legitimize policies driven by power and social constructions, scientific rationales are used when the consequences are the same as those dictated by political power and social constructions. For instance, actuarial statistics are used to determine police surveillance. Because more crime is perpetrated by populations and neighborhoods having certain characteristics—racial minorities, teenagers, high school dropouts—certain populations are targeted for more intense policy surveillance (Deflem 1994). These criteria have all the trappings of objectivity but place much greater burdens on some people than others—those most burdened are the least powerful. Further, individuals are chosen not because of their own actions, but because of their membership in a statistically created class. The unfortunate consequence is that this classification system overlaps and reinforces social stereotypes. Deborah Stone has pointed out the way in which clinical reasoning may fortify stereotypes. While the use of diagnostic tools such as "rape trauma syndrome" bolsters the truth claim of women who are constructed as dependents, clinical reasoning that treats women as individual medical cases, rather than as victims of systematic forces, discourages the political mobilization that might change the dependency status. The syndrome also denigrates women whose truthfulness must be subject to independent, outside verification (Stone 1993). At the same time, this sort of clinical reasoning elevates medical expertise as more reliable and objective than the witness of experience.

Under circumstances in which degenerative politics identifies targets in initial policy design, scientific and professional modifications made by strongly professional bureaucracies in the implementation process can correct design errors. In the creaming and relabeling exercises described earlier, agencies can modify the target populations to more closely fit professional criteria for effectiveness. Often target groups so constructed cut across existing stereotypes and create new links between people of different economic, racial, and class lines. The resulting policy is clearly better for the modification. Whether agencies are able to more objectively construe targets depends a good deal on bureaucratic esprit de corps and professional commitment. Consequently, many of the agency characteristics that lend themselves to the excesses in combination with highly integrated scientific communities operate to improve designs that are driven by stereotypes and other social constructions. Ironically, scientists and profession-

als make the greatest contribution to good policy design not when they dominate, but rather when they do not.

Agents and Implementation Structure

The scientific method biases scientists and professionals toward Wilsonian implementation structures where goals are set politically and objective agency officials
with the necessary expertise are given free reign in implementation. Ideally, the
agencies chosen for implementation will base their actions on sound scientific theory and adequate information. To perform their job properly, agencies must employ
many scientists and professionals and contract with others. The details of implementation structure are dictated by the findings of objective studies carried out by
qualified scientists and professionals. Because the only knowledge reputed by scientists and experts comes from sound theory and replicable experiments, scientists
and professionals have a preference for centralized administrative frameworks
where directions from above are carried out in the field.

The typical administrative structure in policy areas where professionals and
scientists have preponderant influence places national agencies heavily staffed by
scientists and professionals at the apex of the implementation chain. This chain
emerges by design of the implementing agency. Control is placed where there are
fewer political persons and generalists and the largest cluster of persons with scientific and professional credentials. Lower-level agencies at the state and local levels are staffed by kindred professionals and scientists who receive directives and
resources from colleagues higher up. This structure holds up whether the professionals or scientists are from physical or social sciences.

Where scientists and professionals are at odds with a bureaucracy that is weak
and dominated by interest groups, a grassroots implementation model which allows
for more innovation by local actors may be favored. While science ordinarily reinforces bureaucratic power, there are instances in which science provides powerful
arguments for groups challenging prevailing policies. Only when such groups actually prevail in legislative arenas is it likely that such grassroots implementation
structures actually find their way into designs, however. Because this involves politics in which powerless groups supported by science must prevail, such incidences
are rather rare.

Tools

Scientists and professionals have great confidence that, given the proper support,
they and their colleagues can come up with solutions. Therefore, policies directed
toward themselves as agents and targets strongly favor capacity-building tools that
provide personnel and resources to put science into practice. The kind of policy
designs that come out of policy communities in concert with professional bureaucracies utilizes grants and subsidies and authorizes positions and appropriate funds

for scientific analysis and research project management. Scientists and professionals within agencies or target groups are treated with respect, and their choices are anticipated to be the right choices. Authoritarian tools and sanctions directed at scientists and professionals are extremely rare.

From the perspective of the physical and natural sciences, people behave in ways that are not highly predictable; therefore, from a scientific perspective, ordinary people are a poor means through which to deliver policy results. For this reason, the social sciences—those sciences concerned with human subjects—are not so highly regarded and are less often employed in policy designs than are the physical and natural sciences. Scientists favor predictable instruments in policy design. They prefer not to rely on human agency to solve problems. Therefore, they choose policy tools that make human agency irrelevant and behavior modification unnecessary. They desire policy tools based on scientific reason and technology.

Professionals and scientists have been very inventive at finding technical policy solutions. To solve problems of pollution, the scientific and professional community would opt for new waste treatment technologies and the invention of new pollution-free product manufacturing methods. Far more funds will be allocated to these technological solutions than to behavioral scientists' studies of how people might be induced to pollute less. To cure cancer problems introduced by smokers, science and technology favor the manufacture of low-tar nicotine tobacco products rather than behavioral strategies leading to less demand for tobacco. To cure drug use, the technological perspective would rely on methadone or other substitutes for harmful drugs. Rather than driver education or more stringent traffic laws, the scientific and professional perspective would prefer engineering designs that make highways safer or new car equipment like air bags and antilock brakes. Rather than teaching people not to eat junk food, scientists would prefer to invent additives that make junk food more healthful. Rather than modifying the behavior of naughty children in school, professionals are turning to drugs that calm unruly students. Rather than disciplining children not to watch violent programs on television, new devices are invented that enable parents to preprogram their TVs.

Several examples come to mind from the field of water policy. Rather than expecting the public not to choose homes in the floodplains, dams, levees, and other flood control projects have been designed to keep rivers in their main channels. Rather than imposing water conservation measures prohibiting the use of more water than is delivered naturally, water engineers have designed huge water supply projects that divert rivers from one river basin to another and store water for use when people want it. The loss of natural wetlands to development is countered by environmental restoration projects through which engineers simulate natural processes observed in swamplands. Membranes have been developed to desalinate seawater and remove toxic and other undesirable substances from water, rather than relying on humans to limit their water use or protect their water resources. Through such technological miracles, most people can effortlessly get ample affordable water supplies by merely turning on the tap. Further, through the construction of vast irrigation projects, farmers no longer have to rely on rain and can grow crops in the deserts.

While social science tools are not so highly regarded as those of physical scientists, they are frequently adopted when physical solutions are not available. Moreover, expanding the capacity of social scientists is definitely preferable to relying on laypeople to learn by themselves. Social scientists usually prescribe policy designs that inject professionals as the proximate targets who are first in line to receive benefits. Families on welfare usually are not simply given welfare with no strings attached by government. Instead, economically dependent families become part of the caseload of professional social workers who often have the power to discontinue funds to clients if advice is ignored. Job training programs usually work not by directly funding the jobless to seek an education, but rather indirectly through professional job training programs that receive the government aid. Aid to battered women is filtered through grants to social researchers, health professionals, and professionalized battered women's shelters. It is not at all surprising that the growth in social programs has been accompanied by a bureaucratic explosion.

Rules

A key ingredient in a marriage of professional bureaucracy to science is bureaucracy's need for established rules and science's willingness to supply such research-based rules. The rules are often complex and obfuscated by scientific jargon. Limitations on who can participate in decisions and what kinds of information should be considered are the heart of rules driven by scientific and professional perspectives. When science and professionalism dominate design choices, participation rules tend to be closed and information rules are narrow. Hiring policy specifies minimum qualifications that limit participation to persons with scientific and professional qualifications. Special skills and credentials are made a condition of employment and thus employees are already imbued with professional values before they are hired. Sometimes specific qualifications are written into law. For instance, a certified engineer must be appointed as commissioner to the International Boundary and Water Commission. A physician must be appointed surgeon general. Even more often qualifications emerge from administrative rule making and personnel policies. The Civil Service Administration sets qualifications for the vast majority of federal jobs. To qualify, candidates must demonstrate that they have certain relevant education and experience. The United States Forest Service hires people with forestry degrees. The Fish and Wildlife Service hires biologists and ecologists. The Soil Conservation Service hires agronomists and irrigation engineers. The U.S. Geologic Service is open mainly to geologists and hydrologists. The Census Bureau hires statisticians.

Designs sometimes foster informal linkages or operating rules between university programs and particular agencies. Georgetown University has placed many more than their share of graduates in the foreign service. The six or seven western state universities with range management programs are the recruiting grounds for the Bureau of Land Management. Yale Forestry School has supplied a large number of forest rangers. Agricultural economics departments send many of their graduates to the Agricultural Research Service. This tie sometimes becomes institutionalized. For instance, a few appointees to the Agricultural Extension Service are based in agricultural colleges at state universities to facilitate the transfer of new technologies from the laboratory to the field.

Through the influence of informal operating rules, professionals dominate the cadre of experts to which agencies turn for advice. The National Academy of Sciences receives a large number of grants and contracts to provide advice to and review the work of federal agencies. Committees are set up by recruiting professionals and university professors who are recognized for their knowledge in specific fields. The scientific reputation of the academy is important to lending legitimacy to its advice. Agencies often set up advisory committees dominated by specialists. Not only do these committees provide scientifically based advice, they also legitimize agency actions (Jasanoff 1990). Their scientific prestige is important to public and congressional confidence. Since the 1970s it has become common practice to include members of the public on advisory committees. While broadening the membership improves representativeness of committees, lay members are almost always a distinct minority.

Numerical standards, quantitative decision aids, and standard operating procedures are among the ways in which decision choices are narrowed to options consistent with professional and scientific values. Professional standards and values substitute for open and democratic discussion. For instance, water pollution is scientifically defined in parts per million of this or that substance. These rules are bound to professional instrumentation and sampling procedures. In a context less dominated by scientists and professionals, water pollution might be said to exist when people in the relevant river basin desire uses, such as habitat for trout, for example, in which existing water quality is unsuitable. Instead of technical measurement, this much more open rule requires a discussion of preferences among water users.

Similarly, numbers of rules and procedures narrowly circumscribe participation and relevant information. Scientific research underpins quantitative decision aids through which the fruits of scientific research are brought to bear on routine bureaucratic choices. The number of foraging animals that can be sustained on public lands and the number of grazing permits allowed are based on a formula that takes into account soil type, density of plant cover, extent of invasion of undesirable plants, and the habits and nutritional requirements of particular animal types. Sentencing, parole, release, and intensity of parole supervision guidelines in the criminal justice system are based on statistical analysis of historical data. Complex multiple regression models are tested using historical records of recidivism among a large number of cases. Variables are identified as important criteria and given weights including such characteristics as prior records and the seriousness of previous crimes, age at first offense, drug and alcohol problems, and ties to the community. The importance of individual officials in the justice system and their professional judgment about offenders in particular is greatly downgraded, and responsibility becomes diffuse.

Standard operating procedures institutionalize professional and scientific perspectives into administrative agencies' day-to-day operations. The forest service has a manual that covers many of the decisions the Forest Ranger encounters each day. Even though the national forests may be hundreds of miles away from the head office, decisions are consistent because rangers follow the same rule book (Kaufman 1960). When scientific research performed by scientists inside the service uncovers new information, as it did when it was discovered that natural fires have benefits, rules about putting out fires change. These changes are not always appreciated by the public, which in this case was indoctrinated into the conventional belief that forest fires are bad.

Regulations applied by regulatory agencies like the Environmental Protection Agency often emerge from standard operating procedures that involve consultation within a professional network. Working parties that develop new regulations are drawn from different units within the agency and from among private consultants with industry experience. Working documents containing draft regulations are published in the *Federal Register* and sent out for comment. The participants in this review process are professionals in other agencies, interest groups, and private businesses. Regulations reflect what is believed by participants to be the best practice on the basis of professional experience. Many people affected by regulations do not participate, are not consulted, and would not know how to participate if invited. Processes of rule making are often open only in name.

Rules reinforce the use of disciplinary methodologies and knowledge, and different disciplines have their favorites. Economists want to require benefit/cost analysis, psychologists will desire the use of lab experiments followed by field trials, sociologists will prefer evaluation research based on effectiveness, physicians will prefer diagnostics, and hydrologists create complex models guided by their own concepts such as the hundred-year floodplain, safe yield of aquifers, and acre feet of water rights. Each discipline wishes that its rules would drive decisions, but usually has to settle for having its rules used as rationalizations. For instance, benefit/cost ratios have long been used to rationalize political choices in water resources. To suit political purposes, however, the rule has been modified so that all projects whose benefits exceed the cost are deemed worthy, and many economically questionable secondary and tertiary benefits are included. As a result, many politically acceptable water projects are clothed in the fig leaf of economic respectability.

Rules will often be complex and require someone trained in a specialized discipline to interpret and administer them properly. Risk, defined by the Environmental Protection Agency, is much different from the layperson's sense of vulnerability. Further, rules often require the collection and interpretation of complex data sets and the employment of specialists in information management. Data then tend to take on a life of their own and become a time series that requires continued collection, whether there is immediate utility. The federal government collects and maintains thousands of data sets that include physical and social statistics and information. Streamflow information, for example, goes back many years as do crop reports, bird and other wildlife species counts, employment statistics, data on housing units, poverty levels, FBI uniform crime reports, national crime victimization surveys, and the like. As users of these data sets, professionals and scientists are powerful clientele groups. Common knowledge of this data knits together membership in professional networks and excludes the uninitiated.

Timing rules add to the bulwarks within bureaucracy against broad public involvement in decision making. Long-range plans have rules that require goals to be adopted and actions to be decided on that will not take effect for many years. The time horizon is decades for forest, water, and national park planning. Only those persons who have expertise in the field are likely to express interest so far in advance. While planning documents are useful for professionals, they are often barriers to participation despite the efforts agencies make to get public involvement. By the time the public becomes interested, opportunities to affect decisions have been forgone. Further, planning decisions are often based on professionally prepared scenarios of alternatives based on assumptions the public is in no position to question.

Rationales

Scientific and professional designs excel when it comes to credible logics. Ends and means are closely linked in clear utilitarian rationality. In instrumentally rational terms, the principal flaws exhibited in the scientific and professional policy designs are an overemphasis on investigation and data gathering. Scientists are loathe to draw conclusions with insufficient evidence even when such conclusions are reinforced by common sense. Calling for further study is second nature to researchers. As a consequence, government collects a great deal of information that may not be particularly useful for decision making. A call for further study is often attractive to elected leaders even if information to be gathered does not seem to be very important to the decision at hand. Delay, rationalized on a professional basis, is often politically attractive to elected leaders who are uncertain of the political consequence of choice.

Deference to utilitarian rationality and underemphasis on such nonutilitarian values as justice and democracy have many undesirable consequences in terms of policy design. Government may very effectively deliver goals most people do not share and unwittingly foster popular sentiments of injustice. Scientists and professionals are adept at claiming that whatever they provide is essential for national security, economic well-being, full employment, higher standards of living, competitiveness in the global marketplace, or whatever might be the public preoccupation of the day. The scientific establishment may come to be regarded as a privileged class, even though scientists themselves prefer to think of themselves as antiestablishment by being open to new knowledge regardless of source. However, the new knowledge may not appear to address the condition of the common citizen, and the high status of scientists and professionals may not be regarded as deserved. Scientists and professionals may come to be regarded not as exceptions to the rule of self-interest, but instead as part of the "overclass."

TRANSLATION DYNAMICS: IMPLICATIONS FOR JUSTICE, CITIZENSHIP, AND DEMOCRACY

Just as policies influenced by power and social constructions of target populations send messages to citizens about their status, what can be expected by government, and how they might participate, so do policies framed by scientific and professional perspectives. Similarly, different messages are sent to different people. In this case, scientists and professionals are treated very differently from ordinary citizens by government and learn very different lessons about justice, citizenship, and democracy. While the messages about the meaning of citizenship and the resulting orientations toward government and participation are quite different from those associated with degenerative political contexts, the impact is often negative. Under certain circumstances, a utilitarian rational viewpoint can have a therapeutic effect. Where scientists and professionals have the greatest influence, however, the consequences are damaging to democratic values.

Messages, Orientations, and Participation of Scientists and Professionals

Scientists and professionals are often treated as advantaged targets by degenerative policy designs because they have both political power and a positive social construction. The source of these attributes can be traced to the same social values that are also imbedded in scientific and professional contexts. Contemporary society places great weight on scientific knowledge and technological solutions. Scientific reason is venerated above any other kind of understanding. Those citizens with scientific and professional credentials are led to believe that their approach to problem solving is much better than more "political" approaches. How they come to this conviction is easily explained. Government regularly turns to the scientific and professional community for advice. Scientists and professionals are asked to serve on National Academy of Sciences committees, to testify before Congress, to be expert witnesses in court proceedings, and to conduct studies for administrative agencies. It is not at all surprising that these specialists come to believe that they know what is best for society.

The orientation that scientists and professionals have toward government is deprecatory. They are under no illusion that government will actually act on their counsel. They have many experiences in which their advice is used when it is politically advantageous to electoral politicians and ignored when it is not. To scientists and professionals, the world of politics is often unreasonable and clearly inferior to the professional and academic worlds. While many scientists acknowledge that politics operates by different kinds of reason, they have little respect for political processes that regularly choose what they regard as inferior solutions. To think politically is to concede that all of society is not yet ready to accept scientific rationality, a more evolved kind of reason. While scientists and professionals know that ordinary people often believe that they live in an ivory tower, they are proud of their different and more advanced thought processes. They believe that politics would be clearly better if it were more like science.

While many scientists and professionals would like to ignore politics, they cannot afford to. Their own professional welfare is too closely tied to political decisions. Government is the source of most educational and research funding and is a source of employment for members of the science fraternity. Therefore, they envision themselves as performing a necessary but not altogether high-priority service when they consult with government. Scientists and professionals believe that they give at least as much as they get from politics and government.

Most scientists and professionals see no harm in playing politics, like any other interest group, when the welfare of disciplines and professions is at stake. While scientists and professionals are convinced that they represent the finest and brightest hope for our society, they acquiesce to lobbying like any other interest group when it comes to promoting self-serving policies. After all, what is good for science is undoubtedly good for America, even if playing an unenlightened game is required to achieve scientific and professional goals. Even though scientists and professionals are clearly advantaged as compared to ordinary citizens, they nonetheless feel mistreated and abused by politics. While they know that ordinary citizens do not value their contributions as highly as they themselves do, they imagine that the problem is due to lack of public comprehension. Public understanding of science programs are a high priority of many professional organizations. In the eyes of most scientists and professionals, the problems of politics and government stem from not using the scientific method of decision making. If ordinary citizens and politicians were as wise as scientists, scientific and professionally designed policies could solve most problems. The time that scientists and professionals are forced to spend in public affairs is unfortunately lost to higher scientific pursuits. They have little commitment and less spirit to engage in political reform because politics is not very worthwhile and they are already unduly burdened.

Scientists and professionals are resigned to the misuse and distortion of their methods and findings in politics. Economists, for example, admit that cost-benefit analysis performed by government agencies is far from the pure and rigorous tool they espouse. Though the tool has become flawed in political practice, it is still an improvement over a complete lack of economic discipline. Many other science-based measures and classifications, such as the poverty line, consumer price index of inflation, sole-source aquifers, floodplains, wilderness, wetlands, and hundreds of similar categorizations in current use, are scientifically vulnerable. At the same time, professionals reason, these categories introduce some objectivity into otherwise political judgments. Scientists and professionals are also resigned to the exploitation of professional differences by different sides in political debates. While they may be of the opinion that scientific differences should be settled in peer-reviewed journals, there is nothing wrong with different scientists giving conflicting evidence in political forums. Within some very broad parameters, scientists are free to express their own judgments. The use to which scientific evidence is put in the political arena is not their responsibility. Nor is it the duty of the scientific community to control the public use of science by any of its members. Scientists must stray rather far from professional norms, such as clear plagiarism, as may have been the case in the discovery of the AIDS virus, or misrepresentation, which seemed obvious in the instance of cold fusion, to provoke professional discipline. From a professional perspective, politics is about conflicting opinions, unfortunately not about science.

Scientists and professionals are even resigned to having research agendas largely driven by the availability of governmental grants. Governmental funds have made possible the explosion of higher education in the United States since World War II. While some disciplines, such as the physical sciences, have prospered much more than some others, such as the humanities, inequality in resources is accepted as just. Science has become a matter of finding answers for society, rather than asking bold questions for the benefit of science. Scientists and professionals have come to embrace their own rhetoric that science is about improving public welfare through technical discovery. Funding should go to areas where many scientists will profit, large-scale instrumentation is used, and significant theoretical and practical breakthroughs are likely. The cost to the scientific community of its close ties to government is high. Ultimately the independence and autonomy of science is eroded, and a false image of science is projected to the public.

Scientists and professionals acknowledge that they have been able to shield some policy areas from the intrusion of politics. Government support is necessary to get some important scientific endeavors off the ground, such as the information highway, the fruits of biotechnology, remote sensing of global changes, and many others. However, they are confident these projects will provide many benefits to society and are well worth the public investment. Because these matters are basically scientific matters, they believe it is altogether fitting for science to take charge of policy. More political oversight would clearly introduce illogical, ill-conceived changes. When policy areas become politicized, instrumental rationality is usually lost. When science and professionalism are unleashed to solve problems, like the cure for polio, the Manhattan Project, winning the Cold War, and conquering space, success is more likely.

Messages, Orientation, and Participation of Lay Citizens

The message that ordinary citizens receive from contemporary policy designs that are heavily influenced by science and technology is that the problems they see as most important may not be important at all. Public problems are revealed through apparently objective scientific tests and measures, such as test numbers revealing that drinking water contains excessive contaminants and statistical indications that crime is increasing, drug addiction is worsening, forest fires are increasing, and species are disappearing. Such measures have been developed by scientific networks and professional bureaucracies, which serve to provide seemingly impartial proof that they are addressing important issues. Many problems not experienced by ordinary people get on the agenda. In contrast, the experience of ordinary citizens is subjective, unscientific, and often does not count for much. If everyday problems fail to hold scientific and professional promise or economic profit, they are not subjected to study or measurement; therefore, they cannot be said to really exist as public issues. Regular citizens are often reluctant to testify as to their experiences without the support of scientific data relating to more general experience. Science, therefore, often serves as a filter between people and their government even when it does not itself raise the problems.

In contexts with long histories of scientific and professional dominance, scientific measurement and analysis are prisms through which political reality must pass to be perceived. Further, these same prisms cast lights and shadows not otherwise seen. The general public has been willing to accept the picture of a robust economy that is revealed by economic statistics over the last twenty years, even though most of them have not shared in its prosperity. They are willing to embrace the notion that ours is the best health system in the world, even though many go without health care or worry about the loss of health insurance. Peoples' own experiences, because they are not objectively documented, are all regarded as personal—not public—problems. Problems labeled "private" include: privacy invasion by telephone advertising and unwanted mail solicitations; the absence of down-to-earth amenities such as good, affordable child-care alternatives; and, the incredibly high and practically unattainable skill and knowledge necessary for successful participation in today's economy. One of the reasons government is perceived as so remote is that its agenda reflects concerns of bureaucrats and scientific networks rather than everyday experience.

In many policy-making contexts, problem solving is portrayed as the business of specialists and experts, not ordinary people. If there is evidence that problems are not being solved, it is not the fault of scientists and professionals. Instead, it is the responsibility of politicians who have let political issues interfere with good professional practice. Ordinary people have been conditioned and now accept the idea that there is one objective answer to any particular problem that is better than any other and that specialists, rather than politicians or ordinary people, are best endowed to answer. Political decisions are always inferior because they involve time-wasting discussion and deviate from the ideal solution because of politically motivated compromises.

The technological tools employed in this kind of policy fail to educate or empower ordinary citizens. Policy does not treat the citizens as if they are capable of weighing evidence, considering the values at stake, and making appropriate choices. Instead, people are treated as if they were mere consumers of devices created by others. Their range of action is involuntarily narrowed to serve policy purposes. Citizens themselves do not need to consider their actions to receive policy goals. Citizens therefore gain nothing through the policy experience to make them better evaluators of policy choices. As a consequence, over time citizens become less capable of self-government, and the distance between themselves and the scientists and professional bureaucrats who dominate scientific and professional policies widens.

While most people believe that politics is generally bad, their orientation toward science and technology is generally good. The postindustrial technological information society in which we now live is thought to be advanced and preferable to any previous era or less-advanced society. Human values of happiness, sense of well-being, community, and belonging are emotional and therefore not real. Objective, utilitarian notions of rationality are the only meaningful rationality. Cultivating nonutilitarian values is a luxury not affordable by ordinary people. The ability to empathize, find common ground, and defer one's personal preferences for more public values are not attributes much admired or cultivated by anyone.

The ideology of science is that participation in politics should be knowledgeable, and experts have knowledge while ordinary people do not. Ordinary people do not expect policy making to make everyday sense. They defer to specialists who have studied the issue. While people may feel guilty that they do not participate more in public affairs, they usually feel their background is inadequate to make policy judgments. Even though they sometimes suspect that the participation of experts may be self-serving, they still do not feel qualified to contribute meaningfully to specialized policy debates. While experts may disagree about what should be done, they all seem to reflect knowledge and understanding not possessed by people outside the specialty. The rules guiding participation in policy design are experienced by ordinary people as real barriers against their participation.

Should grassroots mobilization occur in opposition to technical designs, it is portrayed by the scientific community as ill-informed and unreasoning. Grassroots leadership is exposed as amateurish and ignorant. Immediate human experience is discounted as anecdotal and unscientific. Resisters are disadvantaged because they are not able to construct credible logics supported by scientific disciplines. The existence of social conflict or widespread feelings of alienation are not relevant to professional and scientific designs, and such policies do nothing to address them.

SOCIETAL CONSEQUENCES AND PATHOLOGIES

The considerable influence that science and technology hold over policy making appears to be growing rather than diminishing. As the flaws of degenerative political designs have been revealed, depoliticization through science and professionalism is perceived as preferable. Further, elected officials are interpreting more and more policy issues as devoid of opportunity for entrepreneurship and fraught with political dangers. Many issues appear too complex for public involvement and too uncertain for elected politicians to assert leadership. It makes sense for these politicians to turn these policy areas over to the scientists and professionals to govern. Further, as these issues come to be framed in scientific and professional terms, elected leaders are unable to identify a public interest separate from the professional network or community interest. Elected politicians simply have neither the skills nor the motivation to disentangle the implication of issues to the broader public. Further, they fear that specialists will be able to portray them as ignorant and uninformed. Consequently, many policy areas come to be dominated by professional networks or communities.

Citizens in turn feel as if they simply do not have the skill and information they need to participate meaningfully in politics. Political matters seem to involve matters far above their heads and not really very relevant to ordinary life. While they may feel guilty about not participating, they think that they have very little to contribute and that participation would involve an information and learning process they have neither the skills nor inclination to pursue.

There are some circumstances, however, under which professionalized policy designs become more public and democratic. Policy networks have difficulty excluding the public when events occur that their theories do not explain, or when there is unexpected technological change that threatens conventional ideas (Smith 1993). More than any other policy analyst, Dorothy Nelkin (1977, 1984, 1987) has identified and documented the conditions under which scientific and professional hegemony is challenged. Among such circumstances are situations where grassroots groups come to believe that they and their geographic area are being sacrificed to benefit others. For instance, citizens have been able to mobilize in opposition to complicated policy choices such as the location of technical facilities, including power plants, dams, waste treatment facilities, nuclear waste depositories, and the like. In such cases, local citizens gain confidence in their familiarity and interest in place. They come to view the issue in question as an equity rather than technical issue. At the same time, they usually recognize that scientific reasoning is the coin of the realm and hire or otherwise try to attract their own experts.

Another circumstance that facilitates the democratization of technical decision making is the willingness of some experts to take issue with prevailing scientific and technical constructions. The dangers of nuclear power plants became a public issue when the physicist members of the Union of Concerned Scientists stated that in their professional judgments, nuclear energy posed a significant threat to public welfare. Even though some scientific communities are able to contain significant professional differences, in other areas complexes rather than integrated communities exist, and real controversies about values and facts among experts usually widen the arena of participation to include persons outside the field.

Public involvement is sometimes engendered when it appears that prevailing scientific and professional judgments underpinning governmental regulatory decisions will deprive some persons of their rights and freedoms. The backlash termed the Wise Use Movement was spawned by regulations limiting the use of private lands and private use of public lands. In the view of this movement, governmental protection of habitats to protect rare and endangered species and other similar regulatory choices represent a public taking of private rights. Cancer victims have opposed governmental prohibitions of laetrile as treatment, AIDS victims have protested restricted access to promising but unproven drug treatments, and cigarette smokers have protested limitations on their individual freedoms based on scientific studies of secondhand smoke risks. Governmental prescriptions of fluoride in water supplies and prohibitions against saccharine in soft drinks have been resisted as unwanted government paternalism. Some groups have insisted on their rights to engage in natural childbirth, holistic medicine, and the right to die, even though regulatory bodies dominated by physicians have resisted.

Scientific decision making in areas touching on traditional values may provoke citizen resistance. Scientific research or medical treatment—using human fetuses and funded by government or using public facilities—has encountered opposition, as has surrogate and postmenopausal motherhood. The relationship of mothers and their children is at the heart of family values, which are difficult to subsume into the realm of science and technology.

Despite the above examples of citizen mobilization against scientific and professional networks and communities, Nelkin and others have noted the tendency of scientists to close ranks when faced with outside challenges. While some scientists were willing to question the value premises of recombinant DNA research, once there was a serious threat of public regulation, scientists presented a united front. Whatever the merits of the question of biotechnology, scientists agreed that governmentally regulated science would be bad science (Krimsky 1984, pp. 251–80). Once scientists and professionals are unified in resisting popular involvement, their hegemonies are difficult to penetrate.

CONCLUSION

While there is little question that scientific and professional perspectives do have and should have powerful voices in decision making, there are many reasons not to be entirely comfortable with the roles that scientists and professionals have come to play. Scientists and professionals themselves are rueful that their insights are often used only when it is politically expedient and that their tools and findings are frequently distorted. Some scientists and professionals view with alarm the way in which governmental interests have come to dominate the research agenda. Many resent the time and effort demanded by services they feel they must perform for government.

The observers who see scientists and professionals as overly engaged in policy design believe that important value questions, which should be democratically decided, are being controlled by experts. Further, the utilitarian reason science defends has crowded out communicative reason and questions of equity and justice that are not amenable to scientific judgments. Scientific and professional networks, they warn, have colonized government so that there are no public arenas but only bureaucratic maneuvering among privileged specialists.

We have observed that scientists and professionals often contribute most positively to policy designs in areas where their influence is marginal, and they help to counteract the ills sometimes spread by policies designed in response to political power and social constructions of target groups. Only by understanding social constructions of knowledge and focusing on policy content can political scientists make the finer distinctions necessary to understand and appreciate the role of science and professionalism in politics and policy.

7
Conclusions

CONTRIBUTIONS AND LIMITATIONS OF POLICY THEORIES

Policy designs are centrally implicated in the policy problems and governance issues facing the United States at this point in our history. Yet, policy design has remained largely outside the purview of the predominant social science theories applicable to public policy. These theories should be helpful in addressing policy failures and the widespread disconnection of citizens from politics. While each of the theories we reviewed in Chapters 2 and 3 (pluralism, policy science, public choice, and critical theory) contributes to policy designs that could serve democracy better, none provides a framework for analyzing policy content, none offers more than a partial view of the policy design characteristics that support and perpetuate democracy, and none links the elements of designs with their consequences for democracy.

The causal framework provided in Chapter 4 of this book builds on and integrates the most useful and insightful aspects of other policy approaches. Pluralist theory informs us of the importance of political power, mobilization of interests, building of coalitions, voting, and support for democratic structures of government. It emphasizes process over substance, but the significance it attaches to procedural justice, the protection of individual rights and liberties, and the importance of responsiveness and accountability are well-advised. Policy science emphasizes the significance of solving real-world problems. Instead of public policies representing simply a balance among competing interests as pluralism suggests, policy sciences teach the importance of logical policies with credible linkages of means to goals. Efficiency is only one of the measures of good policy, and we argue for alternative ways of measuring efficiency, but this is a standard that should not be disregarded. Public choice contributes greatly by directing attention to which kinds of "goods" government is justified in attempting to produce and which should be left to markets. Although the public choice view of policy making is overly rationalistic and its view of the self-interested citizen is too narrow and even destructive of democratic values, the perspective directly challenges a number of assumptions about how pluralist democracy works in the United States. Several scholars working under the rubric of public choice have provided useful ideas about institutions and the rules that make them flexible, responsive, and long lasting.

Critical theory, more than any of the previous approaches, provides a standard for citizen participation, involvement, and enlightenment. Further, the deconstructive methods of critical theory provide tools with which to unmask the detrimental impacts of social constructions of target groups and the social construction of knowledge. Critical theorists also have contributed with their conception of communicative rationality, guided by communicative ethics, as an alternative to instrumental rationality. Critical theorists, however, have little to offer in terms of concrete policy-making processes or the content of public policies. For this, we have turned to the evolving field of policy design to help identify the elements of public policy and to understand how their variations affect problem solving, democratic values, and citizenship. The emphasis that design theorists have given to context and the ability of human agency to reframe issues, create new social constructions, and modify previous designs to better serve human purposes is both positive and challenging.

The theory of policy design offered here explicates *how* policy designs often fail to serve democracy and offers explanations of *why* the society produces these kinds of policies. As explained in Chapter 4, our theory contends that the contexts giving rise to public policy are socially constructed, and the dynamics that provide the engine for policy action are grounded in a socially constructed world. These social constructions yield interpretations and give meaning to several factors: the conditions of democracy, the events that are implicated in the emergence of an issue, the potential target populations involved in an issue, and the facts and values that come together into a coherent, credible scientific theory explaining causes and consequences. The production of policy designs involves processes of socially constructing several different "realities" into a frame of reference that will permit a politically feasible policy to emerge. The social constructions that arise become embedded in the design itself and have subsequent consequences for issue contexts and conditions of democratic life.

This chapter will reiterate the major concepts and logic of our theory offering comparisons across the two families of designs that were the focus of the previous two chapters. We will then review the major contributions of the book and how they help to answer questions and concerns that have long interested students of public policy, politics, and democracy. The chapter closes with the implications for improved public policy.

CHARACTERISTICS OF POLICY DESIGNS THAT DAMAGE DEMOCRACY

The issue contexts from which policy designs emerge are extremely complex, containing some characteristics that are much researched (such as institutions and political power) and others that are largely ignored (such as the social constructions of target populations and the social construction of knowledge). We have chosen to concentrate our analysis on the relatively understudied impact of the last two and how these interact with institutional cultures and political power (influence). When issue contexts become highly politicized and the dynamics center around the power and social construction of target populations, policy designs usually will treat different target groups quite unequally. These designs carry messages of privilege and disentitlement that are damaging to citizenship and democratic values. In contrast, when problems are viewed as matters of fact-finding and the social construction of knowledge is central, policy designs usually will disrespect the ordinary experience and common sense of citizens and undermine democratic values in deference to expertise grounded in scientific rationality.

These contexts present very different patterns of risk and opportunity to elected officials. When issues are constructed so that it is possible to provide benefits to powerful, positively constructed groups ("advantaged" populations) or devise punishment for weak, negatively constructed people ("deviant" populations), science and professionals are likely to play only a marginal role and then only when their findings converge with the politically advantageous policy. In more risky political situations in which public officials need justifications for bending to the power of groups that have been negatively constructed (as "greedy" or "undeserving"), science and professionalism are often more important. Similarly, in risky political situations where policy makers need justifications for providing beneficial policy to powerless groups who are constructed as undeserving, then science and professionalism will have a stronger role. In risky political situations, as we have explained in the previous chapter, science and professionalism may dominate the policy design process and elements through their largely agreed on approaches to knowledge production and utilization.

The two issue contexts and the types of policy designs that emerge from each, which we explored in the previous two chapters, are often portrayed as dichotomies. However, we expect that many contexts and policy designs are a mixture of both. Some policy areas may change from one to the other over time. Some political institutions may have a culture that favors one or the other style of policy making, but most institutions are capable of both and are able to socially construct issues such that one or the other set of values will dominate the policy development toward that issue. In their pure form the designs are markedly different, but we believe that both kinds are detrimental to democracy.

As we showed in Chapter 5, degenerative policy-making contexts result in policy designs created to enhance political opportunities and avoid political risks rather than designs intended to serve the public interest, solve problems, or make contributions to a more democratic polity. Such designs often are illogical, deceptive, contain divisive constructions of target populations, and systematically overrepresent, oversubscribe, and overfund certain groups in the society (the "advantaged") at the expense of others. These designs send messages, teach lessons, and allocate values that exacerbate injustice, trivialize citizenship, fail to solve problems, and undermine institutional cultures that might be more supportive of democratic designs.

Social groups that lack significant political power are vulnerable to being socially constructed as deviants or as dependents. Demonizing social groups creates opportunity for political capital by inflicting punishment policy on powerless, negatively constructed groups and gaining widespread public acclaim for having done so. By constructing other politically weak groups as dependents whose problems are mainly the purview of the private and philanthropic world, political leaders can shunt their interests aside and concentrate instead on target groups that offer greater political payoffs. By constructing powerful groups as deserving, political leaders create the opportunity to extend favorable legislation and government largesse and receive accolades from the media and the public for their actions. Political opportunism drives the policy agenda and the characteristics of policy designs, exacerbating inequalities across social, cultural, political, and economic spheres.

Divisions along class, race, gender, ethnicity, region, religion, and the like create power available to whomever is able to capitalize on it, including policy makers as well as others. Without these divisions taking on positive and negative valences, public policy would not provide such straightforward and lucrative opportunities for political gain. Those who are able to create, control, and change social constructions are able to generate new political capital for themselves without necessarily crafting policies that either solve problems, provide justice, or support democratic values.

The designing dynamics that lead to such destructive policies grow out of a pattern of risks and opportunities confronted by elected officials and others involved in the policy-making process. Always anxious not be caught in opposition to prevailing values, elected political leaders often succumb to prevailing images and stereotypes—or participate in creating new ones. This is not inevitable. Elected leaders are not simply robots ordered by power and polls to do this or that. Even though policy makers work within institutions that have considerable influence over their behavior, they are not captives of these institutions or the issue context in any deterministic sense, but are capable of human agency and ingenuity. The dynamic process through which issue contexts shape policy designs involves the social construction *of the context itself.* Policy makers and others involved in the designing process will attempt to construct the issue to ensure that values favorable to them will become dominant within the issue context. Negative stereotypes may be reinforced, or previously negatively constructed groups may be more positively reconstructed.

Designing dynamics also allows for the exercise of leadership in modifying institutions. The extent of civility or interpersonal hostility that characterizes the deliberative culture of the institution may be the result of long-standing tradition, but the people within the institution have the capacity to change the character of interpersonal relationships and the forms of deliberation that ensue. Leaders are also influential in how the issues are framed and how the various design elements are themselves portrayed so that policies offering political opportunities and minimizing political risks will appear more or less illogical. Political leaders are capable of unmasking deceptive policies as well as falsely justifying them.

As we argued in Chapter 5, not all designs from degenerative situations are alike. Instead, quite dramatic differences exist in the designs for advantaged, deviant, dependent, and contender target populations. Yet, there are some common design characteristics, including those summarized below.

- Target populations often are selected for benefits or burdens along well entrenched racial, social, economic, and gender divisions that reinforce existing stereotypes. Designs are carefully crafted to distribute benefits and burdens in accord with social constructions. The result is that existing inequalities are exacerbated.
- Advantaged target groups that are already powerful and positively constructed are systematically overrepresented, oversubscribed, and overfunded whereas others who are already disadvantaged are systematically underrepresented, undersubscribed, and underfunded. These designs erode the democratic principle of equal treatment under the law, make equal opportunity impossible to achieve, and ensure that policy is responsive to the few rather than the many.
- Goals and problems to be solved typically are framed so that they converge with and legitimate the distribution of advantages and disadvantages that yield political capital to public officials.
- Policy delivery chains often have multiple agents and targets that provide opportunities for agencies to enlarge their jurisdiction and powerful groups (advantaged and contenders) to capture benefits they might not otherwise have received. Advantaged groups often are selected as proximate targets to receive benefits even though there is little logical connection between them and the presumed public interest goals. Strategic placement within a long policy chain also is a mechanism for allocating benefits to contender groups that then remain largely disguised from the general public.
- Policy tools tend to become increasingly punitive for some groups, and the rules specifying who is included in the groups to be punished are expanded over time, distancing these groups from the capacity they need to become effective citizens. Government becomes mean-spirited as political leaders and those who aspire to take their place search opportunistically for social groups that can be constructed negatively and subjected to punishment, providing an apparently low-cost strategy for political gain.
- There is an overreliance on economic incentives and disincentives as policy tools. Economic incentives reinforce self-interest as the dominant human motivation

and create contexts in which other motivations, such as public regardedness, are destined to lose.

- Capacity-building and learning tools are seldom directed to dependent or deviant groups who might benefit greatly from them. Groups that are politically weak remain politically weak and become a permanent underclass without the social capital needed to sustain political participation and mobility.
- Rationales create or reinforce the deservedness of some groups and the unworthiness or helplessness of others. Rationales and policy logics, however, often are quite arbitrarily chosen and are no more "true" than any one of several other rationales that would justify quite different designs. Rationales too often are masks for hidden agendas that disguise the effects that may realistically be expected and disguise the actual distribution of benefits and costs. Rationales and policy logics often will not stand up to critical scrutiny.
- Assumptions commonly are unreasonable, stereotyping people as to their behavior patterns, positing illogical causal relationships, and presuming that different targets are motivated differently so that some are capable of learning, human agency, or self-help if resources are provided whereas others must always be looked after or threatened.
- Designs have some (or many) illogical connections and are not well worked through so that it is unlikely the policy will have the presumably desired effects.
- Degenerative designs are deceptive for all groups, but especially for contenders, and contain deceptive practices across many of the elements. The rules disguise who the true beneficiaries are; rationales mask the true purposes; tools are misdirected or intentionally made too weak or contradictory to have the presumed effects; and implementation structures are established to ensure that powerful groups can intervene in ways not obvious to anyone except those deeply immersed in the intricacies of the policy itself.

Over the past several decades, the most prominent challenge to prevailing policy-making systems has come from those who believe that policy making should be more scientific, more professional, and less political. There are many who believe public policy would be dramatically improved if scientific and professional policy analysis could be more effective.

In Chapter 6 we explored in some detail the conditions under which scientific and professionalized values will become important in policy design. Observation of policy designs across many different policy arenas reveals that science has a strong hand in many designs and seems to completely dominate others. Yet, pluralist theories of public policy virtually ignore the role of science. Other theories, while decrying its dehumanizing influences, virtually ignore the actual effects of science on policy content and democracy.

Building from the theory of social constructions and policy design presented in Chapter 5, we posit (in Chapter 6) that the influence of science and professionalism in policy design depends, first, on politics, namely, *the extent to which the issue context and possible design elements can be linked together into a clear-cut political opportunity, or whether the context mainly represents political risks to political leaders.* Second, we posit that the influence of science and professionalism will depend on *the cohesion of the scientific community behind an agreed-on theory relevant to the policy.* Third, we argue that the existence of *political institutions* that have been colonized by scientists and professionals will be important in the extent of scientific influence.

When policy makers believe they can strategically manipulate a situation to create significant political capital for themselves, they will keep scientists and professionals out of the initial design process, except when the findings of science support the same policy positions that offer political opportunities. When scientific findings point in the same direction that policy makers want to go, then scientific findings will be used opportunistically to rationalize the policy design and conceal its political characteristics behind complex scientific provisions. When the scientific findings do not support the granting of benefits to advantaged or burdens to deviants, however, scientists and professionals will be excluded from the initial design but may be able to challenge it during implementation, correcting some of the illogical aspects of designs produced in degenerative pluralist contexts. Through selective use of strategies such as net-widening, relabeling, and goal displacement or enhancement, agency professionals may be able to eliminate some of the illogical and deceptive aspects of the design. These strategies may thwart implementation, in the narrow sense of implementation as compliance with statutory intent, but at the same time may actually convert the policy into one that has a realistic hope of achieving a credible goal.

Policy makers are not always able to construct issues in such a way that they promise political payoffs, however, and many contexts present mainly political risks. In these situations, policy makers may find it advantageous to permit scientists and professionals to have a dominant role in policy designs, virtually turning the decisions over to tightly knit policy communities with common disciplinary interests who colonize legislative staffs, interest groups, and implementing agencies. In these circumstances, however, our theory suggests that policy goals over time come to reflect the interests of the scientific community itself rather than the pursuit of public interest goals. Scientific interests may divert attention away from solving problems to focus too heavily on producing new knowledge, more databases, and carrying out more research. Science, in its purest sense, is best at identifying questions to be answered rather than finding answers useful to achieving policy goals. When science and professional values dominate a policy arena, therefore, significant policy design flaws emerge. Some of the common characteristics of scientific and professional designs are:

- Goals reflect scientific and professional interests such as increasing knowledge of the problem and possible solutions; monitoring activities and routines for compliance with standards and rules; gathering information and building data sets;

producing reports; and training professionals. Solving problems becomes secondary to increasing knowledge because knowledge never seems to be sufficient.

- Goals and problems are framed in the language of scientific and professional communities and usually involve topics that are amenable to study with scientific methodologies. In those cases where the public is involved in setting goals, participation is in highly structured planning exercises occurring long before all but the most attentive public is aware and mobilized. Alternatives are framed by professionals with the professionally preferred solution placed favorably as a median point among extremes.

- Except when scientists and professionals themselves are targeted for benefits, these types of policy designs favor "objective" and automatic selection criteria including statistically created classes, clinical diagnoses, and other quantitative decision-making procedures that have been developed from scientific studies. As a result, mobilization on the part of target groups is discouraged. Target groups seldom gain capacity and are not much involved in solving their own problems.

- Discretion in the implementation structure is placed where professionals dominate, often in the heavily staffed central offices of agencies. However, study commissions whose membership overrepresents scientists and professionals with only token public representation are frequently designated as preferable to "political" problem solving.

- While science-driven policy designs favor capacity-building tools when scientists and professionals are targets, the tools directed at other target groups often make human behavior modification irrelevant. Tools are based on technological fixes that automate the delivery of solutions, i.e., dams and reservoirs rather than water conservation; food additives and vitamins rather than choice of healthy foods; smokeless tobacco rather than nonsmoking areas. Such tools not only fail to build the capacity of citizens to make wise choices, but they also limit freedom of choice and meaningful participation in the solution of public problems.

- Rules tend to limit participation in policy to those with professional and scientific qualifications. Rules also constrain the types of information that can be considered to that which requires expertise. Numerical standards and standard operating procedures narrow options to those consistent with the preferences of scientific and professional communities. Rules also tend to be complex and require specialized training to properly interpret.

- Rationalizations emphasize the ability of science and professionals to solve problems and underemphasize nonutilitarian values such as justice and democracy. Scientists and professionals are adept at constructing credible logics connecting whatever they are providing to the accomplishment of widely shared goals such as security and economic progress.

Although the scientific designs differ considerably from those driven by the social construction of target populations, both damage democracy. Public policy has real consequences, and people experience public policy personally and vicariously. When the messages discourage active citizenship that will strengthen and deepen democracy and instead encourage further retreat into a postmodern chaotic political passivity, then the policies are unable to solve problems, promote citizenship, sustain democratic institutions, or serve justice. When policies are illogical, deceptive, or impossibly complex, policies cannot encourage good citizenship, serve justice, or solve problems. When policies allocate values along well-entrenched lines of privilege and disadvantage, justice, democracy, citizenship, and efficiency all are damaged.

Degenerative designs send different messages to different target populations, but these messages encourage most of the target groups to take only their own interests into account in their expectations of government thereby leading to irresponsible citizenship and the demise of community. Dependent populations are the primary exception, such as women and children, who commonly receive messages that they should continue to sacrifice for the common good of others and are encouraged to be altruistic and public-spirited. In degenerative politics "good citizens" too often are expected to sacrifice for the common good all the while being exploited by self-interested, manipulative, strategizing groups and individuals.

The dynamic processes that produce each kind of design appear to contain few if any self-corrective mechanisms and instead lead to an ever-worsening cycle of public policy. More than any other single factor, it is the effects on citizens conveyed through policy designs that thwart the self-correcting mechanisms that many believe pluralism will provide. The messages reinforce the divisive social constructions of target groups into those who are meritorious and deserving and those who are constructed as greedy, violent, or undeserving. Degenerative designs reproduce, reinforce, or even create social constructions of target populations that systematically stigmatize and disempower those who already suffer from disadvantages and at the same time systematically construct others positively to the point that they become convinced they have earned their exalted status in the society and are fully deserving of the advantages they receive.

Active, responsible citizenship is discouraged by degenerative pluralist designs as these either minimize citizen participation or structure participation in such a way that ordinary citizens cannot make a difference. The designs fail to incorporate mechanisms to enhance citizen learning and discourse about the issues, fail to incorporate mechanisms of self-government and mobilization, fail to teach lessons about trade-offs between costs and benefits, and therefore fail to produce public reactions that would lead to self-correction of flaws.

It becomes increasingly difficult, politically, to take any of the kind of policy actions that would alter the direction of these dynamics. Citizens, interest groups, or media who make the effort to deconstruct and critique the social constructions are suspected of having hidden agendas and of simply acting on the basis of self-interest not distinguishable from any other citizen or interest group making claims on government. Leaders who try to combat the features of degenerative politics are subject to similar charges and, finding themselves at odds with prevailing constructions, are defeated at the polls. Persons who would be willing and able to combat the strategic, deceptive, self-interested, and manipulative features of degenerative policy making are those who are open, guileless, altruistic, and ethical. Such people are not likely to be recruited into "politics" as practiced.

Scientific and professional designs are excessively complex and convey the message that understanding of issues is virtually beyond the capacity of ordinary citizens. The value orientations that leave their mark in scientific and professionalized designs convey the message that politics is detrimental to rational public policy as it thwarts the ability of science to find the one right answer. The discourses in such designs disempower laypeople and encourage them to leave public policy to the experts. These messages disparage politics and political leaders, showing them to be self-interested and irrational, thereby feeding the cynicism citizens have toward government. Although there are conditions under which scientific and professional influence are a useful antidote to excessive politicization, this is the exception rather than the rule. As scientific and professional interests increasingly dominate many policy arenas, citizens lose their trust in science and become cynical about the capacity of scientific studies and professional elites to work for the public interest rather than further individual professional careers. Thus, scientific and professional designs discredit both politics and science, showing both to be unreliable processes for achieving a more preferred future. These designs reproduce and exacerbate the negative tendencies within their own context and in that sense thwart whatever self-corrective mechanisms might otherwise be available.

THEORETICAL CONTRIBUTIONS AND APPLICATIONS

Recognizing the Importance of Social Constructions

The significance of social constructions has been all but ignored by mainstream political science. Scholars in the pluralist tradition have concentrated their attention on the influence of political power in shaping policy content. More recently, political scientists have rediscovered institutions and the way in which the rules adopted by institutions and the varying strength of institutions modify behavior and policy designs as well as policy results. Our contribution is to give equal weight to social constructions of target groups and social construction of knowledge as significant factors influencing policy.

Recognizing the significance of social constructions allows us to provide much better answers to some long-standing questions, including Lasswell's (1936) question, *Who Gets What When and How?* Theories of public policy, and a great deal of research, have shown that public policy often reflects the interests of powerful constituency groups. The role of competitive elections, political parties, self-interested behavior by elected officials as well as citizens, and citizen contacting behavior have been offered as explanations. Yet powerful groups do not always win, and weak ones do not always lose. The power theories do not account for the social construction of target populations or the social construction of knowledge. We have shown that the social construction of target populations is at least as important as political power in understanding what kinds of designs will be produced and the effects of these designs on the populace. Scientists and professionals are able, in some circumstances, to socially construct issues so that the policy design appears to reflect logical, means-end reasoning. While lacking many of the attributes of traditional political power, many people trust the scientific and professionalized groups more than government or business leaders. Such powerful social constructions can compensate greatly for the lack of traditional political influence.

Social constructions of target populations also provide a better explanation of the politics of punishment, which is puzzling when only power and institutions are considered. There would appear to be little gain in concentrating so much attention and public money on relatively weak groups such as teenage gang members, drug users, and criminals. However, the great importance of social constructions means that there is much political capital to be gained, and much trouble to be avoided when political actors are able to position themselves in accord with passionately held stereotypes and stigmas.

Social constructions of knowledge explain how scientists and professionals can come to dominate and receive considerable benefits from some policy without appearing to have a great deal of political power. The high regard in which scientific reasoning is held provides a shield to politicians in politically risky situations. As we illustrated in Chapter 6, political leaders all but abandon some issue areas to scientific and professional communities that constitute networks spanning government agencies, universities, private think tanks, and interest groups. The common issue definitions and agreements on applicable solutions that exist in such policy communities monopolize policy discourse and control the choices of policy designs.

Framework to Analyze Policy Content

We have made a contribution to the growing literature in policy design by providing a more comprehensive framework for describing the elements that are common to statutes, regulations, executive orders, programs, and political pronouncements. The absence of such a framework has made it difficult to compare policy design in different contexts, issue areas, levels of government, or countries. As a consequence, the policy learning that could occur through the observation of how different policy designs perform in similar or different contexts has been slow to develop. Elected leaders who might be willing to take on greater agency in espousing policy change do not have the accumulated experience with different choices of designs or design elements to draw on. Political and other social scientists have not had a fine-grained policy variable with which to compare other political phenomena. For example, the framework for studying policy content makes it possible to compare the propensities of different political parties, presidents, or historical eras to favor one or another type of design or design element. Most important, the description of policy elements provided in Chapter 4 (goals, targets, agents and implementation structures, tools, rules, rationales, and assumptions) has enabled us to trace the consequences of policies for citizenship and democracy. Although it has long been recognized that policy causes politics, and others have noted that policies have implications for democracy, tracing how and why effects occur requires a more complete description of policy content such as our framework provides.

A framework for analyzing policy design also contributes significantly to understanding the policy process. By carefully deconstructing policy designs, the analyst is able to uncover variables that (arguably) must have been important in the negotiations over the design elements.

Connecting Citizenship and Democratic Values to Policy

It is an understatement to say that scholars and laypersons alike are interested (and concerned) about the low levels of political participation and the uneven nature of participation. Others before us have shown that the groups who stand to gain the most from political action, such as the poor and minorities, have the lowest rates of participation. Voting in elections, even at the presidential level, is disturbingly low.

Some scholars have posited a generalized alienation from politics and government (attributable to the loss of respect for political leaders and the disrepute ordinary citizens have for government) as the reason for citizen withdrawal from politics. Putnam (1995) has documented a dramatic decline in civic participation in the United States over several decades and has attributed it mainly to the emergence of television and the extraordinary amount of time Americans spend watching television. Others have argued that withdrawal from politics should at least be partly attributed to the increasing technocratic characteristics of politics (Sclove 1995). Government offers complex, technical explanations for policy that are beyond the comprehension of everyone except the experts resulting in the depoliticization of society (Fischer 1990; Habermas 1975; Hawkesworth 1988).

Differential rates of participation among various segments of the population have been attributed to structural impediments, such as complex or difficult-to-meet registration laws, single-day voting at designated places, and complex ballot structures. Alienation of the disadvantaged from the promises of all the candidates is another possible explanation (Gaventa 1980: Piven and Cloward 1988).

The theory of design presented here contends that attitudes and participation are influenced by public policy and helps explain how these linkages take place. Public policy is an important independent variable that shapes citizen orientations and perpetuates certain views of citizenship that are, in turn, linked to differential participation among groups. The social constructions of target populations become embedded in policy and teach different lessons to different groups. Persons who identify with groups portrayed as dependents or deviants fail to mobilize or participate because they have been stigmatized and labeled by the policy process itself. They buy into the idea that their problems are not public problems, that the goals important to them are not part of the "public interest," and that government is not a remedy for their problems. They do not see themselves as legitimate or effective in the public arena, and participation in politics has no rewards. Advantaged groups, on the other hand, are reinforced in pursuing their self-interests through politics because they are taught by policy rationales and other elements that what is good for them is good for the country. Social constructions enhance the efficacy and power of advantaged groups even as they reduce the efficacy and power of the disadvantaged.

The theory of social constructions and policy experiences resulting from different designs helps explain the findings in studies such as Verba et al. (1993) that there are significant differences in attitudes and participation patterns among persons receiving means-tested benefits (AFDC, Medicaid, food stamps, and housing subsidies) compared with those receiving nonmeans-tested benefits (Social Security, Medicare, veterans' benefits, and educational loans). Although their study was intended to probe differences in the message *sent to* public officials, their research supports our contention that persons *receiving* nonmeans-tested benefits will have significantly higher levels of participation of almost every kind compared with those involved in the more demeaning process of proving eligibility for means-tested benefit programs. Their research also shows that persons in means-tested benefit programs were much less likely than those receiving broadly defined benefits to make participatory decisions based on these programs (1993, p. 311).

Science and professionalism reduce participation partly because if scientists and professionals are in charge, it matters little who is elected. But scientific and professionalized designs also reduce participation because they structure the rules of discourse about policy in such a way that citizen points of view do not matter. It is greatly to the advantage of scientific and professional communities for issues to be constructed as extraordinarily complex and subject to discussion only among those who know the specialized language and theories of the disciplines relevant to the issue.

The connection of public policy to citizenship provided in this book is an important antidote to the overly technical, utilitarian, and goal-driven orientation toward public policy adopted by the policy sciences and public choice. The purposes and consequences of policy are seen as broader and more important than merely solving particular problems or satisfying majority self-interest. Public policy in our work takes its rightful place as a primary teacher and messenger about how government treats citizens, whose problems are important and whose are not, the role of government, and the rights and duties of citizens.

Integrating the Differing Approaches to Public Policy

The review of the different major social sciences approaches to the study of public policy and politics presents very different views of the standards for judging good public policy, different understandings of what motivates political behavior and why different kinds of designs emerge, different perspectives on what is the appropriate role of government, and different explanations of how citizens should and do behave. Although each of these literatures has significant flaws, each also offers important insights that have been essential to the construction of the causal theory we present in Chapter 4. Public policy serves multiple roles in a democratic society: It must solve problems as emphasized by the policy scientists; it must support democratic values and institutions with rules and ethics through which communities can engage in collective action for the common good; it must reflect and respond to the mobilization and exercise of political power as emphasized by the pluralists; and it must engage, enlighten, and emancipate citizens and serve justice as the critical theorists contend. None of these perspectives, alone, is adequate to address the crisis of policy and confidence in politics we now experience. Each must be considered as part of a larger causal model as described in Chapter 4.

The causal model we offer provides a comprehensive set of concepts within which each of the major perspectives has its place. The framework invites the members of each scholarly tradition to look beyond the limits of their own literatures and tools of analysis to recognize the importance and contribution of other perspectives. Rather than talking past one another as they are used to doing, our framework invites collaboration and the use of multiple theories in analyzing public policy.

We have also stressed the importance of analyzing the issue context, including the historical development of the policy itself. Not all social science theories, including those we have offered, are equally relevant to every policy area. No amount of theorizing is a substitute for in-depth knowledge of the particular issue context. Policy prescription absent learning from the lessons of previous policy designs cannot be justified.

It is our hope that our work, including our integrative causal model, will encourage much more research into the kinds of policy designs that benefit disadvantaged groups and break down barriers created by stigma. What are the conditions and characteristics of contexts that support such designs? How do negatively stereotyped groups acquire a more positive image? How is it that advantaged groups come to lose their favored position yet hold on to more than their fair share of policy benefits? There are examples of policies in which scientific studies have undercut pervasive, entrenched social constructions and provided an avenue for improved public policy. What are the dynamics of this process, and how is it that the intervention of science can actually create designs for deviants and dependents that enlighten, educate, and empower citizens in some cases?

Studies of particular policy areas over long periods of time are necessary to inform us about how to design policy that will better serve democracy. Nevertheless, it is possible to specify some general rules of thumb for better designs on the basis of the analysis of the many policy examples we have cited here. It is to that task we now turn.

APPLICATIONS TO REAL-WORLD POLICY DESIGN

Movement toward a stronger and deeper democracy requires policy analysis and policy designs that recognize and correct the errors of previous designs. Designs are needed that will achieve a better balance among the multiple values that need to be served including solving problems, being responsive and accountable to the people, serving justice, and encouraging active, empathetic citizenship. The unequal power relationships, divisive social constructions, privileging of scientific rationality and expertise, and the loss of civility in interpersonal relationships within policy-making situations must be avoided. The analysis in this book suggests that there may be some general principles of good design.

1. Construct target groups for benefits and burdens that cut across lines of long-standing social, racial, economic, or other cleavages.

This principle urges policy makers to avoid playing into stereotypes. Goals and rationales should be selected so that policy connects all members of the society, especially dependents and deviants, to the most central values and goals of the community as a whole. In the case of degenerative politics, balance may be improved by designs that cut across prevailing social, economic, racial, and other common stereotypes or normal lines of cleavage. The targets would be persons who may have little in common apart from the crucial role of acting so as to better realize policy goals. The treatment of such diverse targets by government should be determined by generalized notions of how to motivate citizens that accord with the democratic ideal of the rule of law. Consequently, the personal and vicarious experiences of people drawn from vastly different social groups and situations would be similar and should result in members of the target group having the same rather than conflicting orientations toward government. In degenerative contexts, all members of the society—but especially those constructed as "dependent" or "deviant"—would be linked by these kinds of designs to the most highly prized national goals, helping ensure that all persons are equally respected for their potential contributions to the well-being of the society. Policy designs with broadly drawn targets groups who are treated the same within the policy itself are more sensitive to the way people actually will experience the policy and to the messages that are sent about who is worthy and who is not. These kinds of designs work against the grain of divisive social constructions that impart negative messages about whole sectors of the population.

By purposefully designing targets that pull membership from diverse groups so that they have in common a strategic position vis-à-vis policy goals, policy may be able to avoid the divisiveness of increasingly fine distinctions based on race, gender, or other socially constructed categories that are so common in contemporary American politics. Science has an important and positive role in these situations to act as a counterbalance against power and social constructions of targets.

2. Design to ensure public involvement and avoid overly complex and technical designs that empower narrow scientific and professional interests.

In the case of scientific and technical designs, balance should be improved by greater public involvement in decision making. Policies need to be designed to provide a counterweight to elite dominance of decision making and to give greater status to grassroots knowledge in decision making. The impetus toward open, participatory policy designs that characterized the 1970s has been lost and needs to be renewed. The experience of private industry with worker involvement suggests that there are efficiency and effectiveness reasons as well as benefits related to democracy. Again, the contemporary movement toward downsizing, defunding, and decentralizing of government may provide opportunities. Policies need to be designed to encourage self-help efforts such as community policing and neighborhood watches. Private businesses, industries, and voluntary associations can take over where governments are withdrawing from employment training, adult education, and other public projects. Citizen groups can be taught to perform environmental quality monitoring. Public policies can encourage the adoption of more open and accessible technologies. For instance, government should capitalize on its involvement in communications technologies to assure that electronic communications and information highways offer accessible and inexpensive public access.

3. Create designs to encourage and strengthen communicative ethics and communicative rationality across all policy-making contexts in government, the workplace, and civil society.

Policies should be devised to increase public awareness of the importance of communicative ethics, to study the various codes of ethical conduct that might be applied, to provide examples and models that might be adopted, and to suggest enforcement strategies. There are many types of policy tools and rules that could be used to encourage ethical behavior without having to "mandate" ethics—such as grants, studies, commissions or task forces, resolutions, and model statute development.

Even though short-term risks and rewards dictate otherwise, political leaders can adopt policy designs with elements that encourage civility. Leadership and the exercise of human agency in creating policy designs can result in the selection of rules that encourage open participation. Rationales can be chosen that grant respect and dignity to the common sense of ordinary citizens. Tools that build the capacity of citizens to solve problems can be selected, not just for advantaged groups, but especially for dependents and deviants. The selection of more democratic design elements can improve the operation of political institutions. Communicative rationality can be adopted into the formal and informal rules and procedures of legislative bodies, including the U.S. Congress, so that greater weight is given to the substance and content of argument and less to the role and power of the advocates. Communicative reason rather than authority and expertise should guide discussions. A plethora of management strategies are available to improve communicative ethics within legislative, executive, and judicial organizations as well as in the civil society and workplace. These include retreats, team-building exercises, and greater emphasis on cooperation and the interests of the organization.

4. Cultivate a sense of community through designs that favor the creation of civic organizations.

The much discussed demise of the civic culture must become a concern of public policy, and designs can be found to encourage, support, and facilitate neighborhood-based, civic-minded organizations at the local level.

A vibrant civil society in which citizens regularly interact and develop mutual trust is fundamental to democracy (Barber 1984; Mansbridge 1990a, 1990b; Putnam 1993, 1995; Reich 1991). Many commentators call for a return to a more communal sense of values and the creation of associations that are based on shared values and communicative ethics rather than hierarchy and control (Etzioni 1992, 1993; Forester 1985a). The total quality management movement of Edward Demming (see Aguayo 1990) and Stephen Covey (1991) argues for greater involvement of workers in the operation of private corporations and the substitution of a much more cooperative culture for the self-interested competitive features of capitalism and politics. Public policies that employ self-governing entities in the implementation structure and policies that build the capacity of targets and encourage action independent of government are generally beneficial to democracy.

Policies are needed that help construct a common stake among citizens with diverse backgrounds by providing arenas for direct communication by participants. Service-learning programs that are becoming increasingly popular in U.S. higher education circles help ensure that the educated elites of society have an understanding of how to engage others within the community without simultaneously disempowering them (Barber 1992). Programs that provide tax credits or deductions for college education in exchange for community-based service work may well be beneficial to citizenship and simultaneously provide the encouragement and financial resources to youth who otherwise would not have access to higher education.

Volunteerism is a democratic virtue not just for the young, however. Policies are needed that encourage and reward public service by everyone, including those who themselves are the recipients of help. It may be possible to establish public service centers or registries that link those with the impulse to give and those who need help in jointly designed and executed action strategies. These forms of overarching projects help avoid the hierarchical power relationships characterized by traditional forms of volunteerism where the "haves" provide "help" to the "have-nots."

Privatization of governmental functions, decentralization, and the turning over of authority to self-governing collectivities may have negative effects if undertaken simply as a way for government to abdicate responsibility for those who lack the political clout needed to claim government largesse, all the while continuing the pattern of protection and subsidies to powerful well-regarded constituents. On the other hand, privatization and decentralization are not always detrimental and may offer some opportunities for the emergence of public-sphere organizations that can build trust and support a strong civic sector. It must be recognized, however, that nongovernmental groups who fill the policy vacuum left by government downsizing, decentralization, and privatization may be narrow and exclusive. They may be more likely to represent selfish rather than collective interests. While government may utilize such groups, it must retain the authority to insist on openness, fairness, and service to the general welfare.

5. Design for context, draw from multiple theories, and analyze from multiple perspectives.

No one theory of public policy is sufficient. Public choice, pluralism, policy sciences, and critical theory all have insights but alone will not be an adequate guide to future policy choices. The consequences of policy go beyond the instrumental goals to the implicit messages about what government does, whose problems are "public" problems, and what status the citizen has. Many analysts need to be working at all levels of society within their own specialities to fit designs into context. Therefore, the design profession should not be hierarchical or centralized. Caseworkers are as important to design as are legislators and agency officials. University-based analysts must learn about contextual issues from policy makers and deliverers at all levels so that theoretically inspired designs embody real-world experience with real-world contexts. There is no idealized model deducible from general principles. At the same time that designs must be fit into a context, they must contain elements that will transform the context toward one that is not degenerative but more nurturing for the kinds of policies that engage and give agency to people thereby strengthening democracy.

6. Design policies that build capacity, inform, empower, and facilitate self-governance and learning rather than policies that manipulate through slogans or symbols.

Policies must assist in the task of creating a vision of politics and citizenship in which "good politics" is synonymous with "good government" and both depend fundamentally on "good public policy." This requires citizens able and willing to grasp the complexities of public policy and engage one another in finding the most appropriate designs taking into account all relevant interests.

7. Avoid designs that rely on deception for support.

Political leaders must acknowledge an ethical responsibility to eschew all forms of deception and return politics to an ethical, honored pursuit. Deceptive and strategic maneuvering should be replaced with discursive processes through which the elements of design are openly negotiated so that compromises reflect a communicative rationality rather than secret "deals" that have been made. Every policy design should clearly state what it will actually do, how it will be done, who will be affected, and why it should be undertaken by government. Policies should not be mysterious texts comprehensible only to scientists and professionals or providing lucrative opportunities for lawyers and litigation.

Whether public policy in the future will follow the degenerative pattern of the past several decades or undergo a course correction that will bring U.S. democracy closer to its own ideals may depend at least partially on the success of policy theory and analysis. Policy analysis needs to deconstruct policy designs making clear the degenerative characteristics, exposing deception and other flaws to a wide public audience, and teaching citizens and leaders better lessons about possible alternative futures. Theories of public policy need to provide a better vision of democratic possibilities, better explanations of how and why antidemocratic elements come to be embedded in policy designs, and better explanations as well as interpretations of how designs impact democratic life.

References

Abramowitz, Alan I. 1989. The United States: Political culture under stress. In *The civic culture revisited,* edited by Gabriel Almond and Sydney Verba. Newbury Park, Calif.: Sage.

Achinstein, Peter, and Stephen F. Barker, eds. 1969. *The legacy of logical positivism.* Baltimore: Johns Hopkins University Press.

Aguayo, Rafael. 1990. *Dr. Deming: The American who taught the Japanese about quality.* New York: Simon & Schuster.

Alexander, Ernest R. 1982. Design in the decision-making process. *Policy Sciences* 14:279–82.

Almond, Gabriel. 1989. The intellectual history of the civic culture concept. In *The civic culture revisited,* edited by Gabriel Almond and Sidney Verba. Newbury Park, Calif.: Sage.

Almond, Gabriel, and Sidney Verba. 1963. *The civic culture.* Princeton, N.J.: Princeton University Press.

Anderson, Charles W. 1993. Recommending a scheme of reason: Political theory, policy science, and democracy. *Policy Sciences* 26:215–27.

Anderson, James E. 1984. *Public policy making.* Madison, Wis.: CBS College Publishing.

Arizona Republic. 1993. Rights groups takes issue with "crack" terms, August 26, sec. A, p. 2.

Arizona Republic. 1995. Drug offenders crowd prisons, December 4, p. 1.

Arizona Republic. 1996. Drug enforcement differs by race, February, 27, p. A5.

Arnold, R. Douglas. 1990. *The logic of congressional action.* New Haven, Conn.: Yale University Press.

Arrow, Kenneth. 1951. *Social choice and justice.* New York: Wiley.

Aucoin, Peter. 1971. Theory and research in the study of policy making. In *The structure of policy making in Canada,* edited by G. Bruce Doern and Peter Aucoin. Toronto: Macmillan.

Babst, Gordon A. 1979. Public policy theory and analysis. In *Public policy in Canada,* edited by G. Bruce Doern and Peter Aucoin. Toronto: Macmillan.

_____. 1996. Social construction theory: Theoretical foundations and application issues in policy studies. Paper presented at 1996 annual conference of the American Political Science Association, August 31, San Francisco.

Axelrod, Richard D. 1987. *The evolution of cooperation.* New York: Basic Books.

Bachrach, Peter, and Morton S. Baratz. 1961. Two faces of power. *American Political Science Review* 56:947–52.

Baker, Susan Gonzalez. 1993. Immigration reform: The empowerment of a new constituency. In *Public policy for democracy,* edited by Helen M. Ingram and Steven Rathgeb Smith. Washington, D.C.: Brookings Institution.

Balz, Don. 1993. NRA changes lobbying strategies. *Washington Post,* October 25–31, national weekly edition.

Baquet, Dean, with Diana B. Henriques. 1993. Abuses plague programs to help exports of agricultural products. *New York Times,* October 10, sec. A, p. 1.

Barber, Benjamin. 1984. *Strong democracy.* Berkeley: University of California Press.

——. 1992. An aristocracy of everyone. New York: Ballantine Books.

Bardach, Eugene. 1977. *The implementation game.* Cambridge: MIT Press.

Barry, Brian. 1989. *Democracy, power, and justice.* Oxford: Clarendon Press.

Baumgartner, Frank R., and Bryan D. Jones. 1993. *Agendas and instability in American politics.* Chicago: University of Chicago Press.

Becker, Gary S. 1976. *The economic approach to human behavior.* Chicago: University of Chicago Press.

Beer, Samuel H. 1977. Political overload and federalism. *Polity* 10:5–17.

Benhabib, Seyla, and Drucilla Cornell, eds. 1987. *Feminism as critique: On the politics of gender.* Minneapolis: University of Minnesota Press.

Bentley, A. F. 1908, 1949. *The process of government.* Bloomington, Ind.: Principia Press.

Berejikian, Jeffrey. 1992. Revolutionary collective action and the agent-structure problem. *American Political Science Review* 86(3):647–57.

Berger, Peter L., and Thomas Luckmann. 1967. *The social construction of reality: A treatise in the sociology of knowledge.* Garden City, N.Y.: Anchor Books/Doubleday.

Berk, Richard, Robert F. Boruch, David L. Chambers, Peter H. Rossi, and Ann D. Witte. 1985. Social policy experimentation: A position paper. *Evaluation Review* 9(4): 387–429.

Berkowitz, Edward D. 1991. *America's welfare state.* Baltimore: Johns Hopkins University Press.

Berman, Paul. 1980. Thinking about programmed adaptive implementation. In *Why policies succeed or fail,* edited by Helen Ingram and Dean Mann. Beverly Hills, Calif.: Sage.

Bernstein, J. M. 1995. *Recovering ethical life.* New York: Routledge.

Berry, Jeffrey, Kent Portney, and Ken Thomson. 1993. *The rebirth of urban democracy.* Washington, D.C.: Brookings Institution.

Best, Joel. 1989. *Images of issues: Typifying contemporary social problems.* New York: Aldine De Gruyter.

Boborow, Davis B., and John S. Dryzek. 1987. *Policy analysis by design.* Pittsburgh: University of Pittsburgh Press.

Bok, Derek. 1982. *Beyond the ivory tower: Social responsibilities of the modern university.* Cambridge: Harvard University Press.

Bortner, M. A. 1988. *Delinquency and justice: An age of crisis.* New York: McGraw Hill.

Bortner, M. A., and Linda Williams. 1997. *Youth in Prison: We the people of unit four.* New York: Routledge.

Bortner, Peg, Carol A. Burgess, Anne L. Schneider, and Andy Hall. 1993. *Equitable treatment of minority youth.* Phoenix, Ariz.: Governor's Office for Children.

Boruch, Robert F., and Werner Wothke, eds. 1985. *Randomization and field experiments.* San Francisco: Jossey Bass.

Box, Richard C. 1995. Critical theory and the paradox of discourse. *American Review of Public Administration* 25(1):1–19.

Brewer, Garry D., and Peter deLeon. 1983. *The foundations of policy analysis.* Homewood, Ill.: Dorsey Press.

Brown, Clifford A. 1995. Social construction and enactment: Gender and racial integration of the U.S. armed forces. University of Arizona, typescript.

Brown, Robert D. 1995. Party cleavages and welfare effort in the American states. *American Political Science Review* 89(1):23–33.

Buchanan, James M., and Gordon Tullock. 1962. *The calculus of consent.* Ann Arbor: University of Michigan Press.

Campbell, D. T. 1969. Reforms as experiments. *American Psychologist* 24:409–29.

Campbell, Donald, and Julian C. Stanley. 1963. *Experimental designs for research.* Chicago: Rand McNally.

Cater, Douglas. 1959. *The fourth branch of government.* Boston: Houghton Mifflin.

Cetina, Karin Knorr. 1995. Laboratory studies: The cultural approach to the study of science. In *Handbook of science and technology studies,* edited by Sheila Jasanoff, Gerald E. Markle, James C. Petersen, and Trevor Pinch. Newbury Park, Calif.: Sage.

Champagne, Anthony, and Edward J. Harpham. 1984. *The attack on the welfare state.* Prospect Heights, Ill: Waveland Press.

Cobb, Roger, and Charles Elder. 1983. *Agenda-building and democratic politics.* Baltimore: Johns Hopkins University Press.

Cohen, Steven, and Sheldon Kamieniecki. 1991. *Environmental regulation through strategic planning.* Boulder: Westview.

Coleman, James S. 1992. Democracy in permanently divided systems. *American Behavioral Scientist* 35(4/5):363–74.

Collins, Patricia Hill. 1989. The social construction of invisibility: Black women's poverty in social problems discourse. *Perspectives on Social Problems* 1:77–93.

Copp, David, Jean Hampton, and John E. Roemer, eds. 1993. *The idea of democracy.* Cambridge: Cambridge University Press.

Cordes, Colleen. 1997. Congressional earmarks for colleges increased by 49% for fiscal 1997. *Chronicle of Higher Education,* March 28, 1997, p. A36.

Covey, Stephen R. 1991. *Principle-centered leadership.* New York: Simon & Schuster.

Coyle, Dennis, and Aaron Wildavsky. 1986. Social experimentation in the face of formidable fables. In *Lessons from the income maintenance experiments,* edited by Alicia Munnell. Washington, D.C.: Brookings Institution.

Cozzens, Susan E., and Edward J. Woodhouse. 1995. Science, government, and the politics of knowledge. In *Handbook of science and technology studies,* edited by Sheila Jasanoff, Gerald E. Markle, James C. Petersen, and Trevor Pinch. Newbury Park, Calif.: Sage.

Cronbach, Lee J. 1980. *Toward reform of program evaluation.* San Francisco: Jossey-Bass.

Currie, Eliot. 1985. *Confronting crime.* New York: Pantheon Books.

Dahl, Robert A. 1961. *Who governs?* New Haven, Conn.: Yale University Press.

_____. 1969. The behavioral approach in political science: Epitaph for a monument to a successful protest. In *Behavioralism in Political Science,* compiled by Heinz Eulau. New York: Atherton Press.

_____. 1982. *Dilemmas of pluralist democracy.* New Haven, Conn.: Yale University Press.

_____. 1989. *Democracy and its critics.* New Haven, Conn.: Yale University Press.

_____. 1993. The behavioral approach in political science: Epitaph for a monument to a successful protest. In *Discipline and history: Political science in the United States,* edited by James Farr and Raymond Seidelman. Ann Arbor: University of Michigan Press. Article originally published 1961.

Dahl, Robert A., and Charles E. Lindblom. 1953. *Politics, economics, and welfare.* New York: Harper.

Dalton, Russell, and Manfred Kuechler. 1990. *Challenging the political order: New social and political movements in western democracies.* Oxford: Oxford University Press.

Daneke, Gregory A. 1990. A science of public administration. *Public Administration Review* 50(May/June):383–92.

Dawes, Robyn M. 1980. Social dilemmas. *Annual Review of Psychology* 31:169–93.

Dawson, Richard E., and James A. Robinson. 1963. Inter-party competition, economic variables, and welfare policies in the American states. *Journal of Politics* 57:426–48.

Deflem, Mathieu. 1994. Surveillance and the laws of the population: Historical foundations of governmentality in criminal statistics. Paper presented at annual meeting, Law and Society Association, Phoenix.

deHaven-Smith, Lance. 1988. *Philosophical critiques of policy analysis: Lindblom, Habermas, and the great society.* Gainesville: University of Florida Press.

Denhardt, Robert B. 1981. *In the shadow of organization.* Lawrence: University Press of Kansas.

_____. 1984. *Theories of public organization.* Monterey, Calif.: Brooks/Cole Publishing.

Deutsch, Morton. 1985. *Distributive justice.* New Haven, Conn.: Yale University Press.

Diamond, Irene, ed. 1983. *Families, politics, and public policy.* New York: Longman.

Diamond, Larry, and Marc F. Plattner, eds. 1993. *Capitalism, socialism, and democracy revisited.* Baltimore: Johns Hopkins University Press.

Diesing, Paul. 1991. *How does social science work? Reflections on practice.* Pittsburgh: University of Pittsburgh Press.

Dimock, Marshall. 1992. The restorative qualities of citizenship. *Public Administration Review* 52(January/February):21–25.

Dionne, E. J. 1991. *Why Americans hate politics.* New York: Simon & Schuster.

_____. 1993. Scandalous acts. *Washington Post* Wire Services. *Tribune Newspaper* (Tempe, Ariz.), November 20, sec. A, p. 13.

_____. 1996. *They only look dead: Why progressives will dominate the next political era.* New York: Simon and Schuster.

Dodge, Robert. 1993. Death of superconducting super collidor. *Dallas Morning News,* October 24, p. 1.

Doern, G. Bruce, and Peter Aucoin, eds. 1979. *Public policy in Canada.* Toronto: Macmillan.

Doern, G. Bruce, and V. Seymour Wilson. 1974. *Issues in Canadian Public Policy.* Toronto: Macmillan.

Dolbeare, Kenneth M., and Russell M. Lidman. 1985. Ideology and policy research: The case of Murray's losing ground. *Policy Studies Review* 4(May):587–95.

Donovan, Mark C. 1994. Social constructions of people with AIDS: Target populations and United States policy, 1981–1990. *Policy Studies Review* 12(3/4):3–29.

Downs, Anthony. 1957. *An economic theory of voting.* New York: Harper and Row.

Dror, Yehezkel. 1971. *Design for policy sciences.* New York: American Elsevier.

Drucker, Peter. 1995. Really reinventing government. *Atlantic Monthly 275(2):*49–61.

Dryzek, John S. 1983. Don't toss coins in garbage cans: A prologue to policy design. *Journal of Public Policy* 3:345–67.

_____. 1987. *Rational ecology: Environment and political economy.* Oxford: Basil Blackwell.

_____. 1990. *Discursive democracy.* Cambridge: Cambridge University Press.

_____. 1996a. *Democracy and capitalism.* Cambridge: Cambridge University Press.

_____. 1996b. Political inclusion and the dynamics of democratization. *American Political Science Review* 90(3):475–87.

Dryzek, John S., and Jeffrey Berejikian. 1993. Reconstructive democratic theory. *American Political Science Review* 87(1):48–60.

Dryzek, John S., and Brian Ripley. 1988. The ambitions of policy design. *Policy Studies Review* 7(summer):705–19.

Dryzek, John S., and Doug Torgerson. 1993. Democracy and the policy sciences: A progress report. *Policy Sciences* 26:127–37.

Dunn, William N. 1982. Reforms as arguments. *Knowledge: Creation, Diffusion, Utilization* 3(3):293–326.

Dunn, William N., and Rita Mae Kelly, eds. 1992. *Advances in policy studies since 1950.* New Brunswick, N.J.: Transaction Publishers.

Duvall, Tim. 1995. Organ transplant policy: Failures and suggestions for reform. University of Arizona, typescript.

Dye, Thomas. 1966. *Politics, economics, and the public: Policy outcomes in the American states.* Chicago: Rand McNally.

Easton, David. 1965. *A systems analysis of political life.* New York: John Wiley and Sons.

_____. 1991. Political science in the United States. In *The development of political science,* edited by David Easton, John Gunnell, and Luigi Graziano. New York: Routledge.

Easton, David, John Gunnell, and Luigi Graziano, eds. 1991. *The development of political science.* New York: Routledge.

Edelman, Murray. 1964. *The symbolic uses of politics.* Urbana: University of Illinois Press.

_____. 1988. *Constructing the political spectacle.* Chicago: University of Chicago Press.

Edwards, Ward, and J. Robert Newman. 1982. *Multiattribute evaluation.* Newbury Park, Calif.: Sage.

Elmore, Richard F. 1987. Instruments and strategy in public policy. *Policy Studies Review* 7(1):174–86.

Elster, Jon. 1986. *Rational choice.* New York: New York University Press.

Elster, Jon, and Karl Ove Moene. 1990. *Alternatives to capitalism.* Cambridge: Cambridge University Press.

Engeldorp Gastelaars, Ph. van, Slawomir Magala, and O. Preuss. 1990. *The Frankfurt School: How relevant is it today: Critics and critical theory in Eastern Europe.* Rotterdam: University Press.

Erikson, Robert S., Gerald C. Wright, Jr., and John P. McIver. 1989. Political parties, public opinion, and state policy in the United States. *American Political Science Review* 83(3):729–50.

Etzioni, Amitai. 1992. On the place of virtues in a pluralistic democracy. *American Behavioral Scientist* 35(4/5):530–40.

_____. 1993. *The spirit of community.* New York: Crown Publishers.

Eulau, Heinz, comp. 1969. *Behavioralism in political science.* New York: Atherton Press.

Ezrahi, Yaron. 1991. *The descent of Icarius.* Cambridge: Harvard University Press.

Farber, Daniel A., and Philip P. Frickey. 1991. *Law and public choice.* Chicago: University of Chicago Press.

Farr, James, and Raymond Seidelman, eds. 1993. *Discipline and history: Political science in the United States.* Ann Arbor: University of Michigan Press.

Fay, Brian. 1987. *Critical social science.* Ithaca, N.Y.: Cornell University Press.

Feigl, Herbert. 1969. The origin and spirit of logical positivism. In *The legacy of logical positivism,* edited by Peter Achinstein and Stephen F. Barker. Baltimore: Johns Hopkins University Press.

Ferraro, Kathleen J., Peg Bortner, Katherine Miller, and James Riding. 1994. In *Reflections on homelessness in Maricopa County: Preliminary report of the research project for homeless people.* Tempe: College of Public Programs, Arizona State University.

Ferris, James, and Elizabeth Graddy. 1986. Contracting out: For what? With whom? *Public Administration Review* 46(July/August):332–45.

Fesler, James William, and Donald F. Kettl. 1991. *The politics of the administrative process.* Chatham, N.J.: Chatham House.

Fischer, Frank. 1980. *Politics, values, and public policy: The problem of methodology.* Boulder: Westview Press.

————. 1985. Critical evaluation of public policy: A methodological case study. In *Critical theory and public life,* edited by John Forester. Cambridge: MIT Press.

————. 1990. *Technocracy and the politics of expertise.* Newbury Park, Calif.: Sage.

————. 1992. Participatory expertise: Toward the democratization of policy studies. In *Advances in policy studies since 1950,* edited by William N. Dunn and Rita Mae Kelly. New Brunswick, N.J.: Transaction Publishers.

————. 1995. *Evaluating public policy.* Chicago: Nelson Halls.

Fischer, Frank, and John Forester, eds. 1993. *The argumentative turn in policy analysis and planning.* Durham, N.C.: Duke University Press.

Fischoff, Baruch, S. Lichtenstein, P. Slovic, S. L. Derby, and R. L. Keeney. 1981. *Acceptable risk.* Cambridge: Cambridge University Press.

Fisher, Roger, and William Ury. 1981. *Getting to yes.* Boston: Houghton Mifflin.

Fishkin, James S. 1991. *Democracy and deliberation: New directions for democratic reform.* New Haven, Conn.: Yale University Press.

Forester, John. 1985a. Critical theory and planning practice. In *Critical theory and public life,* edited by John Forester. Cambridge: MIT Press.

————, ed. 1985b. *Critical theory and public life.* Cambridge: MIT Press.

Forester, John. 1989. *Planning in the face of power.* Berkeley: University of California Press.

Fraser, Nancy. 1987. What's critical about critical theory? In *Feminism as critique: On the politics of gender,* edited by Seyla Benhabib and Drucilla Cornell. Minneapolis: University of Minnesota Press.

Freeman, J. Leiper. 1965. *The political process: Executive bureau–legislative committee relations.* New York: Random House.

Freire, Paulo. 1983. *Pedagogy of the oppressed.* New York: Continuum Press.

————. 1994. *Pedagogy of hope.* New York: Continuum Press.

Froman, Lewis A. 1967. *The congressional process: Strategies, rules, and procedures.* Boston: Little, Brown.

Fukuyama, Francis. 1992. *The end of history and the last man.* New York: Free Press.

Furlong, Elizabeth A. 1994. Agenda setting and policy design of the National Center for Nursing Research legislative amendment. Paper presented at the annual meeting of the American Political Science Association, September 1–4, New York.

Gaventa, John. 1980. *Power and powerlessness*. Urbana: University of Illinois Press.

Gilpin, Robert, and Christopher Wright. 1964. *Scientists and national policy-making*. New York: Columbia University Press.

Ginsberg, Benjamin, and Elizabeth Sanders. 1990. Theodore J. Lowi and juridical democracy. *PS: Political Science and Politics* 23(December):563–65.

Giroux, Henry A., ed. 1991. *Postmodernism, feminism, and cultural politics: Redrawing educational boundaries*. Albany: SUNY Press.

Giroux, Henry A., and Peter L. McClaren, eds. 1989. *Critical pedagogy, the state, and the cultural struggle*. Albany: SUNY Press.

Godwin, R. Kenneth. 1993. Using market-based incentives to empower the poor. In *Public policy for democracy*, edited by Helen M. Ingram and Steven Rathgeb Smith. Washington, D.C.: Brookings Institution.

Goodin, Robert E. 1993. Democracy, preferences and paternalism. *Policy Sciences* 26:229–47.

Gormley, William. 1990. *Controlling the bureaucracy*. Madison: University of Wisconsin Press.

Gottlieb, Robert. 1993. *Forcing the spring: The transformation of the American environmental movement*. Washington, D.C.: Island Press.

Gramlich, Edward M. 1981. *Benefit cost analysis of government programs*. Englewood Cliffs, N.J.: Prentice-Hall.

Gray, Tara, Clark R. Larsen, Peter Haynes, Kent Olson. 1991. Using cost benefit analysis to evaluate correctional sentences. *Evaluation Review* 15(4):471–81.

Green, Donald, and Ian Shapiro. 1994. *Pathologies of rational choice theory: A critique of applications in political science*. New Haven, Conn.: Yale University Press.

Green, Phillip, ed. 1993a. Democracy as a contested idea. In *Key concepts in critical theory: democracy*. Atlantic Highlands, N.J.: Humanities Press.

_____. 1993b. *Key concepts in critical theory: Democracy*. Atlantic Highlands, N.J.: Humanities Press.

Greenberg, David H., and Philip K. Robins. 1986. The changing role of social experiments in policy analysis. *Journal of Policy Analysis and Management* 5(2):340–62.

Greenberg, George D., Jeffrey A. Miller, Lawrence B. Mohr, and Bruce C. Vladeck. 1977. Developing public policy theory: Perspectives from empirical research. *American Political Science Review* 71(3):1532–43.

Greider, William. 1992. *Who will tell the people: The betrayal of American democracy*. New York: Simon & Schuster.

Grogan, Colleen. 1994. Political-economic factors influencing state medicaid policy. *Political Research Quarterly* 47(3):589–622.

Habermas, Jurgen. 1975. *Legitimation crisis*. Translated by Thomas McCarthy. Boston: Beacon Press.

_____. 1989a. The public sphere. In *Jurgen Habermas on society and politics, a reader,* edited by Steven Seidman. Boston: Beacon Press.

_____. 1989b. Social action and rationality. In *Jurgen Habermas on society and politics, a reader,* edited by Steven Seidman. Boston: Beacon Press.

_____. 1989c. The tasks of a critical theory of society. In *Jurgen Habermas on society and politics, a reader,* edited by Steven Seidman. Boston: Beacon Press.

Hall, Andy. 1992. Listening to the voiceless: Women in street prostitution and the feminist democratic project. Unpublished dissertation. Tempe: Arizona State University.

Ham, Christopher, and Michael Hill. 1984. *The policy process in the modern capitalist state*. New York: Harvester Wheatsheaf.

Hamilton, Alexander. 1962. *Federalist I.* New York: Mentor Books.

Hardin, Garrett. 1968. The tragedy of the commons. *Science* 162:1243–48.

Hardin, Russell. 1982. *Collective action.* Baltimore: Johns Hopkins University Press.

Hausman, Jerry A., and David A. Wise, eds. 1985. *Social experimentation.* Chicago: University of Chicago Press.

Hawkesworth, M. E. 1988. *Theoretical issues in policy analysis.* Albany: State University of New York.

Hawkins, Stephen. 1993. *Black holes and baby universes and other essays.* New York: Bantam.

Hays, Samuel P., and Barbara D. Hays. 1987. *Beauty, health and performance: Environmental politics in the United States, 1955–1985.* Cambridge: Cambridge University Press.

Hecht, Stacey. 1996. Unequal targets: Explaining welfare innovation in the states. Prepared for the 1996 annual conference of the American Political Science Association, August 31, San Francisco.

Heclo, Hugh. 1974. *Modern social politics in Britain and Sweden: From relief to income maintenance.* New Haven, Conn.: Yale University Press.

Heidenheimer, Arnold J., Hugh Heclo, and Carolyn Teich Adams. 1983. *Comparative public policy.* New York: St. Martin's Press.

Heilbroner, Robert. 1993. *21st century capitalism.* New York: Norton.

Held, David. 1980. *Introduction to critical theory.* Berkeley: University of California Press.

____. 1987. *Models of democracy.* Stanford, Calif.: Stanford University Press.

Held, David, and Christopher Pollitt. 1986. *New forms of democracy.* Newbury Park, Calif.: Sage.

Heller, Agnes, and Ferenc Feher. 1988. *The postmodern political condition.* Cambridge: Polity.

Hempel, Carl. 1969. Logical positivism and the social sciences. In *The legacy of logical positivism,* edited by Peter Achinstein and Stephen F. Barker. Baltimore: Johns Hopkins University Press.

Henry, William A., III. 1994. *In defense of elitism.* New York: Doubleday.

Hicks, Alexander M., and Duane H. Swank. 1992. Politics, institutions, and welfare spending in industrialized democracies, 1960–82. *American Political Science Review* 86(3):658–74.

Hjern, Benny. 1982. Implementation research—the link gone missing. *Journal of Public Policy* 2:301–8.

Hofferbert, Richard I. 1986. Policy evaluation, democratic theory, and the division of scholarly labor. *Policy Studies Review* 5(February):511–19.

Hogarth, Robin M., and Melvin W. Reder. 1986. *Rational choice: The contrast between economics and psychology.* Chicago: University of Chicago Press.

Holzner, Burkart. 1968. *Reality construction in society.* Cambridge, Mass.: Schenkman.

Hood, Christopher C. 1986. *The tools of government.* Chatham, N.J.: Chatham House.

Huntington, S. P. 1991. *The third wave: Democratization in the late twentieth century.* Norman: University of Oklahoma Press.

Ianello, Kathleen. 1992. *Decisions without hierarchy: Feminist interventions in organization theory and practice.* New York: Routledge.

Imwalle, Laurence. 1994. The politics of base closures and realignment: An analysis of alternative policy designs. University of Arizona, typescript.

Ingraham, Patricia. 1987. Toward more systematic consideration of policy design. *Policy Studies Journal* 15(June):611–28.

Ingram, Helen M. 1978. The political rationality of innovation: The clean air act amendment of 1970. In *Approaches to controlling air pollution,* edited by Ann F. Freidlaender. Cambridge: MIT Press.

_____. 1990a. Implementation: A review and suggested framework. In *Public administration: The state of the field,* edited by Aaron Wildavsky and Naomi B. Lynn. Chatham, N.J.: Chatham House.

_____. 1990b. *Water politics: Continuity and change.* Albuquerque: University of New Mexico Press.

Ingram, Helen M., Nancy K. Laney, and David M. Gillilan. 1995. *Divided waters.* Tucson: University of Arizona Press.

Ingram, Helen M., and Dean E. Mann. 1980. *Why policies succeed or fail.* Newbury Park, Calif.: Sage.

Ingram, Helen M., H. Brinton Milward, and Wendy Laird. 1991. Scientists and agenda setting: Advocacy and global warming. Paper presented at annual meeting, Association for Public Policy Analysis and Management, Bethesda, Md.

Ingram, Helen M., and Anne L. Schneider. 1990. Improving implementation by framing smarter statutes. *Journal of Public Policy* 10(1):67–88.

_____. 1991. The choice of target populations. *Administration and Society* 23(3):333–56.

_____. 1993. Constructing citizenship: The subtle messages of policy design. In *Public policy for democracy,* edited by Helen M. Ingram and Steven Rathgeb Smith. Washington, D.C.: Brookings Institution.

_____. 1996. Public policy, science and social constructions. Presented at the 1996 annual conference of the American Political Science Association, August 31, San Francisco.

Ingram, Helen M., and Steven Rathgeb Smith, eds. 1993. *Public policy for democracy.* Washington, D.C.: Brookings Institution.

Jagger, Alison. 1983. *Feminist politics and human nature.* Potowa, N.J: Rowman Allanheld.

Jasanoff, Sheila. 1990. American exceptionalism and the political acknowledgement of risk. *Daedalus: Proceedings of the American Academy* 119(4):61–81.

Jasanoff, Sheila, Gerald E. Markle, James C. Petersen, and Trevor Pinch, eds. 1995. *Handbook of science and technology studies.* Newbury Park, Calif.: Sage.

Johnson, James. 1993. Is talk really cheap? Prompting conversation between critical theory and rational choice. *American Political Science Review* 87(1):74–86.

Juvenile Justice and Delinquency Act. U.S. Code. Vol. 42, sec. 72 (1974).

Kahneman, Daniel, Paul Slovic, and Amos Tversky. 1982. *Judgment under uncertainty: Heuristics and biases.* Cambridge: Cambridge University Press.

Katzmann, Robert. 1990. The American legislative process as a signal. *Journal of Public Policy* 9(3):287–306.

Kaufman, Herbert. 1960. *The forest ranger: A study in administrative behavior.* Baltimore: Johns Hopkins University Press.

Kelly, Rita Mae, and William N. Dunn. 1992. Some final thoughts. In *Advances in policy studies since 1950,* edited by William N. Dunn and Rita Mae Kelly. New Brunswick, N.J.: Transaction Publishers.

Kelman, Steven. 1987. *Making public policy: A hopeful view of American government.* New York: Basic Books.

Kelso, William. 1978. *American democratic theory: Pluralism and its critics.* Westport, Conn.: Greenwood Press.

Kemp, Ray. 1985. Planning, public hearings and the politics of discourse. In *Critical theory and public life,* edited by John Forester. Cambridge: MIT Press.

Kennon, Patrick E. 1995. *The twilight of democracy.* New York: Doubleday.

Key, V. O. 1961. *Public opinion and American democracy.* New York: Knopf.

Kingdon, John. 1984. *Agendas, alternatives and public policies.* Boston: Little, Brown.

Kirkhart, Larry. 1971. Toward a theory of public administration. In *Toward a new public administration,* edited by Frank Marini. Toronto: Chandler Publishing.

Kleinberg, Howard. 1992. Defense contracts become licenses to defraud public. *Tribune Newspapers* (Tempe, Ariz.), November 20, sec. A, p. 13.

Kolderie, Ted. 1986. The two different concepts of privatization. *Public Administration Review* 46(July/August):285–92.

Krimsky, Sheldon. 1984. Regulating recombinant DNA research. In *Controversy: Politics of technical decisions,* edited by Dorothy Nelkin. Newbury Park, Calif.: Sage.

Kyle, Ken. 1996a. Scientific expertise, social constructions and the question of homeless policy. Paper presented at the 1996 annual conference of the American Political Science Association, August 31, San Francisco.

_____. 1996b. A bum rap: The homeless as a social construct? Paper presented at annual conference, Western Political Science Association, March 21, San Francisco.

Landy, Marc. 1993. Public policy and citizenship. In *Public policy for democracy,* edited by Helen M. Ingram and Steven Rathgeb Smith. Washington, D.C.: Brookings Institution.

Lasswell, Harold. 1936. *Who gets what, when, and how?* New York: McGraw Hill.

_____. 1971. *A preview of the policy sciences.* New York: American Elsevier.

Latour, Bruno, and Steve Woolgar. 1979. *Laboratory life: The social construction of scientific facts.* Newbury Park, Calif.: Sage.

Leighley, Jan E., and Jonathan Nagler. 1992. Socioeconomic class bias in turnout, 1964–1988: The voters remain the same. *American Political Science Review* 86(3):725–36.

Leonard, Stephen. 1990. *Critical theory in political practice.* Princeton, N.J.: Princeton University Press.

Lewis, Darrell R., David R. Johnson, Tsuey-Hwa Chen, Ronald N. Erickson. 1992. The use and reporting of benefit-cost analyses by state vocational rehabilitation agencies. *Evaluation Review* 16(3):266–87.

Lieberman, Robert C., Helen M. Ingram, and Anne L. Schneider. 1995. Social construction. *American Political Science Review* 89(2) 437–45.

Light, Paul C. 1995. *Thickening government.* Washington, D.C.: Brookings Institution.

Lindblom, Charles E. 1959. The science of muddling through. *Public Administration Review* 19(2):79–88.

_____. 1977. *Politics and markets.* New York: Basic Books.

_____. 1979. Still muddling, not yet through. *Public Administration Review* 39(November/December):517–26.

_____. 1982a. Another state of mind. *American Political Science Review* 76:9–21.

_____. 1982b. The market as prison. *Journal of Politics* 44:324–36.

_____. 1983. Reply to John Manley. *American Political Science Review* 77:390–92.

_____. 1988. *Democracy and market systems.* Oslo: Norwegian University Press.

Lindblom, Charles E., and David K. Cohen. 1979. *Usable knowledge: Social science and social problem solving.* New Haven, Conn.: Yale University Press.

Linder, Stephen H., and B. Guy Peters. 1985. From social theory to policy design. *Journal of Public Policy* 4(3):237–59.

_____. 1987. A design perspective on policy implementation: The fallacies of misplaced prescription. *Policy Studies Review* 6(February):459–76.

_____. 1988. The analysis of design or the design of analysis. *Policy Studies Review* 7(summer):738–50.

____. 1992. A metatheoretic analysis of policy design. In *Advances in policy studies since 1950,* edited by William N. Dunn and Rita Mae Kelly. New Brunswick, N.J.: Transaction Publishers.

Lipset, Seymour Martin. 1963. *Political man.* New York: Doubleday.

Lipsky, Michael. 1980. *Street level bureaucracy.* New York: Russell Sage Foundation.

Lipsky, Michael, and Steven Rathgeb Smith. 1989. When social problems are treated as emergencies. *Social Service Review* 63(March):5–25.

Lowi, Theodore J. 1964. American business, public policy, case-studies, and political theory. *World Politics* 16:677–715.

____. 1972. Four systems of policy, politics, and choice. *Public Administration Review* 11:298–310.

____. 1979. *The end of liberalism.* New York: Norton.

Luke, Timothy W. 1989. *Screens of power: Ideology, domination and resistance in an information society.* Urbana: University of Illinois Press.

Lukes, Steven. 1974. *Power: A radical view.* New York: Macmillan.

MacRae, Duncan. 1979. Policy analysis for public decisions. North Scituate, Mass: Duxbury Press.

Majone, Giandomenico. 1989. *Evidence, argument, and persuasion in the policy process.* New Haven, Conn.: Yale University Press.

Manley, John F. 1983. Neo-pluralism: A class analysis of pluralism I and pluralism II. *American Political Science Review* 77:370–89.

Mansbridge, Jane J. 1990a. The rise and fall of self-interest in the explanation of political life. In *Beyond self-interest,* edited by Jane J. Mansbridge. Chicago: University of Chicago Press.

____, ed. 1990b. *Beyond self-interest.* Chicago: University of Chicago Press.

Marcuse, Herbert. 1964. *One dimensional man: Studies in the ideology of advanced industrial society.* Boston: Beacon Press.

Marini, Frank, ed. 1971. *Toward a new public administration.* Toronto: Chandler Publishing.

Marks, Gary, and Larry Diamond. 1992. Seymour Martin Lipset and the study of democracy. *American Behavioral Scientist* 35(4/5):352–62.

Marshall, T. H. 1964. *Class, citizenship, and social development.* New York: Doubleday.

Marston, Sallie A. 1993. Citizen action programs and participatory politics in Tucson. In *Public policy for democracy,* edited by Helen M. Ingram and Steven Rathgeb Smith. Washington, D.C.: Brookings Institution.

May, Peter. 1991. Reconsidering policy design: Policies and publics. *Journal of Public Policy* 2(11):187–201.

Mazmanian, Daniel A., and Paul A. Sabatier. 1983. *Implementation and public policy.* Glenview, Ill.: Scott, Foresman and Company.

McCool, Daniel C. 1994. *Command of the waters: Iron triangles, federal water development, and Indian water.* Tucson: University of Arizona Press.

____. 1995. *Public policy theories, models, and concepts.* Englewood Cliffs, N.J.: Prentice-Hall.

McDonnell, Lorraine. 1994. Persuasion as a policy instrument: The case of student assessment. Paper presented at the American Political Science Association meeting, September 1–4, New York.

McFarland, Andrew S. 1993. *Cooperative pluralism: The national coal policy experiment.* Lawrence: University Press of Kansas.

McKenzie, Evan. 1994. *Privatopia.* New Haven, Conn.: Yale University Press.

McLaren, Peter. 1995. *Critical pedagogy and predatory culture.* New York: Routledge.

Meier, Ken. 1994. *The politics of sin: Drugs, alcohol, and public policy.* Armonk, N.Y.: M. E. Sharpe.

Miller, David. 1989. *Social justice.* Oxford: Oxford University Press.

Miller, David, and Michael Walzer, eds. 1995. *Pluralism, justice, and equality.* Oxford: Oxford University Press.

Miller, Trudi C. 1989. The operation of democratic institutions. *Public Administration Review* 49(November/December):511–21.

_____. 1991. Political design science: A synthesis of traditional political values and behavioralism. *Research in Public Administration* 1:49–78.

_____. 1992. Toward a science of democracy. In *Advances in policy studies since 1950,* edited by William N. Dunn and Rita Mae Kelly. New Brunswick, N.J.: Transaction Publishers.

_____, ed. 1984. *Public sector performance: A conceptual turning point.* Baltimore: Johns Hopkins University Press.

Mills, C. Wright. 1956. *The power elite.* Oxford: Oxford University Press.

Mitchell, Jerry. 1987. Policy community politics: An explanation for the inconsistencies in disability policy. Ph.D. diss., University of Arizona.

Mitchell, Timothy. 1991. The limits of the state: Beyond statist approaches and their critics. *American Political Science Review* 85(1):78–96.

Moe, Terry. 1990. Political institutions: The neglected side of the story. *Journal of Law, Economics, and Organization* 6(1):213–53.

Mohr, Lawrence. 1988. *Impact analysis for program evaluation.* Chicago: Dorsey Press.

Mucciaroni, Gary. 1995. *Reversals of fortunes, public policy and private interests.* Washington, D.C.: Brookings Institution.

Mueller, Dennis. 1981. *Public choice.* Cambridge: Cambridge University Press.

Mukerji, Chandra. 1989. *A fragile power: Scientists and the state.* Princeton, N.J.: Princeton University Press.

Mulcahy, Aogan. 1995. Claims-making and the construction of legitimacy: Press coverage of the 1981 Northern Irish hunger strike. *Social Problems* 42(4):449–67.

Murray, Charles. 1984. *Losing ground: American social policy, 1950–1980.* New York: Basic Books.

Nachmias, David, and Chava Nachmias. 1987. *Research methods in the social sciences.* New York: St. Martin's Press.

Nelkin, Dorothy. 1977. *Technological decisions and democracy.* Newbury Park, Calif.: Sage.

_____. 1987. *Selling science: How the press covers science and technology.* New York: W. H. Freeman and Co.

_____, ed. 1984. *Controversy: Politics of technical decisions.* Newbury Park, Calif.: Sage. *New York Times.* 1993. Requiem for the supercollider, October 24, sec. E, p. 14, op-ed piece.

Offe, Claus. 1985. *Contradictions of the welfare state: Disorganized capitalism.* Cambridge: Cambridge University Press.

O'Hear, Anthony. 1980. *Karl Popper.* London: Routledge and Kegan Paul.

Olson, Mancur, Jr. 1965. The logic of collective action. New York: Schocken Books.

Orbell, John, Alphons J.C. van de Kragt, and Robyn M. Dawes. 1988. Explaining discussion-induced cooperation in social dilemmas. *Journal of Personality and Social Psychology* 54:811–19.

Orbell, John Mol, Peregine Schwartz-Shea, and Randy Simmons. 1984. Do cooperators exit more readily than defectors? *American Political Science Review* 78:147–61.

Ostrom, Elinor. 1985. An alternative perspective on democratic dilemmas. *Policy Studies Review* 4(February):412–17.

____. 1990. *Governing the commons.* Cambridge: Cambridge University Press.

____. 1991. Rational choice theory and institutional analysis: Toward complementarity. *American Political Science Review* 85(1):237–43.

____. 1992a. *Crafting institutions for self-governing irrigation systems.* San Francisco: Institute for Contemporary Studies.

____. 1992b. Policy analysis of collective action and self-governance. In *Advances in policy studies since 1950,* edited by William N. Dunn and Rita Mae Kelly. New Brunswick, N.J.: Transaction Publishers.

____. 1996. Institutional analysis. Presented at the 1996 annual conference of the American Political Science Association, September 1, San Francisco.

Ostrom, Elinor, James Walker, and Roy Gardner. 1992. Covenants with and without a sword: Self-governance is possible. *American Political Science Review* 86(2):404–17.

Ostrom, Vincent. 1973. *The intellectual crisis in American public administration.* Tuscaloosa: University of Alabama Press.

Ostrom, Vincent, and Elinor Ostrom. 1971. Public choice: A different approach to the study of public administration. *Public Administration Review* 31(March/April):203–16.

Ostrom, Vincent, Charles M. Tiebout, and Robert Warren. 1961. The organization of government in metropolitan areas: A theoretical inquiry. *American Political Science Review* 55(December):831–42.

O'Toole, Laurence J. 1987. Policy recommendations for multi-actor implementation: An assessment of the field. *Journal of Public Policy* 6(2):181–210.

Page, Edward. 1992. *Political authority and bureaucratic power: A comparative analysis.* 2d ed. New York: Harvester Wheatsheaf.

Palumbo, Dennis, J., and Marvin A. Harder, eds. 1981. *Implementing public policy.* Lexington, Mass.: Lexington Books.

Parenti, Michael. 1988. *Democracy for the few.* New York: St. Martin's Press.

Paris, David C., and James F. Reynolds. 1983. *The logic of policy inquiry.* New York: Longman.

Pateman, Carole. 1970. *Participation and democratic theory.* Cambridge, Mass.: The Press Syndicate of the University of Cambridge.

____. 1989. The civic culture: A philosophic critique. In *The civic culture revisited,* edited by Gabriel Almond and Sidney Verba. Newbury Park, Calif.: Sage.

Perry, James, ed. 1991. *Research in public administration.* Vol. 1. New York: JAI Press.

Petracca, Mark P. 1990. Politics beyond the end of liberalism. *PS: Political Science and Politics* 23(December):566–69.

____. 1991. The rational choice approach to politics: A challenge to democratic theory. *Review of Politics* 53(2):288–319.

Phillips, Anne. 1991. *Engendering democracy.* University Park: Pennsylvania State University Press.

Phillips, Kevin P. 1990. *The politics of rich and poor: Wealth and the American electorate in the Reagan aftermath.* New York: Random House.

____. 1993. *Boiling point: Republicans, Democrats, and the decline of middle-class prosperity.* New York: Random House.

____. 1994. *Arrogant capital: Washington, Wall Street, and the frustration of American politics.* Boston: Little, Brown.

Piven, Frances Fox, and Richard A. Cloward. 1988. *Why Americans don't vote.* New York: Pantheon Books.

Popper, Karl. 1966. *The open society and its enemies.* 2 vols. Princeton: Princeton University Press.

Pressman, Jeffery, and Aaron Wildavsky. 1973. *Implementation*. Berkeley: University of California Press.

Price, Don K. 1964. The scientific estate. In *Scientists and national policy-making,* edited by Robert Gilpin and Christopher Wright. New York: Columbia University Press.

———. 1965. *The scientific estate*. Cambridge: Harvard University Press.

Public Broadcasting System. 1995. Newt Gingrich interviewed by Charlie Rose, July 6.

Putnam, Robert D. 1993. *Making democracy work*. Princeton: Princeton University Press.

———. 1995. Tuning in, tuning out: The strange disappearance of social capital in America. *PS: Political Science and Politics* 38:664–83.

Quade, E. S. 1991. *Analysis for public decisions*. New York: Elsevier Science.

Quinn, Dennis P., and Robert Y. Shapiro. 1991. Business political power: The case of taxation. *American Political Science Review* 85(3):851–74.

Ranney, Austin, ed. 1968. The study of policy content: A framework for choice. In *Political science and public policy*. Chicago: Markham Publishing.

———. 1968. *Political science and public policy*. Chicago: Markham Publishing.

Rasmussen, David. M. 1990. *Reading Habermas*. Oxford: Basil Blackwell.

Rauch, Jonathan. 1994. *Demosclerosis: The silent killer of American government*. New York: Times Books.

Rawls, John. 1971. *A theory of justice*. Cambridge, Mass.: Belknap Press.

Reich, Robert, ed. 1991. *The power of public ideas*. Cambridge: Harvard University Press.

Rein, Martin, and Donald Schon. 1993. Reframing policy discourse. In *The argumentative turn in policy analysis and planning,* edited by Frank Fischer and John Forester. Durham, N.C.: Duke University Press.

Rhodes, R. A. W., and D. Marsh, eds. 1991. *Policy networks in British government*. Oxford: Oxford University Press.

Ricci, David. 1984. *The tragedy of political science*. New Haven, Conn.: Yale University Press.

Riker, William H., and Peter C. Ordeshook. 1968. A theory of the calculus of voting. *American Political Science Review* 62:25–42.

Ripley, Randall B. 1966. *Public policies and their politics*. New York: Norton.

———. 1985. *Policy analysis in political science*. Chicago: Nelson Hall.

Rochefort, David A., and Roger W. Cobb. 1993. Problem definition, agenda access, and policy choice. *Policy Studies Journal* 21(1):56–71.

———, eds. 1994. *The politics of problem definition: Shaping the policy agenda*. Lawrence: University Press of Kansas.

Rose, Richard. 1986. *Law as a resource of public policy*. Oxford: Oxford University Press.

———. 1991. Votes and markets: Designing policies to increase the influence of individuals. *Australian Journal of Political Science* 26:277–94.

Roth, Guenther, and Claus Wittich, eds. 1978. *Economy and society: An outline of interpretive sociology*. Berkeley: University of California Press.

Rourke, Francis E. 1984. *Bureaucracy, politics, and public policy.* 3d ed. Boston: Little, Brown.

Sabatier, Paul A. 1987. Top down and bottom-up approaches to implementation research: A critical analysis and suggested synthesis. *Journal of Public Policy* 6(2):21–48.

Salamon, Lester M., ed., assisted by Michael Lun. 1989. *Beyond privatization: The tools of government action*. Washington, D.C.: Urban Institute.

Salisbury, Robert. 1968. The analysis of public policy: A search for theory and roles. In *Political science and public policy,* edited by Austin Ranney. Chicago: Markham Publishing.

Salter, Liora. 1988. *Mandated science: Science and scientists in the making of standards.* Dordrecht, Holland: Kluever Academic Publishers.

Savas, E. S. 1982. *Privatizing the public sector: How to shrink government.* Chatham, N.J.: Chatham House.

____. 1987. *Privatization: The key to better government.* Chatham, N.J.: Chatham House.

Scaff, Lawrence A., and Helen M. Ingram. 1986. Politics, policy, and public choice: A critique and a proposal. *Polity* 19(4):613–36.

Schattschneider, E. F. 1960. *The semi sovereign people: A realist view of democracy in America.* New York: Rinehart and Winston.

Scherer, Klaus R., ed. 1992. *Justice: Interdisciplinary perspectives.* Cambridge: Cambridge University Press.

Schneider, Anne L. 1982. Studying policy implementation: A conceptual framework. *Evaluation Review* 6:715–30.

____. 1986a. Evaluation research and political science: An argument against the division of scholarly labor. *Policy Studies Review* 6(November):222–32.

____. 1986b. The evolution of a policy orientation for evaluation research: A guide to practice. *Public Administration Review* 46(July/August):356–64.

____. 1987. Coproduction of public and private safety. *Western Political Quarterly* 40(4):611–30.

Schneider, Anne L., and Helen M. Ingram. 1988. Systematically pinching ideas: A comparative approach to policy design. *Journal of Public Policy* 8(1):61–80.

____. 1990a. The behavioral assumptions of policy tools. *Journal of Politics* 52(May):511–29.

____. 1990b. Policy design: Elements, premises, and strategies. In *Policy theory and policy evaluation,* edited by Stuart Nagel. New York: Greenwood Press.

____. 1993. Social constructions and target populations: Implications for politics and policy. *American Political Science Review* 87(2):334–47.

Schneider, Joseph. 1985. Social problems theory: The constructionist view. *American Review of Sociology* 11:209–29.

Schneider, Mark, and Paul Teske, with Michael Mintrom. 1995. *Public entrepreneurs: Agents for change in American government.* Princeton: Princeton University Press.

Schram, Sanford. 1993. Postmodern policy analysis: Discourse and identity in welfare policy. *Policy Sciences* 26:249–70.

Schulman, Paul A. 1975. Non incremental policy making: Notes toward an alternative paradigm. *American Political Science Review* 69:1354–70.

Schumacher, John A. 1984. The model of a human being in public choice theory. *American Behavioral Scientist* 28(2):211–32.

Schumpeter, Joseph. 1976. *Capitalism, socialism, and democracy.* London: Allen and Unwin.

Sclove, Richard E., 1983. Energy policy and democratic theory. In *Uncertain power: The struggle for a national energy policy,* edited by Dorothy S. Zinberg. New York: Pergamon.

____. 1992. The nuts and bolts of democracy: Democratic theory and technological design. In *Democracy in a technological society,* edited by L. Winner. Netherlands: Kluwer Academic Publishers.

____. 1993. Technology politics as if democracy really mattered: Choices confronting progressives. In *Technology for the common good,* edited by Michael Shuman and Julie Sweig. Washington, D.C.: Institute for Policy Studies.

Scriven, Michael. 1969. Logical positivism and the behavioral sciences. In *The legacy of logical positivism,* edited by Peter Achinstein and Stephen F. Barker. Baltimore: Johns Hopkins University Press.

Seidman, Steven, ed. 1989. *Jurgen Habermas: On society and politics, a reader.* Boston: Beacon Press.

Shklar, Judith. 1984. *Ordinary vices.* Cambridge: Harvard University Press.

_____. 1990. *The faces of injustice.* New Haven, Conn.: Yale University Press.

_____. 1991. *American citizenship: The quest for inclusion.* Cambridge: Harvard University Press.

Shuman, Michael, and Julia Sweig, eds. 1993. *Technology for the common good.* Washington, D.C.: Institute for Policy Studies.

Simon, Herbert A. 1981. *The sciences of the artificial.* Cambridge: MIT Press.

_____. 1986. Rationality in psychology and economics. In *Rational choice: The contrast between economics and psychology,* edited by Robin M. Hogarth and Melvin W. Reder. Chicago: University of Chicago Press.

Simon, Herbert and Associates. 1992. Decision making and problem solving. In *Decision making,* edited by Mary Zey. Newbury Park, Calif.: Sage.

Simon, Jonathan. 1993. *Poor discipline: Parole and the social control of the underclass, 1890–1990.* Chicago: University of Chicago Press.

Simons, Jon. 1995. *Foucault and the political.* New York: Routledge.

Skocpol, Theda. 1992. State formation and social policy in the United States. *American Behavioral Scientist* 35(4/5):559–84.

Slovic, Paul. 1967. The relative influence of probabilities and payoffs upon perceived risk of gamble. *Psychonomic Science* 9:223–24.

Slovic, Paul, Baruch Fischoff, and Sarah Lichtenstein. 1977. Behavioral decision theory. *Annual Review of Psychology* 28:1–39.

_____. 1982. Facts versus fears: Understanding perceived risk. In *Judgment under uncertainty: Heuristics and biases,* edited by Daniel Kahneman, Paul Slovic, and Amos Tversky. Cambridge: Cambridge University Press.

Smith, Bruce L. R. 1992. *The advisers.* Washington, D.C.: Brookings Institution.

Smith, Steven Rathgeb. 1993. The new politics of contracting: Citizenship and the nonprofit role. In *Public policy for democracy,* edited by Helen M. Ingram and Steven Rathgeb Smith. Washington, D.C.: Brookings Institution.

Smith, Steven Rathgeb, and Michael Lipsky. 1992. Privatization in health and human services: A critique. *Journal of Health Politics, Policy, and Law* 17(summer):233–54.

_____. 1993. *Nonprofits for hire: The welfare state in the age of contracting.* Cambridge: Harvard University Press.

Smith, Steven Rathgeb, and Deborah A. Stone. 1988. The unexpected consequences of privatization. In *Remaking the welfare state,* edited by Michael K. Brown. Philadelphia: Temple University Press.

Solomon, Robert C., and Mark C. Murphy. 1990. *What is justice?* Oxford: Oxford University Press.

Spector, Malcolm, and John I. Kitsuse. 1987. *Constructing social problems.* New York: Aldine de Gruyter.

Sproule-Jones, Mark. 1984. Methodological individualism and public choice. *American Behavioral Scientist* 28(2):167–84.

Steinberger, Peter J. 1980. Typologies of public policy: Meaning construction and their policy process. *Social Science Quarterly* (61):185–97.

Stivers, Camilla. 1990. The public agency as polis: Active citizenship in the administrative state. *Administration and Society* 22(1):86–105.

Stockman, David A. 1986. *The triumph of politics.* New York: Harper and Row.

Stone, Clarence. 1989. *Regime politics.* Lawrence: University Press of Kansas.

Stone, Deborah A. 1988. *Policy paradox and political reason.* Glenview, Ill: Scott, Foresman and Company.

____. 1993. Clinical authority in the construction of citizenship. In *Public policy for democracy,* edited by Helen M. Ingram and Steven Rathgeb Smith. Washington, D.C.: Brookings Institution.

Taylor, Charles, with Amy Guttman, Steven Rockefeller, Michael Walzer, and Susan Wolf. 1992. *Multiculturalism and the politics of recognition.* Princeton: Princeton University Press.

Tribe, Laurence H. 1972. Policy science: Analysis or ideology? *Philosophy and Public Affairs* 1(1):66–109.

Tribune Newspapers (Tempe, Ariz.). 1993. Senate gets tough on gun-related crime, November 10, sec. A, p. 3.

Truman, David. 1951. *The governmental process.* New York: Knopf.

Turque, Bill, Eleanor Gift, Melinda Lin, Bob Cohn, and Daniel Glick. 1993. The politics of crime. *Newsweek,* December 6, pp. 20–22.

Turque, Bill, Rich Thomas, and Peter Annin. 1993. Smashing the super collider. *Newsweek,* November 1, p. 30.

U.S. Congress. 1946. *Atomic energy act of 1946.* 79th Cong., 2d sess. Public Law 585.

U.S. House of Representatives. 1986. Subcommittee on energy conservation and power of the committee on energy and commerce. *American nuclear guinea pigs: Three decades of radiation experiments on U.S. citizens.* 99th Cong., 2d sess. Committee Print 99-NN.

Valelly, Richard M. 1993. Public policy for reconnected citizenship. In *Public policy for democracy,* edited by Helen M. Ingram and Steven Rathgeb Smith. Washington, D.C.: Brookings Institution.

Vanberg, Viktor J., and Roger D. Congleton. 1992. Rationality, amorality, and exit. *American Political Science Review* 86(2):418–29.

Verba, Sidney, and Normah H. Nie. 1972. *Participation in America.* New York: Harper and Row.

Verba, Sidney, Kay Lehman Schlozman, Henry Brady, and Norman H. Nie. 1993. Citizen activity: Who participates? What do they say? *American Political Science Review* 87(2):303–19.

Walzer, Michael. 1983. *Spheres of justice.* New York: Basic Books.

Warner, Jean. 1996. Social constructions in the evolution of youth services policy. Prepared for the 1996 annual conference of the American Political Science Association, August 31, San Francisco.

Watson-Verran, Helen, and David Turnbull. 1995. Science and other indigenous knowledge systems. In *Handbook of science and technology studies,* edited by Sheila Jasanoff, Gerald E. Markle, James C. Petersen, and Trevor Pinch. Newbury Park, Calif.: Sage.

Weber, Max. 1978. Three types of legitimate domination. In *Economy and society: An outline of interpretive sociology,* edited by Guenther Roth and Claus Wittich, p. 215. Berkeley: University of California Press.

Weimer, David L., and Aidan R. Vining. 1989. *Policy analysis: Concepts and practice.* Englewood Cliffs, N.J.: Prentice-Hall.

Weinberg, Daniel H. 1996. A brief look at postwar U.S. income inequality. U.S. Census Bureau, http://www.census.gov:so/hhes/income/incineq/p60asc.html.

Wexler, Philip, ed. 1991. *Critical theory now.* London: Falmer Press.

White, Jay. 1986. On the growth of knowledge in public administration. *Public Administration Review* 46(January/February):15–24.

White, Stephen K. 1988. *The recent work of Jurgen Habermas.* Cambridge: Cambridge University Press.

Wildavsky, Aaron. 1979. *Speaking truth to power: The art and craft of policy analysis.* Boston: Little, Brown.

Wildavsky, Aaron, and Naomi B. Lynn. 1990. Public administration: The state of the discipline. Chatham, N.J.: Chatham House.

Wilson, James Q. 1973. *Political organizations.* New York: Basic Books.

____. 1979. *American government: Institutions and policies.* Lexington, Mass.: D.C. Heath.

____. 1989. *Bureaucracy: What government agencies do and why they do it.* New York: Basic Books.

Wood, Dan B., and Richard W. Waterman. 1991. The dynamics of political control of the bureaucracy. *American Political Science Review* 85(3):801–28.

Wood, Robert. 1964. Scientists and politics: The rise of an apolitical elite. In *Scientists and national policy-making,* edited by Robert Gilpin and Christopher Wright. New York: Columbia University Press.

Woodside, Kenneth. 1986. Policy instruments and the study of public policy. *Canadian Journal of Political Science* 19(December):775–93.

Wright, George. 1984. *Behavioral decision theory.* Newbury Park, Calif.: Sage.

Wyatt, Joe. 1993. Pork barrel science. *New York Times,* October 12, sec. A, p. 23.

Yanow, Dvora. 1993. The communication of policy meanings: Implementation as interpretation and text. *Policy Sciences* 26(1):41–61.

____. 1995. Practices of policy interpretation. *Policy Sciences* 28(2):111.

Young, Iris Marion. 1990. *Justice and the politics of difference.* Princeton: Princeton University Press.

____. 1996. Communication and the other: Beyond deliberative democracy. In *Democracy and difference,* edited by Seyla Benhabib. Princeton: Princeton University Press.

Zey, Mary, ed. 1992. *Decision making: Alternatives to rational models.* Newbury Park, Calif.: Sage.

Index

Apathy of citizens *(continued)*
  scientific and professionalized policy making and, 185–87
Arrow, Kenneth, 39
Arrow's paradox, 42–43
Assumptions, 10, 32, 37, 50, 56, 58, 61, 64, 194
  as an element of design, 2, 99–101
Atomic Energy Act of 1947, 172
Atomic, nuclear energy policy, 170–71
Authority tools, 93

Bargaining and negotiating, 8, 77
  critical theory perspective on, 58–59
  pluralism and, 22, 30
Base Closing Commission, 172
Battered women's programs, 177
Behavior,
  critical theory and, 52, 54, 56
  degenerative pluralism and, 104, 107, 111
  institutional public choice and, 47, 49
  pluralist theory and, 13, 17, 20–21
  policy design theory and, 68–69, 76–80, 82, 93, 97
  policy science theory and, 35
  public choice theory and, 40–42, 50,
  in scientific and professional contexts, 151, 176
Behavioral research, 20
Benefit cost
  analysis, 32–33, 35
  ratios, 99
Benefits and burdens,
  to advantaged groups, 113–16
  better designs for, 203
  to contenders, 116–19
  in degenerative pluralism, 112
  to dependents, 123–25
  to deviants, 120–23
  influence of science in allocation of, 158
  to scientific and professional target groups, 173–74
  selection of targets for, 84–89
  Wilson's theory of, 71–72
Bortner, M. A., x
Boundary rules, 98

Buchanan, James, 39
Bureaucracy. *See* Agencies; Implementation
Bureau of Land Management, 173, 178
  capacity to correct design flaws, 174
  centralized, 48, 175
  choice of tools and, 175
  control of, 25
  dangers of, 36
  growth of, 154
  implementation and, 175
  need for established rules, 177
  policy analysis and, 35–36
  responsiveness of, 16–19
  rules and, 180
  science and, 154
  selection of goals and, 171
Business interests, 15, 23–24, 74–75

Calculus of Consent, The, 39
Campaigns, 17
Campbell, Donald, 30
Capacity building tools, 94, 194
  when scientists are targets, 173–75
Career politicians, 17
Causal analysis, 34
Causal theory of design. *See* Policy design theory
Circular majority. *See* Arrow's paradox
Citizen cynicism, 198
Citizen orientations, 5, 200–201
  degenerative pluralism and, 140–45
  scientific and professionalized pluralism and, 181–85
Citizen panels, 34
Citizenship, 3, 5–7, 190, 192–94
  critical theory and, 63, 65
  degenerative policy designs, effect on, 140–45
  education for, 184–85
  empathy as central component, 81
  implementation, effect on, 92
  importance of in improved designs, 206
  passive, 152
  pluralist theory and, 14, 19–23, 26
  policy design and, 5–7

Empirical research *(continued)*
   in pluralism, 19, 25–26
   in public choice, 47, 48
Empower
   in policy design theory, 79
   role in critical theory, 51
Enlightened self interest, 47
Enlightenment, 21
Environmental policy, 5, 34, 83, 100
Environmental protection agency, 165, 179
Evaluation research, 31
   types of evaluations, 33
Experimenting society, 30
Expertise. *See also* Scientific and
      professional designs
   critical theory and, 55
   policy sciences and, 35–38
   in scientific and professionalized
      contexts, 150–88, 198

Fairness
   in pluralist theory, 28
   in policy design theory, 79–80, 83, 85,
      87–88, 92, 99–100
   in public choice theory, 42
Family and women's policies, 52
Federal Deposit Insurance Corporation,
   118
Federal Reserve Board, 172
Fish and Wildlife Service, 177
Food stamp policy, 138
Forest lands grazing policy, 178
Forest service, 179
Framing of issues, 73, 102, 111–12,
   151–52, 186, 193. *See also* Agenda
   setting
Frankfurt School, 51
Free riders, 43

Gender, 17, 19, 33, 36, 50
   justice and, 92
   policy and, 192–93
Genome project, 172
Global climate change, 154, 171, 173
Goal displacement, 195
Goal enhancement, 164, 195
Goals, 2

balance among goals, 84
choice of, 112–13, 171–73
definition and types of goals, 83–84
in scientific and professional designs,
   195–96
Good policy designs. *See also* Standards
      for judging public policy
   ideas for improvement, 203–7
Governance, 4
Government growth, 45–46
Government inefficiency, 40–44
Grants, 175
Grassroots implementation model, 175

Habermas, Jurgen, 53–56
Hidden agendas, 56, 194. *See also*
   Deception
Hierarchy,
   critical theory and, 59
   policy tools and, 93
   public choice and, 40
   within scientific community, 157
Higher education policy, 137
Homelessness, 157
Homosexuals, policy toward, 120, 133
Hortatory policy tools, 95, 131
Housing policy, 84
Human agency, 5, 77
   critical theory and, 52
   institutional public choice and, 47
   role in improving policy design, 193–94,
      204
   social constructions and, 9
Human genome project, 167
Human nature
   critical theory assumptions about, 54
   policy design perspective, 68–69
   public choice theory of, 39
Human organ transplants, 168–69

Ideal speech situation, 53, 56, 62
Identity, 19
   social construction of target populations
      and, 110–11
   target populations and, 86–87
Illogical designs and policy, 126, 183, 192,
   197